STORIES FROM THE WAR
WHAT GOD IS DOING AMID THE ISRAEL-HAMAS CONFLICT

MICHAEL NATT

ENDORSEMENTS

This compilation and anthology of stories regarding the Israel-Hamas war serves as a unique commentary of the tragic events that broke out on Oct. 7, 2023. It provides a 360 view, a personal, historical, spiritual, and prophetic perspective that is typically hidden from the public conversation. This book will not only educate you but inspire and challenge you.

> PASTOR RICH KAO PRESIDENT, FIVE STONES IMPACT

"Michael Natt sheds a prophetic light on the poignant human and historical experiences amidst the Israel-Hamas conflict. With deep insight from his beloved Jewish heritage and Biblical knowledge. Michael offers a nuanced perspective on what God is doing in the midst of chaos."

> CLEM FERRIS ITINERANT TEACHING AND PROPHETIC MINISTRY GRACE CHURCH, CHAPEL HILL, NC

We encourage you to read this new offering by an old-time friend, Michael Natt, and ask the Lord, "What action He would have you take in this season of Israel's dilemma?"

> SHELLY & JUNE VOLK: AUTHORS, ITINERANT TEACHERS, SCOTTSDALE, AZ

CONTENTS

Introduction	xi
1. A Time for War	1
2. My (Almost) Trip to Israel	3
3. Worship on Mount Carmel	5
4. Prophetic Vision	27
5. A Father Wound	29
6. Alexander the Great Visits Jerusalem	33
7. Aliyah	37
8. An Eternal People	43
9. Angels Surround Them	45
10. Arrows	49
11. As the Nations Have Done to Israel	53
12. Athens or Jerusalem	63
13. Awake You Who Sleep	69
14. Beirut, Izmir and Nazareth	71
15. Bombing Auschwitz	73
16. Brace for Impact	81
17. Broken Covenants	83
18. Children in Captivity	93
19. End Time Prophecy	95
20. Finding Real Hope in the Midst of Disaster	103
21. From the River to the Sea	111
22. God Crying Out to Us	115
23. God's Hostage	123
24. God's Plan for Iran	133
25. Hatikvah	139
26. Hebrew Verb Tenses	155
27. If Israel Just Allowed the Palestinians to Have Their Own State	157
28. Ima's Goodies	161
29. In Memoriam	167
30. Indigo Girls	171

31. Iron Swords	175
32. Jewish Humor	177
33. Jews From Arab Lands: The Middle East's Forgotten Refugees	179
34. Justice and Forgiveness	185
35. Miracle at Golan Heights	197
36. Miracles and Martyrs	199
37. Miracles in Gaza	203
38. Miraculously Delivered from Hamas and Abortion	207
39. Moments in History	213
40. New York Stands with Israel	217
41. Our Covenant Declaration with the God of Israel	219
42. Prayer for Peace	227
43. Proclamations on Behalf of Israel	229
44. Rees Howells Intercessor	231
45. Reflections on Chanukah 2023	233
46. Regarding Israel's Enemies	237
47. Serving Holocaust Survivors	239
48. Silver Trumpets and Psalm 91 Bandanas	245
49. The Cry of the Daughters of Israel	251
50. The Danger of Replacement Theology	257
51. The Isaiah 19 Highway	263
52. The Isaiah 62 Fast	265
53. The Nightmare of Jihadi Rape and Murder	271
54. The Spirit of Amalek	285
55. The Way of the Oil דרך השמן	297
56. Try Tears	303
57. 24 Hours of Worship	307
58. Zinzendorf and the Moravians: Messianic Trailblazers	319
59. Zion's Future Glory	327
60. The Last Word on the Middle East	329
About the Author	333

All Scripture quotations, unless otherwise indicated, are taken from the New King James Version of the Bible. Copyright © 1979, 1980, 1982 by Thomas Nelson, Inc., Publishers. Used by permission.

Scripture quotations marked NIV are taken from The Holy Bible, New International Version®, NIV®. Copyright © 1973, 1978, 1984, 2011 by Biblica, Inc.™ Used by permission of Zondervan. All rights reserved worldwide. www.zondervan.com. The "NIV" and "New International Version" are trademarks registered in the United States Patent and Trademark Office by Biblica, Inc.™

Scripture quotations marked NASB are taken from the New American Standard Bible (NASB)®. Copyright © 1960, 1962, 1963, 1968, 1971, 1972, 1973, 1975, 1977, 1995 by The Lockman Foundation. Used by permission. www.Lockman.org.

Scripture quotations marked ESV are taken from the ESV® Bible (The Holy Bible English Standard Version®), copyright © 2001 by Crossway Bibles, a publishing ministry of Good News Publishers. Used by permission. All rights reserved.

ISBN:9798878479240

Copyright © 2024 by Michael Natt

All rights reserved.

No part of this book may be reproduced in any form or by any electronic or mechanical means, including information storage and retrieval systems, without written permission from the author, except for the use of brief quotations in a book review.

FOR MY DAUGHTERS ANNA AND REBECCA

Special thanks to:

Everyone who contributed stories to this book; Abby Reese, Kristina Kaplan and Nicole Green for editing, transcription and interview assistance; Cheryl Natt, the most supportive wife in the world; And to the many lovers of God and lovers of Israel whom I have met over the years.

INTRODUCTION

"Up from the ashes, hope will arise."

The war in Israel started on Simchat Torah, October 7, 2023, and two months later, it was the first night of Chanukah on December 7, 2023. Holding a unique role, like many in the Global Watch—a network of watchmen and intercessors for Israel and the Nations—I received daily updates from numerous leaders in the Middle East.

Bridging the Middle East updates, I was reminded of a profound truth: "To whom much is given, much is required"(Luke 12:48). Therefore, I felt responsible and compelled in my spirit to compile this book about what I have learned and experienced during the last two months. This is my best attempt to tell the stories of the war that I have heard and read about.

It is my hope and prayer that you will learn much in the chapters that follow, and that you will be changed by what you read;

May God open your heart in a greater measure to His heart for the people of Israel.

My heart's desire and prayer to God for Israel is that they may be saved. (Romans 10:1)

CHAPTER 1
A TIME FOR WAR

Seven days you shall keep a sacred feast to the Lord your God in the place which the Lord chooses, because the Lord your God will bless you in all your produce and in all the work of your hands, so that you surely rejoice. (Deuteronomy 16:15)

The Feast of Tabernacles concluded on Shemini Atzeret, Friday, October 6th That day I shared with the Global Watch community from Deuteronomy 16 how this was a time of rejoicing in the goodness of God. When we awoke the next day, October 7th, we were thrust into a new season; it was a time for war.

Blessed be the Lord my Rock,
Who trains my hands for war,
And my fingers for battle. (Psalm 14:1)

It came upon us suddenly, but we were ready to respond to the call to action, starting with 90 hours of continuous worship and prayer. The Lord had prepared us for battle through 21 days of fasting, building community, and dealing with areas in our hearts. As spiritual watchmen, we battle in the heavenlies together:

For we do not wrestle against flesh and blood, but against principalities, against powers, against the rulers of the darkness of this age, against spiritual hosts of wickedness in the heavenly places. (Ephesians 6:12)

CHAPTER 2
MY (ALMOST) TRIP TO ISRAEL

"I want to be with my brothers in Israel at this time. I haven't been there since 2011," I told my wife. "Maybe I'll go there for a couple of weeks, join the prayer team on Mount Carmel, and help out wherever needed."

"Since you'll already be there, why don't you go for six weeks," Cheryl responded.

So, I bought a new suitcase, and started to plan my trip. Until … Cheryl spoke with our daughters Anna and Becky, her two closest friends Kathy and Diane, and our ten-year-old granddaughter Violet. It was unanimous, "Don't go at this time!"

"The five spies giving a bad report" I thought. So, I bargained, and pleaded and prayed.

Cheryl calmly said, "Violet needs you home at this time."

Case closed … for now.

(Two days after God closed the door for me to be in The Land, He put it on my heart to write about it.)

CHAPTER 3
WORSHIP ON MOUNT CARMEL
BY KAREN DAVIS

"RESTORING THE ALTAR OF THE LORD ON MOUNT CARMEL (1 KINGS 18:30)

Positioned on the top of Mount Carmel, Israel, where the prophet Elijah once confronted the false gods of his age, Kehilat HaCarmel (Carmel Congregation) is a Messianic community of Jewish, Arab, and other Gentile worshippers. We have been called to "shout unto God with a voice of triumph," (Psalm 47:1), declaring the victory of the Lord Yeshua over the spiritual darkness of our day. Knowing that the Lord dwells in the praises of His people (Psalm 22:3), our times of corporate praise and worship are a key element in releasing His manifest presence in our gatherings and in the life of our community. As we all drink from the river of life "that flows from the sanctuary" (Ezekiel 47:12), we are empowered for the works of service that bring healing and comfort to the people of Israel. [www.carmelcongregation.org.il; www.karendavisworship.com]

A SHOUT OF VICTORY

When the Lord positioned us on this highest point on Mount Carmel, the Lord spoke to me that our worship was to be characterized by the shout of victory—that we were to take a stand like Elijah did, as he confronted the false prophets, that we were called to spiritually confront the principalities and powers of darkness. We were to be on the offensive, not the defensive.

When my late husband David Davis and I made *aliyah* (immigrated to Israel) back in 1989, the body of Messiah was very small in those days, and there weren't many congregations that were even open to the gifts of the Holy Spirit. So many of the believers were discouraged, and seemed to be just barely "surviving," carrying a sense of defeat. But the Lord said to me, "You need to be proclaiming the victory of the Lord." So, I began to pray, "Lord, we need new music!" asking Him to release songs that would carry the shout of the King, the sound of victory, that would launch the "sword of the Spirit," the Word of God—like a missile of light into the spiritual darkness over Israel.

Engaging in spiritual warfare is essential now for what we are called to in the midst of this multi-front war with Hamas, Hezbollah, and Iran, along with the growing international anti-Semitism. We are facing the most serious scenario we have ever dealt with as a nation since the founding of modern Israel in 1948. Where our worship center is located, near the city of Haifa, on the highest point of Mt. Carmel, we're facing our northern border. Right now, although the main fighting is going on in the south in Gaza, the greatest existential threat to our nation is from the north, from Lebanon and Syria, where the Iranian proxy terror organization Hezbollah is based, with hundreds of thousands of rockets ready to launch major destruction upon us.

Over the years as we've been persevering in worship and prayer, the Lord has faithfully equipped us with new music, "Songs of deliverance." Ephesians 3:10 is one of our key mandates:

> *To the intent that now the manifold wisdom of God might be made known by the church to the principalities and powers in the heavenly places. (Ephesians 3:10)*

This follows in the context of Ephesians Chapter 2 describing the "one new man" of Jew and Gentile, which is a founding vision of our ministry:

> *Having abolished in His flesh the enmity, that is, the law of commandments contained in ordinances, so as to create in Himself one new man from the two, thus making peace. (Ephesians 2:15)*

Ephesians 3:10 underscores the key role of our worship as a mighty spiritual weapon of warfare. In worship, we are celebrating the victory of Adonai Yeshua by faith—not by sight. Just as Asaph, the chief musician, was a seer, so, we, too, need to be taking that position, seeing the victory in the Spirit and declaring it with prophetic praise.

GROWING UP IN AMERICA

Growing up in the Jewish community in Detroit, Michigan, my family were Reformed Jews, which is the most liberal form on Judaism, maintaining Jewish values, but not necessarily believing in God. In actuality the real religion in our household was secular humanism and intellectual achievement. Just about everyone in my family were scientific, intellectual, mathematical types. My dad and grandfather were both successful automotive engineers. We were very much part of the Jewish community, belonging to the synagogue, celebrating all the Jewish holidays, and identifying culturally as Jews.

I began studying piano when I was four years old, and continued to study classical piano for twelve years through high school. I was very deeply moved by the beauty of music, and knew that there must be some kind of "creative force" that was behind the beauty of music and nature. Yet when I would go to the synagogue for services, I didn't experience the reality of God, although I was often moved by some of the beautiful words and songs from the Psalms. But I had an intense need to find God, to find out what is this "creative force" that so moved my soul. So, I began to search through all kinds of New Age practices and Eastern religions, that were circulating in the United States during the counter-culture "hippie" time.

I ended up in New York City where my brother was living as a professional jazz musician. Previous to that, in addition to studying music, I had also studied visual art and painting. I love color! So, I moved to New York City to dive full-time into the arts. I had already practiced close to thirteen years of meditation, using one technique after another. Each time, after a couple years, whatever method I was using just wasn't "working." So, I'd keep searching for something else. I finally got to the place in my life in New York City, where I woke up one morning and nothing was working in my life, in any area. I had exhausted my meditation techniques, and I just had no answers for my life. I was 33 years old when this happened, and I thought, "I need to talk to somebody—someone who might have some good advice."

JOURNEY TO FAITH

The name of one particular friend of mine came to my mind, Camille, and I thought, "Oh, maybe she has some good advice for me. She just seems so happy, and she doesn't even have a boyfriend! Why is she so happy?" Romantic relationships had been a real stronghold in my life and it was one of the things that brought me to the end of myself. After numerous relationships, I finally had a moment of realization one morning, asking myself, "What am I doing with this guy?" It was one of the last straws. "This makes no sense," I thought. "I know this person is not for me."

So I decided to go talk to Camille who lived in my building on the Upper West Side of New York City. She was home, and I just started to pour out my troubles to her. She listened intently and then asked me, "Well, would you like to pray?" I said, "Okay! What are we going to do?" I knew she wasn't Jewish, but I had no idea what I was about to hear. At this point I was only aware of the name of Jesus as a sort of "Christ-consciousness" — a concept we sometimes used in New Age circles — just as we would refer to Buddha, or aspects of other religions.

So as she began leading me in a prayer, the first word I repeated after her was, "Jesus." Well, I thought, I'm a Jewish girl, so even though I've been in the New Age for years and not been in a synagogue in a long time, just saying the name Jesus is so instinctively unpleasant to us as Jews. As Jewish people, we carry a generational trauma at the hands of people who called themselves Christians and use the name of Jesus as they slaughter us. Tragically, through the centuries it's been mainly perpetrated through Christian anti-Semitism. So, for Jewish people, we simply associate the name Jesus with all Christians. These are our enemies. These are the people that want to massacre us. My grandparents immigrated to America from

Russia because Jews were being slaughtered in pogroms (massacres) incited by the Russian Orthodox Church. That's our history and this predates the Holocaust.

Nevertheless, with this in mind, I thought to myself, "Okay I've tried everything, I'll just say His name." So, I said, "Jesus." Then the next line was "I invite you into my heart." The prayer continued with the words, "I ask You to forgive me my sins." I really had no idea what my sins were! I didn't know sleeping with my boyfriend was a problem. I had no understanding of the holiness of God. But I went ahead and said that. Finally, the last line of the prayer was, "And I ask You to save me." After repeating those words, I turned to my friend and I said, "But this couldn't be the only way?" She looked at me and said, "It is. It is the way." The moment she said that, the anointing, the Spirit of truth — the spirit of revelation — pierced my heart. I cannot explain it. It completely bypassed every intellectual and philosophical objection, every prejudice that I had about the name of Jesus. The anointing IS the spirit of truth. And it made no sense. But I somehow knew that I was in the presence of truth and suddenly I remembered a dream that I'd had the very night before, which was really a picture of my long search for truth.

FINDING MESSIAH

I had never read the Bible, so, I didn't know that everything in the dream was in the Bible. When I finished saying this prayer, she gave me a New Testament. I had never read the book, had never even opened it. I had no idea what was in it. She said, "He's in this book. Just take this home, and as you read pray in your own words that God will show you without a shadow of doubt if this is the way." So that's what I did. I went back up to my apartment, and for the next week, every day, I couldn't put it down. I read from Matthew to Revelation, and I began to understand that it's a book written by Jewish people to Jewish people.

Then I started seeing written all of the things that were in my dream. "I am the true light that lights every man." "Satan comes as an angel of light, a counterfeit." "I'm the bread of heaven." In my dream, I had seen a picture of beggar children on their knees with their hands lifted up to heaven, begging for bread. Then at the end of the dream, a curtain was ripped from top to bottom. I was stunned to read in the scriptures that when Jesus was crucified, the curtain of the Temple was ripped to open the way to the Holy of Holies.

Camille started taking me to her congregation that met in a large music studio in Manhattan. She was a comedian, who was working with Jim Henson, creator of The Muppets (she was a very funny person!), and she was part of a gospel revival on Broadway where many people in the performing arts — actors, dancers, singers, musicians, designers and makeup artists — were coming to the Lord.

So, here's me, this Jewish girl, and I didn't have to walk into a church building and see a big cross on the wall and feel strange, because Jewish people are not comfortable walking into a church. It's very foreign to us, like we're walking into enemy territory. But the Lord was so gracious to me, to let me come into this huge music studio that the church was renting. I got gloriously, radically saved — filled with the Holy Spirit, speaking in tongues within two weeks of saying that prayer in Camille's apartment. The love of God began to stream into my life, to heal me, and set me free. Now the same joy that I had seen in my friend, I now had!

Our congregation was very multi-racial, but there was only one other Jewish girl in the congregation, and she became my best friend. I had so many questions, like, "How did our people miss it? Why didn't our rabbis tell us?" She was really there for me, and introduced me to the Song of Solomon which I had never read before. (I now have a whole album called *Israel, My Beloved* with songs based on the Song of Solomon!) As I read it, I entered into a bridal intimacy with the Lord which absolutely transformed my life. I got rid of all my New Age books and objects, and I knew without a shadow of a doubt that Yeshua is "the way, the truth, and the life."

In those early years, I was like an orphan girl. I didn't know anything about walking with the Lord. So, the Lord had to teach me, and He sent me a spiritual mother, a little black lady from Harlem, named Mother Jackson. God knit us together in a very deep way. God had given her a special love for the Jewish people that she had learned from her mother growing up in Richmond, Virginia. Her mother always said, "These Jewish people are God's people. You be good to them." Mother Jackson had never married, so, she didn't have a daughter, and the Lord knit our hearts together like mother and daughter.

She used to bring me to her church up in Harlem, and I vividly recall being the only white girl there, enthusiastically playing my tambourine, which I learned from Mother Jackson. As this newfound joy and the love of God flooded my life, I began witnessing people of all different ethnic backgrounds celebrating the Jewish Messiah. Alongside this new joy, the Lord began to release a sense of deep grief within me for my own people—a sorrow that resonated with His own heart. It felt akin to the pain when a firstborn child doesn't recognize their father. The Lord also says in Jeremiah 31:32, "I was a husband to them," but Israel has been as an unfaithful wife. There have been centuries and centuries of sorrow and grief carried by the Jewish people, and here I was, experiencing the weight of it. I had received the joy of knowing the Lord, and suddenly, I'm experiencing the pain that my own people do not know this joy, this comfort, available to them.

In an all-night prayer meeting, in this multi-racial congregation I had now become part of, the Lord dropped something into my spirit. In the middle of the night, I began weeping for the Jewish people, and out of my innermost being, I started singing the Shema: "Hear O Israel, the Lord, our God, The Lord is one" (Dt. 6:4) which every Jewish child learns. That's what's happening here in Israel during this current war with Hamas, even the most secular Jews are starting to cry out and sing the Shema. As I sang it in the middle of the night, a travail came upon me, and the Lord said to me, "I'm going to take you to the land of your inheritance, and allow you to share this gift of My love with your people."

I had never even been to Israel. New York City, for me, was the center of the universe. I had had no interest in going to Israel or living anywhere else before this happened in my heart. So now I had this promise and a burden in my heart.

MEETING DAVID DAVIS

Surprisingly, soon after, the Lord brought a non-Jewish man into my life, David Davis, who was an actor. At this point Mother Jackson had moved down from Harlem to live with me on the Upper West Side in Manhattan, and she was raising me like a little daughter in the faith. One morning she woke up and said excitedly, "The Lord just told me who you're going to marry!" But I'm thinking, "I'm going to Israel. There's probably some great Israeli believer over there for me." But I went ahead and asked her, "So, who is it?" She responded, "David Davis." And I responded, "Well, nothing is happening between us, we don't even like each other! If this is the Lord, it's going to have to be a miracle."

Two weeks later, David Davis came up to her at one of our midweek meetings (she had been mentoring him too as one of the new believers in the congregation) and asked her to go out for dinner for his birthday. I was standing there next to her, so to be polite, he said, "Oh, well, would you like to come, too?" She and I looked at each other knowing our "secret." So the three of us went out to dinner. As he and I start talking across the table Mother Jackson was unusually quiet. She normally was never quiet, because she had so many stories and testimonies of miracles the Lord had done. She was one of those people that the Word refers to as, "the poor who are rich in faith" (James 2.5). Although having nothing in this world, she was truly rich in faith, having seen and experienced God's miraculous provision and healing for her and her family for decades. So, she always had something to say, but that night she was completely quiet, as we started talking across the table. It was like we were speaking "spirit to spirit"—not at all like the typical male/female dating conversations we were both used to before coming to the Lord. We only talked about our relationship with Jesus, the things He'd been telling us in the word. Amazingly, the Lord spoke to David that night at the dinner table and said, "This is your wife." In the weeks to come we fell madly in love! God just poured His love into us for each other.

Interestingly, two months before that, the Lord had told David to get on a plane and go to Israel. At that time, he was a full professor at Fordham Lincoln Center, Chairman of the Arts department. He was also acting professionally with people like Denzel Washington and Anthony Hopkins, and also was on well-known TV shows. But one night at the pinnacle of his acting career on Broadway, he returned home to his loft apartment in New York and found himself in tears, overwhelmed by an incredible sense of emptiness. "I've achieved my dream.

What does it all mean?" he cried. That's when his earnest search for God began.

An actor friend of his took him to that same fellowship I was attending and that's where he met Jesus. He felt the Lord telling him, "Get on a plane and go to Israel." So, he bought a ticket, flew by himself, rented a car, got a map, opened his Bible, and began seeing biblical prophecy fulfilled everywhere! He also had a powerful encounter with the Lord while in Israel. When he returned to NYC, it was two months later when we had that first dinner out with Mother Jackson. We ended up getting married three months after the dinner. David eventually became an Israeli citizen, living the rest of his life here. God had this amazing plan prepared for us!

Then in 1987, David Wilkerson came back to New York City and started Times Square Church. The Lord specifically called him, saying, "I want you to come back to New York City and raise up a testimony of a church right in the middle of the city."

The Lord directed us to leave the fellowship where we were, and to be part of Times Square Church. God amazingly put us personally under the wing of David Wilkerson and he became our spiritual father. So, my husband started preaching in the Times Square Church street outreach to drug addicts. Meanwhile, he still had his professional acting career, but God was changing his heart and he was losing his desire to be in theater. All he wanted to do was preach the gospel and see lives change, so the Lord gradually called him out of show business completely, and into full-time ministry.

ISRAEL

In the summer of 1988, the two of us decided to take a trip to Israel. It was my first trip there, and both of us were undone. I cried from the moment I put my feet on the soil as we landed in Israel. I sensed deeply, "I've come home." God had already prepared David's heart too about this. At that time, the news had just broken out in the newspapers in Israel about the drug epidemic here among Jews and Arabs, and the Lord said to us, "I want you to open a house for drug addicts, and it will be for Jews and Arabs together."

We went back to New York, and David Wilkerson heard that "something happened to the Davis' in Israel," so he asked us to sit down with him, and tell him what happened. As we shared our hearts we said, "We really believe God's calling us." It witnessed with him and with others there as well. A year later, in 1989, they blessed us and sent us out. So, we packed our bags and moved to Israel and applied for citizenship. Since I had all the Jewish documentation, David, as my spouse, was also able to become an Israeli citizen. We were led to the city of Haifa because the Lord showed us that there were Jews and Arabs living in mixed neighborhoods there, and we could start our work there.

That's where I am now, decades later, sitting here in my apartment right in the middle of the city of Haifa, and our rehabilitation center called House of Victory is just five minutes down the mountain from where I live. In 1990 we started a Bible study in our living room in the apartment where we were living on the top floor of the rehab center. But before we could bring in the drug addicts, the 1st Gulf War started with Saddam Hussein sending scud missiles, targeting our city of Haifa. It was my first war. I'd never run to bomb shelters before.

After that war, we took in our first drug addict, and continued the Bible study. Every week people began filling our living room and into the kitchen and balcony. Soon it was overflowing with people and people started saying to my husband, "Please, will you start a congregation? Please will you be our pastor?" It had not even entered our minds to start a congregation.

BIRTHING A CONGREGATION

We had arrived with a specific vision to establish a residential ministry to afflicted men with backgrounds of substance abuse, but then faced the reality that at that time that there wasn't a congregation in Haifa that was open to the gifts of the Spirit where we could bring our "guys." Knowing that the power of the Holy Spirit was a major key for addicts to walk free, we knew we needed to find a congregation where we and our guys could experience the presence and moving of the Spirit. We realized that the Lord was saying, "You already have a congregation. I'm birthing it, right in front of you."

With another couple, Peter Tsukahira and his wife, we launched Kehilat HaCarmel with our first Shabbat meetings on a property on the very top of Mount Carmel, formerly owned by the Anglican church. They had an old building that was used as a retreat center, with a little upper room that they used as their chapel. In that little room our fledgling congregation started to grow. There were people all over the Haifa area hungry for the Word of God who were looking for a place where the Holy Spirit was free to move. We were carrying the message imparted to us by David Wilkerson—a message centered on the walk of holiness and the power of the Holy Spirit. And people were truly longing for this message.

Very quickly we outgrew the chapel. So the Anglicans graciously let us move downstairs to their salon, and when we outgrew that room, they let us cut big arched openings into their dining room, doubling the size of our seating. They were doing everything possible to make room for us, as we kept growing and growing, until we had nowhere to go. Eventually their board met in England, and they decided to give us the back part of their land on the property where there was nothing but a big bedrock. We were literally given the top of the mountain! This is geographically the highest point on Mount Carmel. I remember my husband saying, "If someone wants to give you the top of Mount Carmel, you should take it!"

Of course, we had no money to build a building! But we thought, "We're just going to have to believe God for this because if He's giving us the top of the mountain, surely He will provide for us to build a building." So, we joyfully received the gift, and the Lord began sending in funds from all over the world. We had over 500 volunteers from close to 50 nations come to help us build. David, with his theatrical background, always tended to see things through his sense of drama. He had also actually designed theaters in the past. So, we said, "Okay, what should this building look like? What is our script? What's the drama?"

THE VISION

The "script" we followed was 1 Kings 18, recalling Elijah's dramatic encounters on Mount Carmel. The altar of the Lord was laying in ruins, symbolizing Israel's idolatrous state, in their mixture of serving both God and Baal. Elijah performed a prophetic act by rebuilding the altar with twelve stones, restoring the Lord's altar on Mount Carmel. Subsequently, in the famous confrontation, the prophets of Baal poured water on the stones, waiting for the true God to answer by fire. It was an astonishing and pivotal confrontation. Elijah brings a short prayer, "Answer me, Lord, that this people will know that You are God in Israel." Then the Lord came and burnt up the stones and manifested Himself as "the God who answers by fire."

The Lord said to us, "I'm calling you to restore an altar of true worship of the God of Abraham, Isaac, and Jacob, and Messiah Yeshua on this mountain, and I am still the God who answers by fire." We know that God inhabits the praises of His people, and our mandate is to be a dwelling place for His Spirit. As we offer up living sacrifices on the altar, we believe He will again manifest Himself as the God who answers by fire. We pray that as Israelis walk into this sanctuary, they will experience the power and presence of God.

It says in 1 Kings 18, they fell on their faces and said, "The Lord, He is God. The Lord, He is God." That's what we're contending for; that's what we're believing the Lord for. We designed and crafted the altar using twelve large stones extracted from the bedrock of this mountain, from the piece of land allocated to us. When you enter the sanctuary, you'll see twelve large rocks encircling our round altar. We designed it with a large skylight right over the altar to represent the open heaven and the fire coming down.

The worship center is a semi-circular building with double doors around the walls. There are twelve little windows on the doors that represent the twelve stones that were on the breastplate of the priests that went into the Temple as they made offerings on behalf of the people of Israel. Our sanctuary is a place of intercession, as we function in our calling as a priesthood before the Lord. That is our nation's destiny to be a kingdom of priests — but it is also the call upon the body of Messiah worldwide. As the worship director of the congregation, I understood our position on top of this mountain, and that our worship was to be characterized by the shout of victory. We needed to be those people that can hear the joyful sound (Ps. 89:15). And so, in His faithfulness, the Lord began to pour out upon us new music that carried the sound of victory.

HOUSE OF VICTORY

This brings me to the present time. Our House of Victory rehabilitation center is still the "heartbeat" of our ministry and is going strong. The vision the Lord gave us for that program was Isaiah 58:6-7, which says

> *"Is this not the fast that I have chosen:*
> *To loose the bonds of wickedness,*
> *To undo the heavy burdens,*
> *To let the oppressed go free,*
> *And that you break every yoke?*
> *Is it not to share your bread with the hungry,*
> *And that you bring to your house the poor who are cast out;*
> *When you see the naked, that you cover him,*
> *And not hide yourself from your own flesh? (Isaiah 58:6-7)*

As we endeavor to be faithful to our founding vision, we also hold fast to the following verse that promises, "Then your light shall break forth like the morning…and the glory of the Lord shall be your rear guard" (v.8).

Over the years, we have been able to establish many other kinds of humanitarian outreaches, and all of this is in operation now during the war. We have a food and clothing distribution center called Hadar HaCarmel ("the glory of Carmel") in the lower part of Haifa. Another miracle donation given our congregation is a large conference/community center called Beit Yedidia ("house of God's friends"), located in central Haifa, close to where I live. It is currently filled with Ukrainian refugees living there. It's become a place of hope and refuge, where we are able to serve hot meals for needy people, hold outreaches to Holocaust survivors, and also offer housing for displaced people due to the Hamas war. Also many kinds of midweek Bible studies, youth meetings, and discipleship training sessions are taking place at Beit Yedidia.

At the top of the mountain, we are called to be a "house of prayer for all nations" (Isaiah 56:7) and we are open to receive intercessors and worshippers from the nations to stand with us on behalf of the salvation of Israel, and to join with us in piercing the darkness with prophetic praise in our ongoing intercessory worship watches. Carved out of the bedrock under our sanctuary, is our Elijah Prayer Cave where we also hope to multiply our watches in the future.

A SHIELD OF FAITH

As we stand on the top of Mount Carmel and "launch" our declarations in songs of praise and adoration, our worship becomes a "shield of faith" to hold back the "fiery darts of the enemy," (Ephesians 6:16), which in our case are the deadly rockets of Hezbollah aimed at us from our northern border.

Our "one new man" worship team is comprised of Jews and Arabs and other Gentiles. The Lord has called us to build unity in the body in the Land through worship and we endeavor to be pro-active in initiating events where we can worship together as Jews and Arabs in the land.

In the Nazareth area in Galilee, there is a wonderful house of prayer led by Rania Sayegh called HOPE (House of Prayer and Exploits) with young "on fire" spirit-filled Israeli Arab believers, who also understand the prophetic scriptures regarding the nation of Israel. Since the October 7 massacre by Hamas, they have been meeting almost every night, interceding for the hostages, IDF soldiers, and the people of Gaza, and standing as watchmen on guard over our northern border. We have just come together with them recently in our worship center on Mt

Carmel to unite in worship, in Arabic and Hebrew, to intercede pre-emptively to thwart the enemy's fiery attacks from the northern border. These attacks are particularly targeted at Haifa as one of the major cities in northern Israel, but the impact would extend across Galilee, affecting everyone in the region.

ONE NEW MAN

The term "one new man" of Ephesians Chapter 2, as mentioned earlier, holds a profound significance for us, particularly reflecting the unity between Jew and Arab in this land. Through the blood of Jesus, He dismantled the enmity between us, fashioning us into a singular entity—a new and unified identity. We have felt God's heart for this, and it had been a mandate very specifically for our congregation. This is particularly critical now for all of us as the body of Messiah in the Land to operate as the "ekklesia" in the authority that flows from true unity.

Many Israeli Arabs who have embraced faith in Yeshua still find it difficult to grapple with what scripture says about Israel. Each of us carries our own historical narratives, having experienced numerous conflicts and adversities. I remember an incident from the early years when an Arab drug addict from the Old City of Jerusalem, who had been involved in terrorist activities targeting Israeli policemen, found salvation through our program. Remarkably, with great trepidation he entered our House of Victory where Jewish Israeli men–his "enemy—were also struggling with substance abuse. But there he met and surrendered his life to Jesus and the love of God filled his heart for these Jewish men who were now becoming his brothers in the Lord.

The same thing happens when a Jewish drug addict finds the love of Jesus. It's only through the love of God that we're able to forgive and true reconciliation takes place. We can't do that in our own nature. As a Jew when you've had your people blown up in terrorist attacks, it's very hard to love Arabs, and this is a genuine struggle for Jewish Israelis. For the Israeli Arabs, some of their families lost property in the Independence War in 1948 and many of them have grown up hating the Jews, hearing the stories from their grandparents. However, when we function as the unified "one new man" in this land, the Lord summons His body to step into our role as a kingdom of priests. As the "ekklesia," we take up the weapons of our spiritual warfare which include the mighty weapons of praise and worship. When we're proclaiming the scriptures in song, we're piercing and pushing back the darkness. Even when we dance with joyful Israeli dancing, it's "celebration warfare." We're putting the enemy under our feet, claiming victory over the enemy, victory of light over darkness.

We had the most incredible worship time recently in one of our monthly Rosh Chodesh celebrations, which mark the beginning of a new month in the biblical calendar. Just as we observe weekly Shabbats, the Bible speaks about the new moons which are the monthly cycle. For the past couple of years, we've begun incorporating into our annual rhythm these monthly celebrations and worship nights. This particular Rosh Chodesh fell during Hanukkah, the Festival of Lights, in the midst of the current Hamas war. Our kids participated like a mighty spiritual army, raising gorgeous banners, dancing, and proclaiming scriptures about the victory of light over darkness.

At this difficult time, our children learning how to throw off fear. Much of the warfare we have to deal with is also our own hearts. We need to drive out our own discouragement, hopelessness, and despair, in the face of the enemy. We see the whole world turning against us now. We see what appears to be an impossible situation. Many of our kids are traumatized in the process. In reality our whole nation is in trauma right now.

THE WARRIOR BRIDE

The term "warrior bride" was impressed upon my spirit by the Lord while I was producing my album called "The Lord Roars from Zion." The subtitle of that album is "Songs of the Warrior Bride." It was while working on that album that this phrase came to me. To be a warrior bride describes what we're called to as the body of Messiah—resting in our Beloved, and warring in the Spirit. The deep, intimate connection with the Lord as His bride serves as the bedrock of our relationship with Him, as well as the cornerstone of any ministry we engage in. It is in the secret place with Him where we receive impartation directly from His presence.

The scripture says, "strength and beauty are in His sanctuary," so as we commune with Him and come into that secret place, we're clothed with strength and then we emerge enabled to engage in the battles. Because we are in the end times, everything seems to be accelerating, with the "birth pangs" getting stronger. We need to understand our fundamental identity as the bride of Messiah, preparing the way for His return. We want to bring as many people as we can into the kingdom to be part of that bridal company. There are battles to be fought all the way to the end, that will require great perseverance. We must balance between resting and warring, or we won't be able to "run the race with endurance" (Hebrews 12:1) if we're not resting in the Beloved.

The Gentile church worldwide is being called to play a role in the narrative of the redemption of the Jewish people, beckoning the Jewish bride back to the Lord God of Israel, her husband. This task will necessitate collaboration between Jewish and Gentile believers. Personally, my encounter with faith occurred as a result of being stirred to jealousy by my Gentile friend Camille in New York City. Observing the life of Jesus manifested through her stirred something within me that I had never seen before. Everything else was just misconceptions about who Jesus was until I saw the living Jesus in her life even though she never preached to me until the day I knocked on her door. It was amazing.

It says in Romans 11:11; "That the Gentiles branches who were grafted in to the tree of Israel, have been called to provoke the Jewish people to jealousy." With what's going on right now in this war, and as anti-Semitism rages in the nations, the Lord is drawing a plumb line in His body with regard to how we treat Israel. More than ever before this is a time for the Gentile church to show the face of Jesus toward the Jewish people, and not be part of the demonic movement to "wipe Israel off the map."

BEHOLDING HIS GLORY

The closing track on my *Yeshua* album, one of my earlier albums, is called "Behold His Glory." It's a very short song based on Psalm 27:4 and 2 Corinthians 3:18:

> *My desire, my one desire,*
> *Is to behold Him*
> *To behold the beauty of the Lord, "Noam Adonai"*
> *And to dwell in His temple all the days of my life*
> *And that we may all, with unveiled face,*
> *Behold His glory*
> *And we shall be changed*
> *by the Spirit of the Lord.*

We will go "from glory to glory" and "strength to strength" (Psalm 84:7) because we've been in the presence of the Lord, transformed by reflecting His image.

When we move forward in answer to the call of the Lord, we only need to be obedient to take the first steps He shows us. I never could have fathomed how far the Lord has brought us, all that He has accomplished as we've tried to remain faithful to the "heavenly vision." Over my 35 years in Israel, I've witnessed tremendous growth in the body, new congregations, so many new evangelistic endeavors, including various online outreach videos resulting in many Israelis finding faith in the Lord.

The ongoing war and trauma is causing Israelis to question, "Where's our hope?" "Where is our security?" While we fervently pray for our IDF's victory and protection over the Land, we all recognize that it's "against all odds" and beyond our human capability. Many who haven't sought God before are now earnestly calling out to Him. We are believing the words of Jeremiah 29:13, that they will seek Him and find Him when they seek Him with all of their hearts.

(Karen Davis is Co-Founder and Worship Director at Kehilat HaCarmel, https://www.carmelcongregation.org.il/ a Messianic congregation located on the top of Mount Carmel, Israel, where her late husband David served as Founding/Senior Pastor for 25 years. https://karendavisworship.com)

CHAPTER 4
PROPHETIC VISION
BY DAVID DAVIS

Where there is no revelation, the people cast off restraint. (Proverbs 29:18)

Revelation means "prophetic vision." Revelation only results from a consistent intimate fellowship with God. Paul prayed for the church that we would receive revelation, or "all wisdom and spiritual understanding. (Colossians 1:9) The difference between gathering information and receiving divine revelation is of the utmost importance. Without prophetic vision we will be lost in a spiritual wilderness or "perish" (KJV). To be "prophetic" simply means to understand what is in God's heart now-the-hour in which we live.

Our vision needs to be continually updated with God's purposes. What is God saying now? The New Testament consistently teaches that the fundamental nature of life in the Spirit involves a disclosure of spiritual "mysteries" that cannot be fully comprehended by human intellect. Prophetic revelation is the antithesis of humanism. God's mysteries can only be spiritually discerned, or revealed by the Spirit. For instance, Jesus called the kingdom of God "the mystery." (Mark 4:11) His kingdom was being revealed to His disciples. A biblical mystery is a secret or hidden truth that can only be known by revelation. Paul wrote of the "mystery of God," (Colossians 2:2) as well as the mystery of the Church, (Ephesians 3:3), and the mystery of Israel. (Romans 11:25)

It has been said that the longest distance between two points is the distance between the head and the heart. In these last days we desperately need to move from information to revelation—or from the preconceived to the prophetic.

(Davis, David. *The Elijah Legacy*. Alachua, FL: Bridge Logos Foundation, 2009. Pages 2-3.)

CHAPTER 5
A FATHER WOUND

For this reason I bow my knees to the Father of our Lord Jesus Christ, from whom the whole family in heaven and earth is named. (Ephesians 3:14-15)

ISHMAEL'S WOUND

"Imagine you are fourteen years old, dearly beloved by your father. One morning you wake up, and your father whom you adore, gives you a piece of bread and some water and sends you away from your home, away from his presence, forever. Overnight, you are left alone, homeless and fatherless; left to wander in the desert; left to hunger and thirst, left to die. That was Ishmael's experience after the birth of Isaac.

What was the level of pain triggered in Ishmael's heart that day? What were the kinds of questions that went through his mind? How intense were the emotions of confusion, betrayal and abandonment? Abraham's decision must have broken his heart. It must have created a very deep "father wound": a wound of separation from the father he no longer had and a wound of longing to return home, to be with family again.

Perhaps the only thing that made sense to him at that moment was that the source of all his pain was this new little baby. It was his fault. Hatred and revenge must have been bearing down on his heart. Perhaps he may have even had thoughts like, "One day, I will come back, get rid of this new baby and take back my inheritance."

MIDDLE EASTERN WOUND

Doesn't this sound like the sentiment within the Middle East today? Doesn't this resonate with the cries rising from the Israeli/Palestinian conflict? Perhaps, what is happening there today is, in some part, a manifestation of that ancient wound that was opened in Ishmael's heart thousands of years ago; a wound that is, unfortunately, still bleeding in the hearts of millions.

I believe that this "father wound" manifests itself later with the pillar of Islam, denying the Fatherhood of God and the Sonship of Jesus Christ. One of the most foundational verses in the Qur'an, called by many as the 'Essence of the Quran", states, "God is one. He is absolute; He has not given birth and was not born, nor does He have an equal." This is not only a statement of monotheism, but emphasizes that God is not, nor can He be approached as, a father-the exact opposite of the essence of the gospel!" [1]

ISHMAEL'S LETTER TO ISAAC

I was born of the bondwoman, and the law cast me out, but the grace of Jesus Christ has brought me in. I was deprived the blessing of Abraham, but now in Messiah Jesus, I am the seed of

Abraham, and an heir according to the promise in Galatians 3:29.

Oh, I grew up without a father in the wilderness, but now your God is my Father. I had no inheritance from my father, but now I have obtained an inheritance that you have not, because I am a son and an heir of God through Christ.

I received the righteousness of the law without the law through faith (Romans 3:21-28). And to you was the glory revealed on the mount through the face of Moses, but to me the exceeding glory is unveiled in the face of Jesus.

To you was given the ministration of condemnation, but to me the ministration of righteousness. Is it not time that we should believe in the same God, and the Messiah He sent to us. Let's get together, and be brothers and sisters in Christ. [2]

> *Behold what manner of love the Father has bestowed on us, that we should be called children of God! (1 John 3:1a)*

---

1. (Shadi. *Israel Born in Egypt Raised in Iran*. London, UK.: PublishU, 2023. Pages 76-78.)
2. By Steven Masood

CHAPTER 6
ALEXANDER THE GREAT VISITS JERUSALEM

The king's heart is in the hand of the Lord, Like the rivers of water; He turns it wherever He wishes. (Proverbs 21:1)

Alexander the Great spared Jerusalem in his conquest of the Middle East, and allowed the Jews to continue their ceremonial laws. The following is the historical account.

"SIEGES OF TYRE AND GAZA"

So, Alexander came into Syria and took Damascus. When he had obtained Sidon, he besieged Tyre, when he sent all epistle to the Jewish high priest, to send him some auxiliaries, and to supply his army with provisions; and that what presents he formerly sent to Darius, he would now send to him, and choose the friendship of the Macedonians, and that he should never repent of so doing.

But the high priest (in Jerusalem) answered the messengers, that he had given his oath to Darius not to bear arms against him.

Additionally, he said that he would not transgress this while Darius was in the land of the living. Upon hearing this answer, Alexander was very angry. Though he determined not to leave Tyre, which was just ready to be taken, yet as soon as he had taken it, he threatened that he would make an expedition against the Jewish high priest, and through him teach all men to whom they must keep their oaths.

So, when he (Alexander the Great) had, with a good deal of pains during the siege, taken Tyre, and had settled its affairs, he came to the city of Gaza, and besieged both the city and him that was governor of the garrison, whose name was Babemeses.

JOURNEY TO JERUSALEM

Now Alexander, when he had taken Gaza, made haste to go up to Jerusalem. Jaddua the high priest, when he heard that, was in an agony, and under terror, as not knowing how he should meet the Macedonians, since the King was displeased at his foregoing disobedience.

He (Jaddua) therefore ordained that the people should make supplications, and should join with him in offering sacrifice to God, whom he besought to protect that nation, and to deliver them from the perils that were coming upon them.

Whereupon God warned him in a dream, which came upon him after he had offered sacrifice, that he should take courage, and adorn the city, and open the gates. He was also told that the rest should appear in white garments, but that he and the priests should meet the King in the habits proper to their order, without the dread of any ill consequences, which the providence of God would prevent. Upon which, when he rose from his sleep, he greatly rejoiced, and declared to all the warning he had received from God.

And when he (Alexander) understood that he was not far from the city, he went out in procession, with the priests and the multitude of the citizens. The procession was venerable, and the manner of it different from that of other nations. It reached to a place called Sapha, which name, translated into Greek, signifies a prospect, for you have thence a prospect both of Jerusalem and of the temple.

And when the Phoenicians and the Chaldeans that followed him thought they should have liberty to plunder the city, and torment the high priest to death, which the king's displeasure fairly promised them, the very reverse of it happened.

MEETING THE HIGH PRIEST

For Alexander, when he saw the multitude at a distance, in white garments, while the priests stood clothed with fine linen, and the high priest in purple and scarlet clothing, with his mitre on his head, having the golden plate whereon the name of God was engraved, he approached by himself, and adored that name, and first saluted the high priest. The Jews also did all together, with one voice, salute Alexander, and encompass him about; whereupon the kings of Syria and the rest were surprised at what he had done and supposed him disordered in his mind.

DANIEL'S PROPHECIES

And when he (Alexander) had given the high priest his right hand, the priests ran along by him, and he came into the city. And when he went up into the temple, he offered sacrifice to God, according to the high priest's direction, and magnificently treated both the high priest and the priests.

And when the Book of Daniel was showed to him, wherein Daniel declared that one of the Greeks should destroy the empire of the Persians, he supposed that himself was the person intended. And as he was then glad, he dismissed the multitude for the present. The next day he called them to him, and bid them ask what favors they pleased of him; whereupon the high priest desired that they might enjoy the laws of their forefathers and might pay no tribute on the seventh year. He granted all they desired.

And when they entreated him (Alexander) that he would permit the Jews in Babylon and Media to enjoy their own laws also, he willingly promised to do hereafter what they desired. And when he said to the multitude, that if any of them would enlist themselves in his army, on this condition, that they should continue under the laws of their forefathers, and live according to them, he was willing to take them with him, many were ready to accompany him in his wars.

So, when Alexander had thus settled matters at Jerusalem, he led his army into the neighboring cities." [1]

After Alexander met the High Priest, he "offered sacrifice to God according the High Priest's direction," (Flavius Josephus) and he afforded them to right to live according to the laws of Moses. This was God's hand at work to prepare the Jewish people for the coming of their Messiah.

---

1. (https://www.biblestudy.org/bibleref/antiquities-of-jews/alexander-the-great-visits-jerusalem.html)

CHAPTER 7
ALIYAH
BY JOSIE SILVER, NOVEMBER 20, 2023

*I am the L*ORD*, and there is no other;*
I form the light and create darkness,
I make peace and create calamity;
*I, the L*ORD*, do all these things.' (Isaiah 45:6b-7)*

October 7, 2023, Israel experienced, a calamity, and so I am assuming, that there is a reason for this calamity. Because God said, I am the Lord that do all these things." He certainly knows about it, and maybe He has allowed it, therefore there is a reason, I believe there will be redemption from this calamity and another season of peace that will settle on Israel again.

Aliyah cannot be separated from Israel, salvation, and the return of Messiah. I personally believe that there will be a huge wave of Aliyah, a return of Jewish people coming from Europe and America primarily, in these coming days, and maybe within the next year, because of what we see happening all over the world since October 7, 2023

The global hatred of Jews is a virulent hatred, and the attempted acts of harm, destruction, even death, and acts of terror towards God's people is called anti-Semitism. Avner Boskey describes it as "a war between the god of Islam and the God of Israel." It seems the Islamic spirit has risen up, it's awakened, across the whole world, like never before.

I believe that Jews are actually safer here in Israel. That sounds really ironic, considering everything that is going on, and even could be seen as a bit crazy. We could see it as a modern day "Jabotinsky warning." Before the outbreak of the Second World War, Ze'ev Jabotinsky warned that the Jewish people were facing destruction and called to the Diaspora Jewry to "exterminate the Diaspora before it exterminated them." Now is the time to pack up and come home while they can.

This requires prayer, because our people really still don't want to come back. I don't want to see my people being harmed out there in the nations, but it is becoming a very real possibility.

We were in Montreal, Canada a few years ago, and our host took us to the local Jewish community. I was initially completely impressed. It had everything there that you could imagine! The Jewish people in this area could live there it was so good. As I was walking around, and thinking how amazing it was, I was apprehended by the Holy Spirit, and as clear as day, I heard the Holy Spirit say to me, "It's a trap!" And immediately, I knew what it meant. It's a trap because Jews outside of Israel feel safe in these Jewish communities because they've got everything there that they need. It's like little Israel in their city, or their town, or their community, and they can hide in there and be Jewish.

However, I believe these communities are going to be attacked. God forbid, and we pray that they won't be, but they could be a target just like the kibbutzim were a target on October 7, 2023.

These communities are dangerous, and they are a trap.

This is a point of prayer that those Jews who are feeling safe in these communities will now not feel safe. I've heard Jewish people in America say, they don't feel safe anywhere now. So, it is time to "Come home."

I can't tell people to come back to Israel, to make Aliyah. It's got to be a God experience. It's got to be something that's been awakened in the spirit of the person.

I was with an Israeli friend this morning, and she's asking questions "Where is God? Why do the Jews have to suffer so much? It's difficult being a Jew today. It's not safe out there." She doesn't want to travel anymore. And I said to her, "We are safer here." She agreed with that, that we are safer here.

Her son-in-law had gone to Europe last week on a business trip. They were a delegation of five Israelis, and when they arrived in their place of business, they were greeted by Israeli security.

They were told by the Israeli security when they were taken back to the hotel in the evening, do not go outside at night, or in the morning. They were there for five nights. They could not go out in the morning or in the night to enjoy the city. They were picked up in the morning and returned in the evening by Israeli security.

A friend's son-in-law had been in Italy prior to October 7, 2023, also on a business trip. They walked around at night enjoying, sitting in cafes and restaurants, no problem.

Everything has changed now out there in the world for Jewish people. It's time to come home.

Pray daily for the Zionist dream, desire and witness to awaken, in Jewish people around the world, and to consider, make inquiries, about returning to their God given homeland.

In Psalm 137:1, it says:

> *By the rivers of Babylon,*
> *There we sat down, yea, we wept*
> *When we remembered Zion.*
> *We hung our harps*
> *Upon the willows in the midst of it.*
> *For there those who carried us away captive asked of us a song,*
> *And those who plundered us requested mirth,*
> *Saying, "Sing us one of the songs of Zion!"*

Jews are weeping today when they think about or remember Zion (Israel). They are remembering their nation, and what is happening there.

I thought about the terrorists and the plunderers in the kibbutzim who committed those murderous acts. They were so happy and so joyful, and laughing like it was a wedding party, like it was a birthday party, like they were at a comedy show. I believe there are plunderers out there today who are laughing at and mocking the Jewish people, and making their plans.

Today is unlike other times in the history of the Jewish people, when Jewish refugees sought asylum from oppression and destruction, but were turned away by many nations and sent back to the gas chambers.

Today we have a homeland, Israel, given by God Himself for every Jewish person to come and dwell in.

Our people need to come home.

I will bring back the captives of My people Israel;
They shall build the waste cities and inhabit them;
They shall plant vineyards and drink wine from them;
They shall also make gardens and eat fruit from them.
I will plant them in their land,
And no longer shall they be pulled up
From the land I have given them,"
Says the Lord your God. (Amos 9:14-15)

CHAPTER 8
AN ETERNAL PEOPLE

And I will establish My covenant between Me and you and your descendants after you in their generations, for an everlasting covenant, to be God to you and your descendants after you. (Genesis 17:7)

"All things are mortal but the Jew. All other forces pass, but he remains." (Mark Twain)

"We are an eternal people

Because we have an eternal God

Who wrote and gave us an eternal word

And gave us an eternal homeland

And who gave us an eternal kingdom

And who gave us an eternal language

And who gave us an eternal city

Who gave us eternal headquarters

And who gave us an eternal hope

And who gave us eternal promises

And who gave us an eternal future

And who gave us an eternal covenant

That cannot be destroyed crushed or removed

And gave the eternal Messiah to Israel and the whole world

So, El-Shaddai, we say that You are the eternal keeper, the eternal guardian of Israel, the Holy One." (Josie Silver)

CHAPTER 9
ANGELS SURROUND THEM

The people who sat in darkness have seen a great light, And upon those who sat in the region and shadow of death Light has dawned. (Matthew 4:16)

In the midst of Israel's intensifying war with hell's fury that is burning through Jihadi blood-thirsty Islam, His heavenly light is shining in the darkest of places.

The following is a translation and retelling of a personal testimony of a believing Messianic wife and mother whose family lived in one of the worst hit Israeli communities along the Gaza border.

On Saturday morning, October 7th, a third of their village's population was slaughtered, mutilated, beheaded, burned alive and raped in their homes while countless others including babies, children and the elderly were violently grabbed and taken into the Hamas dungeons of Gaza where no one has seen or heard from them since. This is her story retold:

"We got up in the early morning hours because of the sounds of missile explosions all around us. After a while, during a brief calm when the missile launches stopped, we checked our son's room who was next to ours while hearing gunshots outside the home. We could not believe that it was happening in our own home kibbutz, and tried to lay low until help came.

By around 7:30 AM, we received a message from the kibbutz' security team that Hamas terrorists had broken into the community and were ravaging homes. Being a disciple of Jesus and part of a regional prayer circle, I began sending urgent prayer requests to my prayer group chat room. Everyone was asking, "Where is the army? Why isn't anyone coming to help us?"

As soon as her prayer group began to cry out to God, at the very same moment, she felt like "something" enveloped her and she started to pray and raise her hands to heaven in adoration. Going back to her mobile phone to check on other communities around them, she realized how widespread the attack was as other kibbutzim in the region also were reporting gruesome attacks and mayhem. With no immediate help arriving, the only option was to lay low and hide.

"Watching a live stream through our home security cameras, we saw that at around 10:30 AM a number of armed terrorists came near our house. Roaming and pillaging the neighborhood, it seemed as if these murderers were moving in a different direction and away from the house, but then they turned back toward us. We heard them hollering and singing wildly outside our windows, and then there was a big bang inside the house and we understood that the terrorists had broken in and were inside our home.

At that very moment, as danger was nearing, I sensed God's deep peace rising in my heart, so much so that I couldn't feel any fear at all. My unbelieving husband was bewildered and fear stricken, knowing that the door to our in-house bomb shelter (which served as their make-shift safe room that morning) was not the standard bomb-shelter bullet-proof door."

As many Israelis do during seasons of calm when there is no war, they had removed the heavy metal door and stored it elsewhere while replacing it by a standard regular door that was easier to handle but offered no protection at all.

"I continued to send messages to my prayer group, asking them to continue praying in light of the family's worsening situation. Based on the number of horrifying messages arriving from neighboring settlements, we understood that there was no one coming to rescue us and that our family was facing armed Jihadi murderous terrorists on our own.

Still hiding in our safe-room, I could see through the security cameras that the terrorists, now inside, were busy opening the fridge looking for food, demolishing furniture, and rummaging through closets for loot. Then, one of the armed brutes approached our son's room, next to the room we were hiding in, so we quickly sent him a phone message to stay very quiet so as to not draw any attention to himself. That terrorist never entered our son's room though he stood in front of his door, looking straight at it...

Another one of the terrorists now approached our shelter, stood right in front of it and looked at the fragile door we hid behind, yet he didn't touch the handle or try to open the door. It was then that I realized what was actually happening. The Hamas invaders had opened every possible door in the house looking to slaughter our family, except the doors to our rooms. It was as if God had blinded them, and though they were looking straight at the doors leading to our rooms, they could not see them at all.

The terrorists stayed in the house, pillaging and destroying our belongings for another forty minutes before they left to continue the massacre elsewhere."

Sometime later, according to this praying mother, Israeli forces arrived to fight and overtake the burning and ruined village from the remaining Hamas forces. When the family finally heard Hebrew spoken outside, they came out miraculously safe. Thanks be to God!

(Reuven Doron Prayer Report November 3 2023)

CHAPTER 10
ARROWS

*Behold, children are a heritage from the Lord,
The fruit of the womb is a reward.
Like arrows in the hand of a warrior,
So are the children of one's youth.
Happy is the man who has his quiver full of them;
They shall not be ashamed,
But shall speak with their enemies in the gate. (Psalm 127:3-5)*

*Out of the mouth of babes and nursing infants
You have ordained strength,
Because of Your enemies,
That You may silence the enemy and the avenger. (Psalm 8:2)*

But Jesus called them to Him and said, "Let the little children come to Me, and do not forbid them; for of such is the kingdom of God. Assuredly, I say to you, whoever does not receive the kingdom of God as a little child will by no means enter it." (Luke 18:16-17)

. . .

Children are precious to the Lord, and they are an integral part of His army. They wield mighty weapons in His hand as they worship and pray from their heart. By virtue of their innocence and purity of heart, God is giving them prophetic dreams, visions and songs of praise. Like Samuel, although he was young when he learned to hear the voice of God, God gave him "adult quality revelations" of Himself. Like Elyana, who wrote the following song when she was 11 years old.

ALLEGIANCE

I love You with my weak love

Knowing Yours is stronger than death

I surrender my indifferent heart

Cause I know that your ways are best

I pledge allegiance to my King

The One who created everything

So, I will worship Him alone

'Til He comes down or takes me home

Teach me how to be a lover

Of your burning heart's desires

Jesus, Helper, Savior, Friend

Help me walk them out 'til the end

I/We will live for You alone,

because you are my/our all.

I/We will give everything,

to stand beside you Lord

We pledge allegiance to our King

The One who created everything

So, we will worship Him alone

'Til He comes down or takes us home

(https://www.youtube.com/watch?v=QrblKNfb82I)

CHAPTER 11
AS THE NATIONS HAVE DONE TO ISRAEL

> *Now the Lord had said to Abram: "Get out of your country, From your family And from your father's house, To a land that I will show you. I will make you a great nation; I will bless you and make your name great; And you shall be a blessing.* **I will bless those who bless you, And I will curse him who curses you;** *And in you all the families of the earth shall be blessed." (Genesis 12:1-3)*

God's word is immutable, and forever settled in heaven. (Psalm 119:89). He has magnified His word above all His name. (Psalm 138:2) God cannot lie, He cannot change, and He has made a covenant with Abraham and his seed that will never be rescinded. He has sworn to bless those who bless Abraham's descendants, and to curse those who curse them. In fact, Jesus said:

> *For assuredly, I say to you, till heaven and earth pass away, one jot (the smallest Hebrew letter yad) or one tittle (a small*

part of the Hebrew letter shin) will by no means pass from the law till all is fulfilled. (Matthew 5:18)

The Prophet Jeremiah stated that His covenant with the seed of Abraham is as binding as His commitment to the entire universe:

Thus says the Lord,
Who gives the sun for a light by day,
The ordinances of the moon and the stars for a light by night,
Who disturbs the sea,
And its waves roar
(The Lord of hosts is His name):
"If those ordinances depart
From before Me, says the Lord,
Then the seed of Israel shall also cease
From being a nation before Me forever." (Jeremiah 36:35-36)

It is clear in Scripture that the Lord Himself would scatter the nation of Israel and disperse them among the nations because of their disobedience to Him. And among these nations, they would be persecuted and find no rest.

"Then the Lord will scatter you among all peoples, from one end of the earth to the other, and there you shall serve other gods, which neither you nor your fathers have known — wood and stone. And among those nations you shall find no rest, nor shall the sole of your foot have a resting place; but there the Lord will give you a trembling heart, failing eyes, and anguish of soul. Your life shall hang in doubt before you; you shall fear day and night, and have no assurance of life. (Deuteronomy 28:64-66)

Yet God would judge the nations that abused the Jewish people and preserve the Jewish people through it all.

> *Therefore do not fear, O My servant Jacob,' says the Lord,*
> *'Nor be dismayed, O Israel;*
> *For behold, I will save you from afar,*
> *And your seed from the land of their captivity.*
> *Jacob shall return, have rest and be quiet,*
> *And no one shall make him afraid.*
> *For I am with you,' says the Lord, 'to save you;*
> *Though I make a full end of all nations where I have*
> *scattered you, Yet I will not make a complete end of you.*
> *But I will correct you in justice,*
> *And will not let you go altogether*
> *unpunished.' (Jeremiah 30:10-11)*

God would then correct the Jewish people, and restore them to their land:

> *Again the word of the Lord came to me: 'Son of man, when the people of Israel were living in their own land, they defiled it by their conduct and their actions. Their conduct was like a woman's monthly uncleanness in my sight. So I poured out my wrath on them because they had shed blood in the land and because they had defiled it with their idols. I dispersed them among the nations, and they were scattered through the countries; I judged them according to their conduct and their actions. And wherever they went among the nations they profaned my holy name, for it was said of them, "These are the Lord's people, and yet they had to leave his land." I had concern for my holy name, which the people of Israel profaned among the nations where they had gone.*
>
> *'Therefore say to the Israelites, "This is what the Sovereign Lord says: it is not for your sake, people of Israel, that I am going to do these*

> *things, but for the sake of my holy name, which you have profaned among the nations where you have gone. I will show the holiness of my great name, which has been profaned among the nations, the name you have profaned among them. Then the nations will know that I am the Lord, declares the Sovereign Lord, when I am proved holy through you before their eyes. '"For I will take you out of the nations; I will gather you from all the countries and bring you back into your own land"'. (Ezekiel 36:16-24)*

And after being restored to the Land, they will return to their God and Messiah in the latter days.

> *For the Israelites will live many days without king or prince, without sacrifice or sacred stones, without ephod or household gods. Afterward the Israelites will return and seek the Lord their God and David their king. They will come trembling to the Lord and to his blessings in the last days. (Hosea 3:4-5)*

We are seeing this take place before our eyes! Let's take a brief look through history to see how this has played out.

"Most of Europe severely persecuted the Jews during the Middle Ages. At that point in history, Europe was fractured, largely ignorant, and in constant turmoil. It suffered from devastating plagues and produced little of cultural or intellectual significance.

In the Islamic world, Jews found peace, security, and respect during the Middle Ages. Is it a coincidence that this was the "Golden Age of Islam?"

The British Empire was friendly toward the Jews and even helped to lay the foundation for a Jewish national home in Israel. Two years after signing the Balfour Declaration, it reached its zenith. It was the world's largest empire, "...on which the sun never set."

But after World War I and during World War II, Britain turned its back on the Jews and its promise to us. Between 1945 and 1965, the number of people under British rule outside the UK itself fell from 700 million to 5 million. The once great British Empire became known as "the sick man of Europe." [1]

There are many other examples of nations rising and falling based on their treatment of the Jewish people. In Biblical days, Egypt experienced great blessing and were divinely given a plan to prosper during a time of drought, resulting in their world dominance which was based on the favor that Pharaoh showed to Joseph and the Sons of Israel. Yet a generation later, they suffered a thorough threshing by the Lord through Moses for their mistreatment of the selfsame Sons of Israel.

There are many other examples in history, for example, "In the fifteenth and sixteenth centuries Spain was the dominant nation in Europe, with a high level of culture, a powerful army and navy and an empire that spanned both hemispheres. Within a century of expelling all Jews from her territories, Spain declined to a struggling, second-rate power." [2]

> *For thus says the Lord of hosts: "He sent Me after glory, to the nations which plunder you; for he who touches you touches the apple of His eye. (Zechariah 2:8)*

What about the United States? Haven't they been favorable to the Jewish people? Yes and No. The United States has blessed the Jewish people since its inception more than any other modern nation. During these times, the United States has experienced unparalleled economic and social prosperity and military strength. For example, when President Harry Truman supported the establishment of the State of Israel in 1947, American grew to become the greatest and wealthiest superpower of the Twentieth Century.

However, in recent years, as U.S. administrations have pressured Israel to institute the failed policy of "land for peace," America has become the world's largest debtor nation, their society is in a state of disrepair, they have suffered humiliation in recent military campaigns, and has experienced massive natural disasters.

Historian and author John P. McTernan states, "There is a direct correlation between the alarming number of massive disasters striking America and her leaders pressuring to surrender her land for 'peace.' Costing hundreds of lives and causing hundreds of billions of dollars' worth of damage, dozens of disasters, including devastating earthquakes, raging fires, hurricanes, floods, tsunamis, and tornadoes, have hit America-and always within twenty-four hours of putting pressure on Israel." [3]

When will the nations learn that God is an unmovable force, and He has purposed from all eternity to set His throne in Zion where Messiah will rule all the nations with a rod of iron? (Revelation 12:5)

> *Why do the nations rage,*
> *And the people plot a vain thing?*
> *The kings of the earth set themselves,*
> *And the rulers take counsel together,*
> *Against the Lord and against His Anointed, saying,*
> *"Let us break Their bonds in pieces*
> *And cast away Their cords from us."*
>
> *He who sits in the heavens shall laugh;*

> *The Lord shall hold them in derision.*
> *Then He shall speak to them in His wrath,*
> *And distress them in His deep displeasure:*
> *"Yet I have set My King*
> *On My holy hill of Zion." (Psalm 2:1-4)*

Messiah will return and set up His kingdom from Jerusalem:

> *And in that day His feet will stand on the Mount of Olives, which faces Jerusalem on the east. (Zechariah 14:4a)*

> *And in the days of these kings the God of heaven will set up a kingdom which shall never be destroyed; and the kingdom shall not be left to other people; it shall break in pieces and consume all these kingdoms, and it shall stand forever. (Daniel 2:44)*

> *Then shall enter the gates of this city kings and princes sitting on the throne of David, riding in chariots and on horses, they and their princes, accompanied by the men of Judah and the inhabitants of Jerusalem; and this city shall remain forever. And they shall come from the cities of Judah and from the places around Jerusalem, from the land of Benjamin and from the lowland, from the mountains and from the South, bringing burnt offerings and sacrifices, grain offerings and incense, bringing sacrifices of praise to the house of the Lord. (Jeremiah 17:25-26)*

> *Then the seventh angel sounded: And there were loud voices in heaven, saying, "The kingdoms of this world have become the kingdoms of our Lord and of His Christ, and He shall reign forever and ever!" (Revelation 11:15)*

Whoever tries to contradict His plan or move His established borders will be broken.

> "Behold, I will make Jerusalem a cup of drunkenness to all the surrounding peoples, when they lay siege against Judah and Jerusalem. And it shall happen in that day that I will make Jerusalem a very heavy stone for all peoples; all who would heave it away will surely be cut in pieces, though all nations of the earth are gathered against it." (Zechariah 12:2-3)

And God will enter into judgement with any nation that tries to divide His land:

> I will also gather all nations, And bring them down to the Valley of Jehoshaphat; And I will enter into judgment with them there On account of My people, My heritage Israel, Whom they have scattered among the nations; They have also divided up My land. (Joel 3:2)

At the end of the Age, God will judge between the sheep and the goat nations based on how they have treated God's people Israel.

> "When the Son of Man comes in His glory, and all the holy angels with Him, then He will sit on the throne of His glory. All the nations will be gathered before Him, and He will separate them one from another, as a shepherd divides his sheep from the goats. And He will set the sheep on His right hand, but the goats on the left. Then the King will say to those on His right hand, 'Come, you blessed of My

> *Father, inherit the kingdom prepared for you from the foundation of the world. (Matthew 25:31-34)*
>
> *Then He will answer them, saying, 'Assuredly, I say to you, inasmuch as you did not do it to one of the least of these, you did not do it to Me.' (Matthew 25:45)*

Israel might be lowly and despised among the nations, but the God Who defends them is The Almighty.

---

1. Hyde, Jim & Ariel. Supernatural or just remarkable.
2. Prince, Derek. *The Key to the Middle East*. Bloomington, Minn.: Chosen Books. 2013.
3. McTernan, John P. *As America Has Done to Israel*. New Kensington, Penn.: Whitaker House. 2006.

CHAPTER 12
ATHENS OR JERUSALEM

In this season of Hanukkah, we remember and celebrate an amazing feat when a very outnumbered small group of Zionist, full of zeal for the word of God the everlasting covenant rose up to throw off the shackles of Greek domination over them.

Within Jewish society of that day, there were two groups, a Hellenizing group that was attracted to a Greek culture and Greek philosophy who wanted to do away with the old practices of the old religion like circumcision and Sabbath. Then there was another group of Jews who were faithful to God and the Torah.

Antiochus Epiphanes, the Greek Hellenistic king who ruled the Seleucid Empire which included Judea, went with a combined group of Greeks and Jews to go throughout Judea to different villages and towns and to force the people to offer pagan sacrifices. Then Matthias from the Maccabean family rose up against the Greeks to take back the power from these Jews in Jerusalem who had become Hellenized Greeks. It was an amazing miracle. Once again, God is raising up Zionists to come against a pagan Greek worldview that has taken root in Israel.

A spiritual battle is recorded In Daniel chapter10 where Daniel had to deal with the Prince of Persia, and afterwards God's people would deal with the Prince of Greece. So, these two are tied together into the very end time battles that are taking place right now.

The Prophet Zechariah states:

> *For I have bent Judah, My bow,*
> *Fitted the bow with Ephraim,*
> *And raised up your sons, O Zion,*
> *Against your sons, O Greece,*
> *And made you like the sword of a mighty man." (Zechariah 9:13)*

This spirit is still at work today. The leadership of Israel must stand against the Pagan Greek worldview that would try to say, "Oh if you'll just give us a ceasefire. The nature of man and the heart of man is good. If we just educate people more there will be no more atrocities such as what happened on October 7th." But we see from the history of Nazi Germany, that education is not the answer to this kind of demonic activity, there must be a full uprooting of Hamas even as there was of the Nazis.

Let's take a look back at the history of Greek civilization in ancient times. The following are quotes from the book *Our Father Abraham* by Marvin Miller.

"The Greeks showcased all human talents — literature, drama, poetry, music, architecture, sculpture, etc. They glorified the beauty of the human body, displaying athletic prowess in the Olympics."

"Human passions were venerated, and this meant there were few sexual taboos — even pedophilia. The sexual initiation of a young boy by an older man was considered the highest form of love and vital part of a boy's education."

"The Greeks introduced into human consciousness an idea which is going to come into play as one of the most powerful intellectual forces in modern history — humanism. The human being is the center of all things. The human mind and its ability to understand and observe and comprehend things rationally is the be-all-and-end-all. That idea comes from the Greeks."

"Above all, the Greeks thought that humanism was enlightenment, the highest level of civilization. They had a strong sense of destiny and believed that their culture was ordained to become the universal culture of humanity."

"The Jews had a different vision. The Jews believed that a world united in the belief in one God and ascribing to one absolute standard of moral values — including respect for life, peace, justice, and social responsibility for the weak and poor — was the ultimate future of the human race."

"This Jewish ideology was wedded to an extreme, uncompromising exclusivity of worship (as demanded by the belief in one God) and a complete intolerance of polytheistic religious beliefs or practices. There's only one God and so only one God could be worshipped, end of story."

"To the Jews, human beings were created in the image of God. To the Greeks, gods were made in the image of human beings. To the Jews, the physical world was something to be perfected and elevated spiritually. To the Greeks the physical world was perfect. In short, to Greeks, what was beautiful was holy; to the Jews what was holy was beautiful."

Such disparate views were bound to clash, sooner or later.

And they are clashing today for the heart of Israel. Rick Ridings, founder of the Succat Hallel in Jerusalem, shared these insights on December 8, 2023:

"Israel, just as in the time of the Maccabees, must not cave into the pressure of the pagan Greek influence that was seeking to take away their identity and the word of God from the center of their lives. Just as the Nazis and ISIS were uprooted, it's crucial to recognize that Hamas and Hezbollah are terrorist organizations. Merely pruning them allows for regrowth. To ensure lasting peace, these groups need to be completely uprooted, preventing them from rebuilding infrastructure and acquiring more weapons."

"In order for this to happen, Israel must throw off the pagan Greek thought that thinks man is just basically good in his nature, and if you just have more education somehow, he will suddenly become very good. They need to realize there's only one cure for the evil that lies in the heart of men, and that is through the salvation and the blood of the Lord Jesus Christ. So, as we pray for the leadership of Israel at this time, let's pray that the Maccabean spirit will once again rise in the sons of Zion to throw off the Grecian spirit and once again cleanse and rededicate our nation to God."

> *Now therefore, fear the Lord, serve Him in sincerity and in truth, and put away the gods which your fathers served on the other side of the River and in Egypt. Serve the Lord! And if it seems evil to you to serve the Lord, choose for yourselves this day whom you will serve, whether the gods which your fathers served that were on the other side of the River, or the gods of the Amorites, in whose land you dwell. But as for me and my house, we will serve the Lord."*
> (Joshua 24:14-15)

. . .

1. Wilson, Marvin. Our Father Abraham Second Edition. Grand Rapids, Mich.: Wm. B. Eerdmans Publishing Co. 2021.
2. Some material comes from a Rick Riddings update on December 8.

CHAPTER 13
AWAKE YOU WHO SLEEP
BY JOY GRIFFITHS AND KAREN DAVIS

Awake you who sleep and turn your face to the dawn

Your Messiah has come

Arise from the dead

Lift up your eyes to the light

Your Messiah has come

For behold deep darkness will be over the earth

But the Lord shall arise

His light will be seen in you

His life will be found in you

Messiah has come

Come up to the mountain

Hear the voice of the Lord

Our Messiah will come

The sound of the trumpet shouts again in the land

Our Messiah will come

And the light of all nations will destroy every veil

Yes, the Lord shall arise

Salvation belongs to Him

Nations rejoice in Him

Messiah will come

CHAPTER 14
BEIRUT, IZMIR AND NAZARETH

BEIRUT

Is it not yet a very little while Till Lebanon shall be turned into a fruitful field, And the fruitful field be esteemed as a forest? In that day the deaf shall hear the words of the book, And the eyes of the blind shall see out of obscurity and out of darkness. The humble also shall increase their joy in the Lord, And the poor among men shall rejoice In the Holy One of Israel. (Isaiah 29:11-19)

Beirut was once considered "the Paris of the Middle East." The amazing city by the sea with a French colonial past was known for its East-West blend of culture, and stood at the forefront of fashion, intellectualism and art in the Middle East.

Beirut House of Prayer - Hosting the presence and transforming the nation.

IZMIR

> *Do not fear any of those things which you are about to suffer. Indeed, the devil is about to throw some of you into prison, that you may be tested, and you will have tribulation ten days. Be faithful until death, and I will give you the crown of life. (Revelation 2:10)*

Izmir, sometimes called the "Little Jerusalem" – a place of historical refuge for the Jews, has never lost its candle stick! There has always been a functioning Christian Church in Izmir since the days of John the Apostle who commissioned Polycarp as Bishop of Smyrna. In those days, Ephesus was the first of the seven churches, but now Izmir (Smyrna) is the only one that remains and now has jurisdiction over the entire region of the seven churches.

Izmir House of Prayer - It's a little town with a really big House of Prayer.

NAZARETH

> *The people who walked in darkness*
> *Have seen a great light;*
> *Those who dwelt in the land of the shadow of death,*
> *Upon them a light has shined. (Isaiah 9:2)*

Nazareth was the childhood home of Jesus, and in its synagogue, he preached the sermon that led to his rejection by his fellow townsmen. Today it is the largest Arab city in Israel, located about 15 miles west of the Sea of Galilee.

House of Prayer & Exploit (HOPE) – where the Lord gives precise battle plans.

CHAPTER 15
BOMBING AUSCHWITZ
BY AVNER BOSKEY, DECEMBER 1, 2023

The prophet Isaiah speaks of the emotional umbilical cord between the God of Jacob and His Jewish people: "In all their affliction He was afflicted" (Isaiah 63:9). This divine connection is not merely one of sympathy ('I feel bad for you') but of empathy ('I feel exactly what you are feeling'). The Apostle Paul mirrors both this spiritual truth and this emotional reality when he declares, "I am telling the truth in Messiah; I am not lying! My conscience testifies with me in the Holy Spirit!" (Romans 9:1).

When the Jewish people suffer, we have it on the highest authority that the God of the Jewish people also suffers. Theologically speaking, this means that Jewish suffering has scriptural priority to the heart of God. It's not just an issue of how it fits into a Last Days scenario or onto an eschatological chessboard.

Yet in most cases the nations of the world have a cold heart vis-à-vis Jewish suffering. Jeremiah states it plainly: The nations "have called you an outcast, saying: 'It is only Zion! No one cares for her'" (Jeremiah 30:17).

A quick look at how the Allies responded to Jewish suffering at Auschwitz murder-camp in WWII can help cast light on how the nations are responding to jihadi attacks on the Jewish people in our day.

DOUBTFUL EFFICACY

On April 7, 1944, two Slovak Jewish young men, Rudolf Vrba (age 20) and Alfréd Wetzler (age 17) escaped Auschwitz and made their way to Oscar Krasniansky of the Slovakian Jewish Council in Zilina, Slovakia. They dictated their eyewitness account – the 'Auschwitz Protocols' – of the Nazi murder machine in Oświęcim, Poland (in German, Auschwitz). That report detailed the camp's location, its geography, sketches and information about the layout of the gas chambers, and how prisoners lived and were murdered. It listed the death transports to Auschwitz since 1942, their cities of origin, and the numbers 'selected' for work or the gas chambers. It was a veritable 'smoking gun' – eyewitness proof of the Holocaust apparatus. These Protocols were later submitted as evidence of Nazi genocidal crimes at Nuremberg Trials (November 1945 – October 1946).

On July 29, 1944, Ernest Frischer of the Czechoslovak State Council forwarded a letter through the US War Refugee Board to John McCloy, Under Secretary of War. The letter sat unanswered until August 9, 1944 when Leon Kubowitzki, Head of the Rescue Department for the World Jewish Congress, sent an urgent appeal asking for the US to consider bombing the gas chambers and crematoria at Auschwitz in order to slow down Nazi mass extermination of European Jews. McCloy responded on August 14, 1944, turning down the request:

The War Department had been approached by the War Refugee Board, which raised the question of the practicability of this suggestion. After a study it became apparent that such an operation could be executed only by the diversion of considerable air support essential to the success of our forces now engaged in decisive operations elsewhere and would in any case be of such doubtful efficacy that it would not warrant the use of our resources. There has been considerable opinion to the effect that such an effort, even if practicable, might provoke even more vindictive action by the Germans. The War Department fully appreciates the humanitarian motives which promoted the suggested operation, but for the reasons stated above it has not been felt that it can or should be undertaken, at least at this time.

The military and strategic facts were markedly different than the War Department's 'officialese.' McCloy was flat out lying when he referenced a study regarding the feasibility of bombing Auschwitz, as no such study had been undertaken. As far as practicability: On August 21, 1944, a front-page article in the New York Times described how "500 United States heavy bombers from Italy today . . . bombed the I.G. Farbenindustrie synthetic oil and rubber plant at Oswiecim in Polish Silesia."

In another example, former U.S. Senator George McGovern piloted a B-24 Liberator in December 1944, and his squadron bombed I.G. Farbenindustrie factories (synthetic rubber based on oil) at Buna-Monowitz (Auschwitz III) less than five miles from the main Auschwitz crematoria. In a 2004 interview, McGovern stated: "It would have helped if we had bombed the railroad lines leading to Auschwitz. The purpose of those rail lines was to carry human beings to their death, and we might even have been able to use long-range fighter planes to get down right on the tracks and knock them out . . . We should have hit that junction and disabled it. We should have hit the rail lines, even if we had to go back several times." In 2005, he added: "There is no question we should have attempted . . . to go after Auschwitz. There was a pretty good chance we could have blasted those rail lines off the face of the Earth, which would have interrupted the flow of people to those death chambers, and we had a pretty good chance of knocking out those gas ovens."

Wolf Blitzer's father David was a prisoner at Auschwitz. Here are his comments about the feasibility of bombing Auschwitz:

"The biggest puzzle for me is that they did not bombard the railroads leading to the crematoria. This is the biggest puzzle. We saw the airplanes — in 1944, we saw airplanes bombarding cities. We were laughing, we were happy, we were even praying to God – we could get killed from those bombs, but we couldn't understand why they did not bombard – every day, thousands of people were burned and gassed in the camps, only because they had the possibility to bring those trainloads of people. If those rails had been bombarded, the [Nazis] couldn't have done it so perfectly."

THE INDIFFERENCE OF THE NATIONS

In his cutting-edge work 'The Abandonment of The Jews,' Professor David Wyman argued that the failure to bomb Auschwitz was a result of the Allies' indifference to the fate of the Jews rather than the practical impossibility of the operation. As Jeremiah re-iterates: the nations "have called you an outcast, saying: 'It is only Zion! No one cares for her'" (Jeremiah 30:17).

In September 1944 David Ben-Gurion addressed the issue of the hardness of the nations' hearts, who quickly avert their eyes when Jewish people were being murdered, preferring to focus on other matters:

"What have you done to us, your freedom-loving peoples, guardians of justice, defenders of the high principles of democracy and of the brotherhood of man? What have you allowed to be perpetrated against a defenseless people while you stood aside and let it bleed to death, without offering help or succor, without calling on the fiends to stop, in the language of retribution which alone they would understand. Why do you profane our pain and wrath with empty expressions of sympathy which ring like a mockery in the ears of millions of the damned in the torture house of Nazi Europe? . . . If, instead of Jews, thousands of English, American or Russian women, children and aged had been tortured every day, burnt to death, asphyxiated in gas chambers – would you have acted in the same way?"

Freda Kirchwey, American journalist and social commentator, wrote these words in 1943: "In this country you and I and the President and the Congress and the State Department are accessories to the crime and share Hitler's guilt. If we had behaved like humane and generous people instead of complacent, cowardly ones, the Jews lying today in the earth of Poland and Hitler's other crowded graveyards would be alive and safe; and other millions yet to die would have found sanctuary."

The same cold-hearted and anti-Semitic dynamics which characterized Western leadership in WWII are characterizing an increasing number across the globe. This is being seen in the speed with which public opinion has turned against Israel – from shock at the Hamas savage atrocities of October 7, 2023, to demonstrators cheering jihadi terrorists and embracing them as freedom fighters (Freiheitskämpfer – a term reminiscent of the German terrorist Baader-Meinhof Gang [Rote Armee Fraktion] back in the 1970's).

THE INDIFFERENCE OF HAMAS

The Allies did not bomb Auschwitz, and so the Jews of Europe continued to be gassed and burned there. Yet those who made the decision to let Nazi genocide continue were able to sleep at night with a 'clear conscience,' not concerned about Jewish casualties. Similarly, in Gaza the jihadi terror group Hamas has made it their habitual 'order of battle' strategy to use Gazan human shields while attacking Israeli civilians with rocket attacks and jihadi fighter land attacks. After committing these double war crimes and atrocities, Hamas and Islamic Jihad are also able to sleep at night 'with a clear conscience.' They also are not concerned about Jewish or even Gazan casualties.

Hamas' leaders are willing to fight Israel 'to the last Palestinian Gazan,' while they hole up in their rat's nests of underground tunnels or in luxury hotels in Qatar. Hamas leaders' willingness to sacrifice their own people reminds one of Adolf Hitler's private declaration to Albert Speer at the end of his life on March 18, 1945: "If the war is lost, the nation will also perish. This fate is inevitable. There is no necessity to take into consideration the basis which the people will need to continue a most primitive existence."

Hamas is playing puppet-master to the world, stirring up anti-Israeli violence and anti-Jewish rage, while sacrificing its own people. Israel is manfully trying to avoid Gazan civilian casualties while rightfully destroying Hamas rocket launchers, squads and jihadi armories. In the meantime, a demonized hand is stirring up violent demonstrations against the Jewish people across the globe, bringing down upon the nations the curse of the God of Jacob according to Genesis 12:3.

Here is an enlightening May 13, 2018 quote from former Commander of British Forces in Afghanistan, Colonel Richard

Kemp: "Hamas has followed this strategy many times in the past, firing rockets at Israeli civilian communities and constructing under the border sophisticated attack tunnels from which fighters would storm into the heart of Jewish communities and carry out mass murder and abduction. Thousands of Palestinians have died, including human shields that are so central to Hamas' strategy, as the IDF has been compelled to forcefully defend its people. The world has often reacted with horror and outrage blaming Israel for the bloodshed provoked by Hamas – just as intended."

Kemp also notes: "While political leaders such as Joe Biden and Rishi Sunak have so far consistently resisted calls for Israel to cease fire, they constantly say that Israel must observe the laws of war and minimize civilian casualties. They know that is exactly what the IDF is doing, and their words amount to posturing to appease elements of their electorates that oppose support for Israel. They should know better than to provide cover for Hamas and its supporters in this way."

The speed at which the nations have pivoted against Israel, and the pustulating wound of anti-Semitic violence smearing across the planet – these are prophetic markers of both encroaching darkness and great spiritual harvest.

(https://davidstent.org/bombing-auschwitz-2/

Avner and Rachel Boskey live in the Beersheva region of Israel and are dedicated to stirring up the creative arts, worship, intercession, evangelism and the prophetic gifts within a Jewish and Israeli matrix.)

CHAPTER 16
BRACE FOR IMPACT
BY SHIRLEY MOMBERG

Surely the Lord God does nothing, Unless He reveals His secret to His servants the prophets. (Amos 3:7)

On June 23, 2023, Shirley Momberg received this word from the Lord:

"For two days, I've heard the words "Brace for Impact." I keep getting a sense of an airplane with passengers on board. The pilot and the cabin attendant are giving instructions to brace for impact. Passengers are to remain seated, bent over with their faces as close to their legs as possible, feet firmly on the floor, and their hands on their heads. I am reminded of Elijah – the way he prayed. (1 Kings 18:42, James 5:16-18)

Something is coming! Something is happening!

One who scatters is coming against you. Brace yourselves! Call out your forces! **Prepare your defenses and man the fortifications!** Keep watch up and down your streets. Strengthen your back – **prepare for battle. Strap your war belt around your**

waist. Summon and gather all the strength you can." (Nahum 2:1)

> *Stay dressed for action and keep your lamps burning, and be like men who are waiting for their master to come home from the wedding feast, so that they may open the door to him at once when he comes and knocks. Blessed are those servants whom the master finds awake when he comes. Truly, I say to you, he will dress himself for service and have them recline at table, and he will come and serve them. If he comes in the second watch, or in the third, and finds them awake, blessed are those servants! But know this, that if the master of the house had known at what hour the thief was coming, he would not have left his house to be broken into. You also must be ready, for the Son of Man is coming at an hour you do not expect. (ESV)*

So, we prayed; so, we prepared; and so, we were ready for October 7th and the season of war that lay ahead of us.

(Shirley Momberg is recognized as a strong prophetic voice relevant to both the church and the marketplace.)

CHAPTER 17
BROKEN COVENANTS

Now there was a famine in the days of David for three years, year after year; and David inquired of the LORD. And the LORD answered, "It is because of Saul and his bloodthirsty house, because he killed the Gibeonites." (2 Samuel 21:1)

There are several principles illustrated in Israel's broken covenant with the Gibeonites that can help us understand how to recover when a breach has occurred in the past.

1. GOD DEFENDS COVENANTS

Paul writes that one of the characteristics of many people in the last days is that they will be truce-breakers (2 Timothy 3:3 KJV). Whether in marriage or church relationships, we often excuse ourselves much too easily from the covenants and commitments we have made.

Although the covenant that Joshua made with the Gibeonites was ill advised and against God's stated will, it was nevertheless perpetually binding.

> *We have sworn to them by the LORD God of Israel; now therefore, we may not touch them. (Joshua 9:19)*

It is the one *who* swears to his own hurt and does not change that may abide in God's tabernacle. (Psalm 15:4) If we have a string of broken commitments in our life, we might find ourselves outside of the blessing of God.

One of the reasons Israel was under a curse was marital unfaithfulness.

> *Because the LORD has been witness*
> *Between you and the wife of your youth,*
> *With whom you have dealt treacherously;*
> *Yet she is your companion*
> *And your wife by covenant. (Malachi 2:14)*

I realize that some people have been victims of other's unfaithfulness and broken promises. Nevertheless, we need to do what we can to remain faithful to our commitments.

> *If it is possible, as much as depends on you, live peaceably with all men. (Romans 12:18)*

2. THE HOLY SPIRIT IS SENSITIVE

Paul tells us in Ephesians 4:30, "Do not grieve the Holy Spirit of God." The Holy Spirit is depicted as a dove. As illustrated in Noah's releasing of two birds after the Flood, the dove was more sensitive than the raven, and would not rest just any place (Genesis 8:9). We cannot dismiss issues that God is dealing with and assume that He will remain in our midst.

Sometimes we can be like Samson and not even realize that the Lord's presence has departed.

> *Then she called, "Samson, the Philistines are upon you!" So he awoke from his sleep, and said, "I will go out as before, at other times, and shake myself free!" But he did not know that the LORD had departed from him. (Judges 16:20)*

Consider as well that all the churches in the Book of Revelation continued to function as churches. They worshipped, taught the Scriptures, and perhaps functioned in the supernatural, but the Lord was displeased with most of them. Therefore, it is not too difficult to see how the following scenario can occur:

> *Many will say to Me in that day, 'Lord, Lord, have we not prophesied in Your name, cast out demons in Your name, and done many wonders in Your name?' And then I will declare to them, 'I never knew you; depart from Me, you who practice lawlessness!' (Matthew 7:22-23)*

If we don't remain sensitive to the Lord, we may become resistant to His conviction and develop a hardness of heart. This can ultimately lead to reprobation and result in an untimely fall. Therefore, we need to respond correctly to God's correction. We have a choice between which of these proverbs will mark our destiny:

> *He who is often rebuked, and hardens his neck, Will suddenly be destroyed, and that without remedy. (Proverbs 29:1)*

> *Turn at my rebuke; Surely I will pour out my spirit on you; I will make my words known to you. (Proverbs 1:23)*

3. SOULISH ZEAL FOR GOD CAN CAUSE GREAT DAMAGE

Perhaps I should call this "Saulish" zeal, for much of Saul's works and the fruit of his life was soulish rather than spiritual. Many throughout church history have acted like Saul in their religious zeal and have inflicted great harm on many people.

Martin Luther, for example, grew impatient with the Jewish people's lack of response to the gospel, and made some unfortunate statements which set in motion a justification for persecution that lasted 400 years.

> *He urged that synagogues should be set on fire, their homes smashed and destroyed. Jews should be banned from the roads and markets, their property seized, and then these poisonous envenomed worms should be drafted into forced labor and made to earn their bread by the sweat of their noses.*

Thank God for the genuine repentance and reconciliation that the German church has initiated toward the Jewish people that has resulted in a greater measure of God's blessing. Similar repentance and reconciliation has occurred between Anglo and Hispanic, Anglo and African American, and Anglo and Native American peoples. We simply can't sweep the oppression, injustice and atrocities of the past under the rug and continue with business as usual. God is putting His finger on these issues so that we can come clean before Him and each other. Reconciliation is the path to His blessing, His manifest presence and His glory. Jesus said that reconciliation even precedes worship.

> *Therefore if you bring your gift to the altar, and there remember*

that your brother has something against you, leave your gift there before the altar, and go your way. First be reconciled to your brother, and then come and offer your gift. (Matthew 5:23-24)

4. JUDGMENT OCCURS IN GOD'S TIMING

Saul had committed the offense against the Gibeonites around 30 years previously, but God chose the appropriate time during David's reign to impose the consequences.

Because the sentence against an evil work is not executed speedily, therefore the heart of the sons of men is fully set in them to do evil. (Ecclesiastes 8:11)

This is a mystery! God can act immediately and decisively (i.e. Ananias and Sapphira in Acts 5), or He can wait a generation or more to execute His judgments. Regardless of the timing, we must deal with things immediately as He brings them to our attention.

For the time has come for judgment to begin at the house of God; (1 Peter 4:17)

For if we would judge ourselves, we would not be judged. (1 Corinthians 11:31)

He sometimes delays judgment in order to give us time to repent (Revelation 2:21), so let us therefore be zealous and repent (Revelation 3:19). If we hear his voice, let us not harden our hearts (Hebrews 3:15) or disregard it (Hebrews 12:25).

5. IT SOMETIMES TAKES AWHILE FOR US TO UNDERSTAND WHAT GOD IS DOING

David was a discerning, God-fearing and faithful shepherd, yet it took him three years to come to understand that there was a correlation between the famine in the land and God's judgment upon the nation for the sins of the previous leader.

The sadder truth is that some people never get the message and continue in a state of rebellion for many years and miss God's purpose for their life.

6. INNOCENT PEOPLE ARE AFFECTED BY THE SINS OF LEADERS

It was Saul's sin that resulted in God's judgment on the entire nation. Therefore, James states that teachers (by implication leaders) are subject to a stricter judgment. (James 3:1)

David, the current king of Israel, was innocent of this crime, yet it was his responsibility to fix the problem. However, there was another situation where David sinned and as a result the Lord sent a plague upon Israel, and 70,000 men of Israel perished (1 Chronicles 21). A pretty stiff price to pay for the sin of a leader!

In this incident, we are clearly told that Satan stood up against Israel, and moved David to number the people (1 Chronicles 21:1). Satan was the instigator, but David was the perpetrator. We can't blame the devil when God's people fall, just as a football team can't blame the opposing team for sacking the quarterback. We as God's people need to take responsibility for the welfare of our leaders. The enemy wants to bring down the quarterback (spiritual leader), so we need to provide the necessary blocking and tackling (prayer cover) for them. Satan knows that if he can strike the shepherd, the sheep of the flock will be scattered (Matthew 26:31).

7. WE NEED TO SEEK GOD'S FACE

David was committed to hearing from God and doing whatever He said.

> *I will hear what God the LORD will speak. (Psalm 85:8)*

Too often we present our agenda to God rather than listening to Him, receiving His instructions and obeying Him. Our relationship with God must take us beyond praying for our needs to seeking His face.

> *And you will seek Me and find Me, when you search for Me with all your heart. (Jeremiah 29:13)*

8. RECONCILIATION IS REQUIRED TO RESOLVE PAST OFFENSES

David had to seek out the Gibeonites and ask them what needed to be done to resolve the problem. Their request was demanding, but appropriate for the offense committed against them.

> *"What shall I do for you? How shall I make amends so that you will bless the LORD's inheritance?" (2 Samuel 21:3)*

> *They answered the king, "As for the man who destroyed us and plotted against us so that we have been decimated and have no place anywhere in Israel, let seven of his male descendants be given to us to be killed and exposed before the LORD at Gibeah of Saul—the Lord 's chosen one." (2 Samuel 21:5-6)*

David was not defensive but was quick to respond and comply with their request.

> *Agree with your adversary quickly, while you are on the way with him, lest your adversary deliver you to the judge, the judge hand you over to the officer, and you be thrown into prison. (Matthew 5:25)*

> *So the king said, "I will give them to you." (2 Samuel 21:6)*

9. WE NEED TO BE CAREFUL HOW WE CARRY OUT GOD'S JUDGMENTS

God was willing to withhold judgment on a large population (Sodom and Gomorrah) if He had found ten righteous people in the cities (Genesis 18:32-33). He holds back His judgment in our day so that innocent people (wheat) are not inadvertently affected.

> *The servants said to him, 'Do you want us then to go and gather them up?' But he said, 'No, lest while you gather up the tares you also uproot the wheat with them. (Matthew 13:28-29)*

Likewise, David was decisive, yet careful in how he implemented God's judgment, so that his covenant with Jonathan was honored.

> *The king spared Mephibosheth son of Jonathan, the son of Saul, because of the oath before the LORD between David and Jonathan son of Saul. (2 Samuel 21:7)*

10. GOD'S MERCY SUPERSEDES HIS JUDGMENT

Mercy triumphs over judgment (James 2:13)

Thank God that He extends to us mercy (not giving us what we deserve) and grace (giving us what we don't deserve). He extends mercy to us when we fall, and grace to us to enable us to stand. It is His goodness that leads us to repentance. (Romans 2:4)

Who could stand if He called us to account for all of our sins and shortcomings! (Psalm 130:3) He deals with us and disciplines us according to His mercy that we might be partakers of His holiness (Hebrews 12:10). He delights to show mercy. (Micah 7:18)

After David had fully carried out the Gibeonite's requirements, God released His blessing upon the nation.

> *They buried the bones of Saul and his son Jonathan in the tomb of Saul's father Kish, at Zela in Benjamin, and did everything the king commanded. After that, God answered prayer on behalf of the land. (2 Samuel 21:14)*

No matter how far a nation has fallen, there is always hope for restoration. Judah spent 70 years in captivity for continually disobeying God, but God had a plan to restore them and enacted it. The nation of Israel rejected their Messiah, but God has a plan to restore them. (Zechariah 12:10). Judgment is a necessary process for restoring the wayward to the Way.

God has committed to His church the ministry of reconciliation. (2 Corinthians 5:19)

> *Those from among you*

> *Shall build the old waste places;*
> *You shall raise up the foundations of many generations;*
> *And you shall be called the Repairer of the Breach,*
> *The Restorer of Streets to Dwell In. (Isaiah 58:12)*

God can release us from the consequences of broken vows. The Jewish people observe a Kol Nidre (all vows) service on the eve of Yom Kippur in which sins are confessed and forgiven.

Yeshua has already paid the price to release us from the curse of breaking the law. We are already forgiven and set free, so He invites us to receive His peace (Yehovah Shalom) and His healing (Yehovah Rapha).

CHAPTER 18
CHILDREN IN CAPTIVITY
BY REUBEN DORON, DECEMBER 13, 2023

Wildest imaginations could not have prepared our therapists, social workers and medical staff for the return of 39 Israeli children who were torn from their cribs and beds and taken to hell barefoot and half asleep. Some were alone, having seen their parents slaughtered in front of their eyes. Others were taken with one parent alive. Within days of the October 7th massacre a brand new, groundbreaking protocol, was born in Israel; one unlike any other country has ever needed or developed before. A protocol to treat captive children and heal their souls from the trauma they suffered.

From day one of the war with Hamas, Israel's medical and psychological services began to develop a program no one ever imagined we'll ever need. Only when the children started coming back did we realize how necessary this protocol is. The children were starved and drugged; locked in damp tunnels and dark attics; coerced and beaten by their captors and by raging crowds; their skin was burned with hot exhaust pipes for identification in case they managed to escape.

Our children were forced to watch the horrifying videos of Hamas terrorists performing their atrocities time and again… the same videos which, after being viewed by adult politicians and journalists worldwide, caused them to exit in tears and often seek therapy. We know some of them personally. The children weren't allowed to go to the bathroom for long periods; they were threatened at gun point when they cried. Some were raped and came back only whispering; others had bruises and lice. They didn't shower for 50 days; they did not see daylight; they drank muddy, salty water.

A few had severe injuries that were treated in terrifying procedures in Gaza hospitals; one underwent surgery without anesthetics; a girl's broken leg was put together backwards by a Hamas physician, and others who were wounded received no treatment at all. Their captors told them that their parents forgot all about them; that they don't want them anymore; that they'll be in those tunnels forever; and that no one is coming to bring them back home.

Caregivers say that they needed to invent new words to help the children express the range and depth of the horrors they experienced while at Hamas captivity. The medical and psychological staff is learning how and what to ask, and especially what not to ask, as they slowly bring these children back to life. Israel, who invented Cherry Tomatoes and Mobileye, the Iron Dome and Waze, now has developed, for the first time ever in human history, a protocol to treat the tortured minds of our captive children.

(Reuven and Mary Lou Doron serve God and His people in Israel. reuven.doron@gmail.com)

CHAPTER 19
END TIME PROPHECY
BY REGGIE KELLY

It should be well known, from the prophetic portions of both testaments, that the age concludes over an international crisis concerning the Land, and Jerusalem in particular. Shepherds and leaders, and witnesses in general are going to need an answer for why this should be so.

As never before, the whole flow of history is moving exactly in the direction that the plain person's plain reading of prophecy would have led them to expect. God Himself has made the issue of Israel, and the so-called, "Jewish question" a watershed of international division.

Just imagine trying to explain the irrevocable election of Israel, based on grace alone, to a generation that is being fast pre-conditioned, almost overnight, to despise the very suggestion of such an unthinkable notion. Talk about a calculated offense!

So yes, how we see the times we're in does indeed come down to a question of one's hermeneutics, but also to a question of the heart.

The pragmatic pastor will want to ask, how is this relevant to the gospel? If a pure gospel is well established in the heart, isn't that enough? Shouldn't such details of prophetic speculation be left to the mystery that God intended, nice to know but not critical, since the sheep will surely make it through, come what may?

Indeed, the gospel and the saving righteousness of Christ is centermost, but this center has a divinely chosen context that must not be neglected, not only for our benefit, but much more importantly the glory that God has invested in His foretold plan, precious to savor at all times, but particularly now, as chaos and deception is about to explode on scale eclipsing anything ever witnessed before.

We must remember, the NT revelation of the mystery of the gospel is built around Christ's coming, departure, and return to Israel, specifically the mount of Olives from whence He ascended. He must return to the place where He was crucified under the placard that said, "This is Jesus of Nazareth, the King of the Jews."

Why end the age just there, in that physical locality? Why has God constructed the end of the age around an ancient land dispute that is divinely calculated to plunge the nations into an insoluble crisis from which none will be able to extricate themselves? (Zechariah 12:2-3). Why would God bind together the issue of the mystery of the gospel with the mystery of Israel?

I would submit that part of the answer is because He fully intended that both comings would be surrounded by an element of mystery designed to elude the pride of self-reliance, just as Paul warns in Romans 11:25. Just as the mystery of Christ's twofold coming so deeply searched and tested Jewish hearts, just so, the mystery of Israel is designed to test and sift the hearts of the nations, even gentile believers.

But there is one important difference. The mystery of Christ's cross and twofold coming was not only hidden from Peter; it was hidden even from the angelic powers. Not so the mystery surrounding the Lord's return.

Those days will not come upon the faithful as a thief, but only upon the unregenerate church and world. We know this because Daniel's prophecy is clear that the vision will be unsealed and known to the wise (maskilim) at the time of the end. They will be doing great exploits, instructing many, and turning many to righteousness, even a vast, countless number that will be saved out of, "the tribulation, the great".

But the larger answer to the question has all to do with the completion of an ancient covenant promise. It is the age ending climax of the "everlasting covenant" that forms the framework of the future. In the larger context of God's eternal purpose in Christ, this is what defines how and why the age ends just as the prophecy of both testaments so fully describes.

With that said, I want to turn to something that will bring us back to this, but hopefully with what I like to call a "plumb line of simplicity" that will align and pull many of the strands together into a coherent clarity. The object will not only be to know what is most important but how best to show others how to make the case from scripture, without getting bogged down in details, in a way that will be accessible for the instruction and equipping of others to equip others.

If observed, I believe God has given us an amazing, and now especially timely, provision to equip the body, not only to escape the manifold forms of end time deception, but to have the Lord's own, personally commended key of interpretation that will enable them to "instruct many" and "turn many" to righteousness" (Daniel 11:32-33; 12:3, 10).

I would like to speak a little on how Daniel aligns and sets in order, not only the end time events, but takes in the whole covenantal framework of the judgments and promises, as traced from Genesis 3:15 to the final perfection of the last two chapters of Revelation.

Daniel is the key to organizing the whole of scripture around the main themes of kingdom, covenant, and mystery. But it is Jesus' Olivet prophecy in particular, and the emphasis He puts on one centermost event, that becomes the key that opens not only Daniel but sets all the prophecies spoken concerning the coming day of the Lord in clearest covenant context.

Referencing and building upon Moses and the earlier prophets, Daniel gives us, not only the timeline and the order of events related to both comings, but he reminds us of the covenant curses that must continue until Israel's everlasting deliverance and final security in the Land, all in glorious analogy to the story of Joseph and his brothers (compare Micah 5:3- with Zechariah 12:10).

Rightly instructed believers will weep with those who weep, not only in their bitter distress, but in the glory that will break upon the beleaguered survivors of Israel when they will look upon Him whom they pierced and say with one voice, "blessed is He who comes in the Name of the Lord!"

In this way, we can begin to see God's mind and purpose behind the great judgments and the unrestrained evils that would be otherwise inexplicable and the occasion for the greatest offense to the natural mind.

But back to my point:

In my experience I found that when I chose to take very seriously Jesus' command to read and understand Daniel's prophecy concerning the abomination of desolation, I was challenged when I saw that this light did not come to him until he first, "Set his heart to understand." Looking to understand this particular event and its full significance, I would be astonished at just how much more this simple obedience would open to discovery in pulling the great strands of biblical themes together. Jesus well knew what this simple obedience would set in motion.

Not only did I discover the event, and the events that follow throughout the second half of the week, I discovered a number of events that would mark and distinguish the first half. What a priceless advantage this first half of the week will provide the body for their readiness for the second half. We will see it coming!

But more than all of this, Daniel became the key to what I like to call, "The glory of the story". This is because Daniel, like no other book, reaches all the way back to Israel's beginnings and outlines the whole sweep of Israel's covenant history of crisis and discipline to its glorious resolution in the kingdom come on earth as it is in heaven.

It is important to note that the abomination of desolation is the very event that Paul was careful to cover during his short, three weeks stay with the Thessalonians. This should underscore the importance he attached to Jesus' Olivet prophecy and his emphasis on Daniel's order of events.

We know this because when the false alarm arose that Christ's return was immediately imminent, he corrected the error by appealing to what he had gone over with them on his earlier visit. "Do you not remember that when I was with you. I told you these things?"

Paul speaks of a coming man who is yet to be revealed. He will be possessed of "all power" of signs, wonders, and cunning deception. He will enter the temple of God in Jerusalem and there exalt himself above all that is called God or that is worshiped. There are some dots we need to connect.

Jesus doesn't mention the man but only this event and its location ("Judea"). Both Paul and Jesus use language that is taken almost verbatim from Daniel chapter 11 where both the man and the event are described within four verses of each other (see Daniel 11:31-37). So, the scripture itself shows us how the dots should be connected.

Manifestly, Paul did not regard knowledge of the basic order of end time events as a matter of no serious concern. Notice Paul's urgent tone when he echoes the Lord's grave warnings concerning the peril of deception on this very matter. "Let no man deceive you by any means!"

You can almost hear the exclamation point.

That sounds like the beginning of Jesus' opening answer to His disciple's question, "what shall be the sign of your coming and the end of the age?" Significantly, Jesus' first words were, "take heed that no man deceive you." Again, the exclamation point. No other theme is so repeatedly reinforced throughout His prophetic discourse.

Paul's response to the error concerning the order of events preceding the Lord's return implies that something far more serious was being threatened than to merely prompt the slackers and busy bodies to return to their day jobs and occupy till He comes.

The abomination of desolation is THE prophetic key to the believer's preparation to instruct many of the meaning, not only of the events of those days, but the great issue of the promise of an "everlasting righteousness" that is the Lord's own righteousness, available to believers now, but promised to come to all the penitent survivors of Israel in that great day The abomination of desolation serves as a crucial prophetic key for believers' preparation. It unveils not just the events of those days but also sheds light on the promise of an "everlasting righteousness"—the Lord's righteousness. This righteousness is accessible to believers presently and is pledged to reach all repentant survivors of Israel in that significant future day. This is the glorious free gift that gives hope and meaning and comfort even in the face of the staggering evil, deception, and suffering of those days, like those we have witnessed very recently. (Zechariah 14:2)

In conclusion, I appeal to the intricate landscape of eschatological possibilities—a realm hard fought and hard won. Yet, amidst this complexity, there exist keys of simplicity that pave a clear path through the maze. I've mentioned one such key, but the discussion on how best to employ this key for equipping the church belongs to another realm of conversation.

Irrespective of your stance—whether you lean towards the preterist view, interpreting the abomination and great tribulation as events of the past, or the classic dispensational perspective, seeing the Olivet prophecy as pertaining primarily to the Jewish context rather than directly applying to the church, which might not be present during that period—my earnest plea is for you to consider the solemn warnings about deception and Jesus' prescribed remedy. Even if approached with a 'just in case' mindset, it's crucial for the sake of your congregations' well-being.

If Jesus put such stress on the relationship of this event to offset some of the prevailing deceptions of "those days", such as the present massive upsurge of antisemitism, just reflect on how regrettable it would be if you had failed to prepare those under your care with at least the means to recognize these things if you might just happen to be sincerely mistaken.

In summary, acquiring a thorough understanding of Daniel's end-time prophecy is an endeavor worth pursuing.

(Reggie Kelly is best known to most of us as a close friend and theological companion of the late Art Katz (1929-2007).

Check out https://mysteryofisrael.org/about/about-reggie-kelly/ for more articles by Reggie)

CHAPTER 20
FINDING REAL HOPE IN THE MIDST OF DISASTER
BY ARIEL HYDE NOVEMBER 19, 2023

How could this happen to us? Why didn't they defend us?

The people of Israel are in the most serious crisis of confidence since our state was founded, and many are asking, "Can we even trust in anyone anymore?"

The good news is, you can. You just need to know where to look.

Israel is a miracle. Look at what's happened here in 75 years: a "start-up nation," prosperity, achievements in many arenas, including in science and security. We've always been proud of "the Jewish mind" and trusted our strong military.

IT ALL COLLAPSED

Until it all collapsed. The horrific massacre on October 7 left all of us in Israel heartbroken, in shock, and traumatized. No one believed the day would come when masses of Hamas terrorists would invade our country so easily.

On that dreadful Shabbat, thousands of Israelis found themselves in a nightmare that lasted for many hours, where barbaric terrorists were burning whole families, kidnapping the elderly and children, raping women, and slaughtering babies. Our souls can't bear the weight and horror of what they experienced – alone, without protection, helpless. More than 1,400 people were murdered, thousands were injured, and over 200 were kidnapped to Gaza.

THE AGREEMENT WAS BROKEN

How can we recover from such a horrible tragedy? Many feel that the agreement between us and our leaders has been broken, because they failed in their primary mission – to protect us.

So where will our help come from? The answer is found in the beautiful psalm: "My help comes from the Lord, the Maker of heaven and earth" (Psalm 121:2).

We appreciate our leaders and military and all they've done for us, but after this tragic failure, can we really trust in them, and them alone? Maybe they're not exactly all-powerful? Maybe all of us as humans aren't as strong, wise, skilled, and good as we often tend to think?

SO WHERE WILL OUR HELP COME FROM?

So where will our help come from? The answer is found in the beautiful psalm: "My help comes from the Lord, the Maker of heaven and earth" (Psalm 121:2).

Many people have a problem with that idea, but if we just look at our own history, we can see that if it weren't for the God of Israel, there's no way we would even be here. Actually, one of the most powerful proofs of the fact that God is faithful and that we can trust Him is that the people of Israel still exist – and live in our land.

God has always fulfilled his promises to his people. Here are just a few examples from his agreement with us, from the covenant He made in the Tanakh (Hebrew Bible):

- God promised that only if the sun, moon, and stars would disappear, then the people of Israel would cease to exist (Jeremiah 31:35-37). And we all know that in spite of all the attempts to destroy us, the people of Israel live.
- God, like a good father, gave us a book of instructions about how to live and succeed, and warned that if we didn't follow them, we'd go into a long exile – and that also happened (Deuteronomy 28:64, Hosea 3:4-5).
- But God also promised that we'd return to our land (Ezekiel 11:17), we'd reestablish our nation (Isaiah 66:8), and revive the Hebrew language (Zephaniah 3:9-10). And here we are in our land, in the State of Israel, speaking Hebrew.

All these miracles haven't happened to any other people in all history — we're the only ones. Have you ever wondered why?

WHAT IS OUR PURPOSE AND DESTINY?

The reason is that God has a purpose and a destiny for us. Listen to this amazing promise of his:

> *"For I will take you from among the nations, gather you out of all countries, and bring you into your own land. Then I will sprinkle clean water on you, and you shall be clean; I will cleanse you from all*

your filthiness and from all your idols. I will give you a new heart and put a new spirit within you; I will take the heart of stone out of your flesh and give you a heart of flesh. I will put my Spirit within you and cause you to walk in my statutes, and you will keep my judgments and do them. Then you shall dwell in the land that I gave to your fathers; you shall be my people, and I will be your God" (Ezekiel 36:24-28).

God is the source of all the love, peace, and security we're searching for.

Wow, what a good father. God has already fulfilled the first part of his promise – miraculously, He gathered us from every corner of the earth and brought us back to Israel. So, we can be absolutely certain that He will fulfill the next stage as well. And now he's inviting us to participate in this miracle.

God is the source of all the love, peace, and security we're searching for, and He wants us to experience all those things. He wants to dwell in us, to fill us with his good Spirit, to give us a new heart.

WHY DO WE NEED A NEW HEART?

But why do we need a new heart? Because – how do we put it lightly – our heart isn't exactly clean. You know: the white lies, the covetousness, the jealousy, the hatred, the pride. God sees how we haven't always honored him, how we've broken our part of the agreement, the covenant with him. So, what do you think? Will a righteous God consider us "not guilty" on Judgment Day?

But the good news is, there is something we can trust in.

According to the Tanakh, we can't trust in our own good deeds, because they can never cancel our evil thoughts and deeds (Isaiah 64:6).

AND NOW FOR THE GOOD NEWS

But the good news is, there is something we can trust in. Look at what God himself says in our Tanakh, in the book of Jeremiah:

> *"Behold, the days are coming, declares the Lord, when I will make a new covenant with the house of Israel and the house of Judah, not like the covenant that I made with their fathers on the day when I took them by the hand to bring them out of the land of Egypt, my covenant that they broke.... For this is the covenant that I will make with the house of Israel after those days, declares the Lord: I will put my law within them, and I will write it on their hearts. And I will be their God, and they shall be my people.... For I will forgive their iniquity, and I will remember their sin no more" (Jeremiah 31:31-34).*

He promised to send the Messiah who would take all of our sin and punishment on himself and die in our place in order to atone for us.

We broke our part of the covenant with God, but He never stopped loving us, and in spite of it all, He wants to give us incredible gifts: He's inviting us to receive forgiveness and to turn a new page in our relationship with Him through this New Covenant.

BUT IT DOESN'T END THERE

So how will God make this covenant? He promised to send the Messiah who would take all of our sin and punishment on himself and die in our place in order to atone for us, just as it's written, "We all, like sheep, have gone astray, each of us has turned to our own way, and the Lord has laid on him the iniquity of us all" (Isaiah 53:6).

But it doesn't end there: God promised that the Messiah would rise from the dead in order to give us a new beginning and everlasting life with Him (Isaiah 53, Psalm 16:10).

Through Yeshua, God made a new covenant with us – it's not a separate religion, but rather the very covenant that the prophets of Israel predicted.

God also foresaw that in spite of hundreds of proofs, the religious leaders of the people of Israel would make a huge mistake and reject the Jewish Messiah. Look at how the Messiah is described in the Psalms: "The stone which the builders rejected has become the chief cornerstone" (Psalm 118:22).

WHEN THE PUZZLE PIECES COME TOGETHER

When you put all the puzzle pieces together that God gave us in order to identify the Messiah, we can see that the only one who fulfills all the criteria is Yeshua, Jesus of Nazareth. The evidence is clear: Yeshua lived his whole life according to the Torah, the builders of religious Judaism rejected him, and Yeshua laid down his life and died for our sin. But God raised Him to life on the third day, proving to us that Yeshua is indeed the Messiah! Hundreds of Jewish people testified that they saw Yeshua alive after He had been buried, and they didn't change their testimony even when they were tortured and killed for it!

Through Yeshua, God made a new covenant with us – it's not a separate religion, but rather the very covenant that the prophets of Israel predicted. What a comfort – Yeshua loved us until death. Through his resurrection He defeated death, and therefore He can grant eternal life to all who believe in him.

You don't have to believe us – these are promises from God himself, and as we've seen, God is always faithful to fulfill his every word. We can trust in him.

WHERE DO WE GO FROM HERE?

So where do we go from here? How can we fulfill our part in this covenant? All we have to do is to realize we've sinned, ask God to forgive us, believe in the God of Israel and in the Messiah, He sent – Yeshua – and decide to follow Him from now on.

We'd be glad to answer any questions you have. And if you'd like to start this new life right now, we're here for you. You're welcome to call or write to us privately. For more videos, and to read the Bible – the Tanakh and New Covenant – and other books for free, visit www.ThinkAgain.Life. For more about our ministry, visit TreeofLifeIsrael.org.

(Tree of Life Ministries Prayer Report 11/19/2023 https://www.treeoflifeisrael.org/)

CHAPTER 21
FROM THE RIVER TO THE SEA
BY ARIEL BLUMENTHAL, NOVEMBER 21, 2023

"From the River to the Sea, Palestine will be free." Many of you have heard or been hearing that rallying cry of the Palestinian narrative. Those from the left politically and with Muslims all over the world, especially in Europe and America, rallying, chanting to see a Palestinian state established not just in the pre-1967 border years, not just in the West Bank in Gaza, but the whole thing from the Jordan River on the East to the Mediterranean Sea on the West. Even American congresswoman Rashida Talib was caught using this phrase which is essentially a call for the destruction of the state of Israel, and to send all of the 7 million Jews for a big long swim in the Mediterranean. She was actually censored for it, but it's become this rallying cry.

It's very interesting, do you know where the original phrase "From the River to The Sea" comes from? Open your Bibles to the Book of Joshua Chapter One.

> *After the death of Moses the servant of the Lord, it came to pass that the Lord spoke to Joshua the son of Nun, Moses' assistant, saying:*

> *"Moses My servant is dead. Now therefore, arise, go over this Jordan, you and all this people, to the land which I am giving to them—the children of Israel. Every place that the sole of your foot will tread upon I have given you, as I said to Moses. From the wilderness and this Lebanon as far as the great river, the River Euphrates, all the land of the Hittites, and to the Great Sea toward the going down of the sun, shall be your territory. (Joshua 1:1-4)*

God is saying to Joshua that the sons of Israel are going to take possession of the land from the river to the sea. But the river is not just the Jordan River, it's the Euphrates River which is half of Iraq. This is one of the biblical definitions of the land of Israel of the inheritance of the sons of Israel which is pretty broad. It basically is from the Mediterranean Sea moving East including what today would be most of Jordan, part of Syria and half of Iraq.

This is something for us to think about. I'm not saying that is what's going to happen as a result of this war, but God is shifting things, and I believe that we're going to see some major changes in the definition in the boundaries of the State of Israel in the coming months, including Judea and Samaria, the West Bank, and in Gaza.

Let's use this as believers to point people to the Bible. Say, "Hey, do you know where that comes from? It comes from the Bible; the Book of Joshua. Do you know that God promised the land to the children of Israel, the Jewish people, more than 3,000 years ago, before there was ever such a thing as Palestine or the Palestinian people? Do you know that according to every modern historical record, the first mention of a Palestinian definition or a Palestinian national identity just started in 1920?"

I'm not saying we can argue about who should have a state, and where it should be. The Palestinian people are a fairly new thing. Again, it doesn't make it right or wrong. Jordan is a new thing. Kuwait is a new thing. The boundaries of a lot of things in the Middle East come from that time in the 1920's, but we want to point people to the Bible. From the River to the Sea, it's all in the Bible, come and see.

(Ariel Blumenthal grew up in a Reform Jewish home. He was searching for meaning in life in Zen Buddhism after college, when he was born again at a church in downtown Tokyo. He made Aliyah in 1998 and co-leads Ahavat Yeshua Congregation in Jerusalem.)

CHAPTER 22
GOD CRYING OUT TO US
BY ARNIE KLEIN, NOVEMBER 26, 2023

Many all over the world are crying out to God. Well beloved, I think God is actually crying out to us and we need to hear what He's saying. When we talk about the prophetic dynamic, for me it means putting together the invisible and the visible and looking at the physical picture and from there, beholding the spiritual reality and understanding from that what needs to happen to affect the physical picture.

The timing of the October 7th attack is unique and remarkable. It happened on the day after the 50th anniversary of the Yom Kippur War, which this year was the feast of Simchat Torah, a day of great rejoicing when the Jewish people traditionally dance with the Torah scroll. This was the day that people are relating to as the worst massacre of Jews since the Holocaust. And what I want to present as a starting point is that this day was not chosen by the enemy, but it was chosen by the Lord to make a statement to us that we might hear something that we have not been able to hear before.

In 1967, when Israel received Jerusalem back for the first time in 3000 years, the Temple Mount was in our hands and we glorified and blessed the Lord for the victory. But within a mere two hours after the Israeli flag was raised over the Temple Mount, our leadership completely surrendered the holy site to our enemies.

Well, we took the city and were really happy about that. But the center of the world, the dwelling place of God's Presence where Isaac was offered up, was of no value to us. Fifty years later in 2017, when the whole nation was rejoicing and dancing in the streets to celebrate the Jubilee anniversary of Jerusalem's return to Jewish hands, Chief Rabbi Meir Lau said, "This is a day of grief because we didn't care about what was most important to the heart of God."

Six years later on Yom Kippur in 1973 came the most devastating attack on Israel to date. Yom Kippur! This is the very day that is focused on the Holy of Holies, the heart of the Temple Mount. How could it be? We quote the verse, "He that watches Israel neither slumbers nor sleeps," but let's look at that in its full perspective. We usually think about that as God's protection, but it's also telling us He's seeing everything, and especially where it has to do with Israel, especially where it has to do with Jerusalem, and especially where it has to do with His Feast days. On the most holy day of all, surely God was right there, and we cannot imagine anything but that He was speaking.

This is not the first time that such a thing has happened. The Temple was destroyed twice on the same day, the 9th of Av. This was a statement from God. He had spoken prior to that through the prophet Habakkuk:

> *Look among the nations and watch – be utterly astounded! For I will work a work in your days which you would not*

> *believe, though it were told you. For indeed I am raising up the Chaldeans, a bitter and hasty nation which marches through the breadth of the earth, to possess dwelling places that are not theirs. (Habakkuk 1:5-6)*

He describes a horrible, brutal, vicious people, and declares that what's about to happen is His doing. So, we ask again now, how do we look at today's situation? How do we think about it? I hear the prayers that are going up asking God to stay the enemy, to bring victory, and all of those things, and I can't get away from what I said before, "We're crying out to God while He's crying out to us." And all that we're crying out to Him says to me that we're not listening.

There's another point, in the Book of Joel, where Joel describes a horrendous, vicious, brutal army coming to bring destruction. It's the day of the Lord! Joel 2:15 calls for a solemn assembly. The Hebrew there means "Stop!" God is emphatically telling us to stand still. Stop. You're not understanding what's going on. You're not seeing what I'm saying. You're not hearing from Me. You're looking at a temporal situation and trying to solve it and fix it from a human perspective. And all the while God is interested in something much, much more.

So here we are at a moment of horror and devastation that takes us back to shades of the Holocaust. It is difficult to speak from the perspective of God's sovereignty because of the horrible suffering that innocent people are going through. It could almost look as though we are ignoring that. But somehow, we need to balance both of these things. We need to understand what we're experiencing in light of what God is saying. I cannot stress enough my belief that what is going on right now is that God is crying out to all who have ears to hear.

The real danger is in the north. Hezbollah is reported to have 150,000 far more sophisticated, far more devastating missiles, than Hamas has. They've not accumulated those missiles for no reason. They surely intend to use them.

What just happened? One of the great questions is how could we -- this nation of such sophistication, of technological brilliance -- how could *we* have been caught unaware like this? We know from captured Hamas operatives, from documents, and from testimonies that this event, this attack, was planned at least a year, up to two years ago.

We look at it and say, "Our Mossad, our intelligence systems, had no idea about that?" Reports said they broke through in some 21 places at the same time, and that it was impossible for us to respond. There was such a breakdown of intelligence and communication.

But now I want to share a thought that we've carried our whole life. To some of you this will be simple to deal with: Israel is the center of the world. It's God's dwelling place, and the Body of Messiah in Israel is the center of Israel. It's the only place, the only group, in which God has a dwelling place. Physical Israel -- what happens on the ground in Israel -- we see as the reflection of the spiritual reality. This is key that we understand this because when we do, we're actually approaching getting an accurate diagnosis of what the problem is and knowing where to go for the solution.

Israel was unprepared. Israel has rejected God. If I would say to you as believers that we as a Body have rejected God, you'd look at me and say, "Where are you coming from? What are you talking about?" But if we connect these two things, and some other dynamics of things that we've heard over the years, we're presenting the thought that God is not really in the center of the Church.

More than 30 years ago I heard the Lord say that He felt neglected because we only come to Him -- primarily His children only come to him -- when we need something from Him. Not necessarily something personal, but anything. We don't abide with Him, come to Him, sit with Him, look to be with Him, just for Him, and He felt neglected. Primarily when we pray, how often in how many prayer meetings, does it happen that before we start to pray, we ask God what He sees? Do we ask him what he thinks? Do we ask Him what He's doing?

I asked a fellow who was in an international position of being connected to intercessory networks all around the world, "How many meetings have you been in like that?" And he said, "Zero." We always seem to be praying according to what the natural situation is. I'm saying that we need to shift, and it's a basic foundational shift. The level to which God is screaming right now is dramatic, and I believe that it wouldn't have come to this point if He hadn't been speaking for a long time and we weren't listening.

In this present situation, we've heard many saying, "This is the spirit of Amalek." And I think, "How interesting that is!" For in Exodus 17, in the first battle that Israel ever fought, the victory, the determination of the outcome, was Moses going up to the mountain with his hands raised up. And from the time I've first looked at that it was obvious and clear. It's a picture of worship! There is nothing written about Moses crying out to God. There is nothing written about Moses praying. He just lifted up his hands holding the rod of God. We simply believe this to be the picture of worship...making a place for the Presence of the Lord.

Another picture is the story of Esther. When Esther went in to the king, she was laying her life down as a living sacrifice, as in Romans 12:1:

I beseech you therefore, brethren, by the mercies of God, that you present your bodies a living sacrifice, holy, acceptable unto God, which is your reasonable service.

It's the picture of worship!

We heard from the Lord years ago that there were things that needed to be changed in the spirit realm that had to do with world principalities and powers, that only He could deal with. And what He said was, "Make a place for Me where I can dwell. And when I come, that spirit will change."

So, beloved, we arrive at the bottom line. We come to the hidden things, the foundations -- that which is the true matter of life and death. Here we are in a bomb shelter where people come for fear of their lives. God has said:

> *Come, my people, enter your chambers, and shut your doors behind you; hide yourself, as it were, for a little moment, until the indignation is past. (Isaiah. 26:20)*

What a picture this is, the message, the call of God! The purpose of our creation is simply to be with Him; He doesn't need us to weed the garden, to fix the problems. He created us for Himself, for fellowship. Oh my, how we've missed it! When the woman poured out the oil on Yeshua's feet, nobody saw what was happening. This was the only time that anyone ministered to the Lord not asking for something in return, and not one of all of the people there understood what was happening. This was about the heart of David being manifest, the heart that was after God. Oh, will we finally hear this call, this cry, the longing of His heart – "Come away with Me"?

The day will come, and we pray that it won't come now, that the Lord will no longer hold back the barrage from the north that will bring hundreds of thousands, if not more, casualties. We say, "Lord, hold it back. Give us more time." And I imagine Him saying, "If I give you more time, what will you do with it?"

And I present to you now what we've been hearing and believing -- what He wants us to do with it. That we would set apart time regularly every week to just *be* with Him, to create a dwelling place for Him. Not to ask Him to do something, but just to be with Him. And I hear Him saying, "You will end up in this sealed room, but the question is, will this room have been prepared as a place of worship? Will it have an eternal atmosphere in it, or will it be a place only of physical protection?"

What a difference that will make! This is the bottom line. We see the two wars, Yom Kippur in 1973 and now, drawing our attention to the Temple Mount, which is about the Presence of God. It's about His dwelling place. It's about intimacy with Him. That's the picture! It is not complicated.

Perhaps if we hear this word and receive it in our hearts, He will hold back the barrage from the north to allow us to become spiritually prepared. That we would be those who so love Him that we love not our lives so much as to shrink from death. For this is the reward of His suffering -- our heart, His dwelling place.

Now you might say, "Well, I have my quiet time with the Lord. I do that." But consider that John 17:22-23 is not about a personal individual experience. That which will reveal Him and His nature and His being to the whole world is a corporate dynamic. This is what we heard 25 years ago. The Lord was saying, "I want you to come to Me as a Body, and be alone with Me together, and wait before Me and listen before Me in a company, in a gathering, and all be together before Me."

This will make an eternal difference, and I know nothing else that can come into this situation and bring peace. The spiritual forces that we've been seeing released over the last years are global in nature. In the battle that we are facing now, Israel will not be destroyed. The Scripture says it. Looking at the end of the book we know we win. But we must not fail to realize that there are multitudes and multitudes of people who will suffer because the spirits of darkness have blinded the minds of the unbelievers (2 Cor.4:4). It is given to us believers, and to us alone, to clear that air...to scatter the spirits of darkness. Not by our works or even by our declarations, but by making a place for the manifest Presence of the Lord which was the result of Moses lifting his hands, and Esther at peril of her life going in before the king.

The seed that falls into the ground and dies when we come to the Lord asking Him for nothing -- just to make a place for Him -- will bear eternal fruit. May the Lord receive the reward of His suffering -- our lives and our hearts, even a dwelling place in Zion. Blessed be the Name of the Lord.

(Originally from New York City, Arni and his wife Yonit now live in the Galilee and lead Emmaus Way)

CHAPTER 23
GOD'S HOSTAGE

Andrew Brunson is an American pastor who was imprisoned in Turkey for two years which inspired global prayers for his safe release. He is the author of the book *God's Hostage*.

The following is an edited transcript of his testimony as told on the broadcast "100 Huntley Street." As we hear Andrew's story, let us continue to pray for the release of all the Israelis who are being held captive by Hamas.

Announcer: We are thrilled to be able to sit down with Pastor Andrew Brunson and just dive deeper into your story. We're so thrilled to have you here. You know, it's in those situations that the whole world is praying for you, you don't know what's gonna happen, and this... actually, you had a little bit of a warning that this was about to happen to you, but you didn't know what. Tell me about that morning that you were shaving three days before you were arrested.

Andrew: I didn't know it was a warning at all. I just heard this phrase, "it's time to come home," and I thought what does that mean, I'm home right now here in Turkey. We've been there 23 years and we had no thought of ever leaving. But it kept echoing in my mind, "it's time to come home, it's time to come home," and as I was held in prison and my time was extended, I just held onto that as a promise from God to me that He would take me home. Of course, when I hear that it's time to come home there's a sense of immediacy to it. It's like I'm saying, isn't it time to take me home? You said you'd take me home. I thought that would be sooner, but He did He did take me home.

Announcer: So, tell me what happened. You have this, "time to go home" thing, and you are then called to the police station. Tell me what was happening at that time and what you expected to happen.

Andrew: So, Noreen and I were called into the local police station, we thought we were going to pick up our long-term residence permits. When we got there, we were shocked when they told us, "We're going to deport you, we're arresting you and holding you for deportation." So, they took us to a deportation center and held us there for 13 days which was very unusual. Usually in America they would be deported in one or two days. Eventually they did release Noreen and then they moved me around to different places, put me into prison, and kept me for two years. So, we had not expected that at all.

Announcer: Tell me what that moment was like. Because you were trying to fight deportation, you're asking for delays, trying to do everything you could, and then all of a sudden you realize I'm not being deported, I'm being arrested. How did that hit you?

Andrew: Well, at the beginning I was crying because I didn't want to be deported. I thought, we've been working here for so long; 23 years, and God had spoken to us to prepare for harvest. And I thought, this isn't possible, you're deporting us, we're supposed to be here. And then after a few days I was crying because they wouldn't deport me. We came to see over time that this was actually part of it. It was an assignment for me to be in prison because so many people began to pray around the world. God had told us to prepare for harvest and actually this was one of the best ways that I could serve that preparation. I was doing nothing, just sitting in prison trying to hold on, and yet people were praying all over the world and that prayer was pouring into Turkey.

Announcer: And when you say the word harvest, for some of those that are watching that are maybe not familiar with that term, it means you're wanting people to come into relationship with Jesus. You feel that God was moving and that people were going to come to know Him in a personal way. I just wanted to clarify that.

Now with Noreen, she is also in prison. Tell me about how it was when she was released, and I guess in a way it was bittersweet, because your wife is getting to be released, but now you're by yourself.

Andrew: Yes, I was very glad that she could get out. And then I also knew that someone would be fighting for me. Up until then we weren't sure that anyone even knew where we were. But I was also very afraid, I had told her just a day before, what I'm really afraid of is that we will be separated and I'll be completely alone and I won't know what's happening to you. And then what I was afraid of actually did happen. We were separated, and I had to steel myself to be all alone. After that they put me into another Detention Center and I was in solitary confinement for fifty days and that was very difficult.

Announcer: And even more difficult, I think in a sense, is when you were moved into a prison cell that was incredibly overcrowded with terrible conditions. So, tell me a little bit about what it was like living in prison.

Andrew: So, they put me in a cell for eight people, but we had over 20 people there. One of the very difficult things was the isolation. I was isolated by culture and life experience and language, but especially isolated by faith because I was the only Christian, and all the other people I was with were very strong Muslims. It was like a 24/7 House of Prayer, but a Muslim House of Prayer, so it was very intense. We never left the cell. It was 24/7 in that room with a lot of people crammed in and I really broke. The isolation of being the only believer throughout my two years in prison, the only believer I had any contact with was Noreen on visits that we were allowed, so that isolation and the fear of not knowing what was going to happen to me... I broke down and I became suicidal over time.

Announcer: What did they say to you in terms of why you were being held? Because I know that's the question. People say, "well, this guy is a missionary." Is that your missionary activities or what were they saying to you?

Andrew: They knew all that we were doing because we did it openly for 23 years. We didn't hide what we did and it was not illegal. But they accused me of many different things. They knew that I was innocent, so this was coming from the very top of the government and I think they arrested me to intimidate other people, to intimidate other missionaries, to intimidate local Christians, Turks. And then it became something political over time, where they wanted to use me to gain concessions from the US. So, the reasons they gave were not really the reasons they were holding me. But they said that I was a terrorist, that I was a military spy, that I had helped to plan and orchestrate an attempted coup. They were all lies, but they were used as propaganda to paint Christians as being traitors and haters of Turks, which is not at all the case. We don't hate Turks, we love Turks.

Announcer: Such a difficult time for you in prison. You mentioned you became suicidal. Just before Christmas, you're out in the prison yard and you were looking at the clothesline. Tell me about that moment.

Andrew: Well, what took me there was a real sense of despair, isolation, and I'm feeling abandoned by God. He never abandoned me, I want to stress that, but I felt that way. I had pursued God's presence for years before and when I went into prison, I expected that I would have this sense of strength, a sense of joy even though it would be difficult, that I'd have a sense of grace, and certainly God's presence. What really surprised me is when that was removed. So, for the two years in prison, I did not have a sense of God's presence and I felt abandoned. And so, I was very confused and I had many questions. I had a lot of doubts, and this is something that especially the first year, where I felt that I was very broken. And in the second year, there was more of a rebuilding that took place.

Announcer: How did you rebuild Andrew? I've met so many that have had these prison experiences, and everybody is different, you know? Some will say, "well I just felt this incredible peace and joy", others, as you share and I think that has been more of the ones that I've heard, is that desperation, this anxiety, depression… So how did you start to get out of it and what did you feel the Lord was doing in that?

Andrew: So, I had a number of very low points and basically, I came to the point where I said, there's very little I can do to fight for my freedom, but I can fight for my relationship with God, and I have to because it's just being suffocated. And so, it was a decision of the will, it wasn't from my emotions, I felt beaten down and very low; just very weak the whole time. But it was a decision- I am going to turn toward God, I will keep my eyes focused on him. And I said, "whatever you do, God, whatever you do or don't do, I will follow you. Whether you speak to me or not, I will follow you. Whether you give me Your presence or not, I will follow you. Whether you release me or not, I will follow you." And after that I began a series of disciplines and of steps where I focused myself on God. One of the important things is, I had all of these doubts and questions, and I came to see that God actually had questions for me. Many believers go into a valley of testing and I was in a valley of testing. And I thought, "the valley of testing is full of dry bones; it's full of the skeletons of people who didn't survive."

Announcer: But you don't actually know you're in that period, or do you?

Andrew: I know that I was in there, absolutely.

Announcer: But I mean in the sense that God was testing you in it. Did you sense that or were you just trying to survive?

Andrew: I won't say that God causes all our problems, but in the midst of those He will test us and I was in the midst of a very intense testing. I thought, I want to survive this. When I say skeletons and dry bones of believers, I'm not talking about going to heaven. They can go to heaven, but I'm talking about a relationship with God. People lose that friendship with God, and I thought, I'm on the verge of that so I'm going to fight for my faith. And I realized that I had questions for God, but He had questions for me. "So, Andrew, are you going to be faithful when you don't feel my presence? Will you continue to love me even if you feel abandoned?" So, I was being tested and I determined that I wanted to come out of that test victorious and be faithful to God. So, I pressed in.

Announcer: You know you actually went all the way to the point where you started thinking that you'd be more impactful for God and his work if you stayed in prison. So that's like a huge arc from where you were thinking, I'd be better if I committed suicide.

Andrew: I didn't want to be in prison, but I came to think, oh no, I see all these people praying for me and maybe I'm more valuable to God in prison than out, so He may keep me in here so that more people will pray. But what I did come to was a battle to say, your will be done, not mine. And if your purposes are best served by my being in prison— I don't want to be here, I want to be with my family and the Turks. The Turkish government had said they wanted three life sentences for me, so I thought I might spend the rest of my life there. I said I don't want to be here, but if my being here will serve your purposes, then I want to serve your purposes and not mine.

Announcer: Wow. Did you know, Andrew, that people were praying for you and did you feel that?

Andrew: I knew it because this is what Noreen would tell me. We were allowed one visit a week through reinforced glass and on phones. And I would ask her every week if people were praying for me. I had such a hunger, a need to know that believers were standing with me. And she would say yes and it's actually growing. And this was an encouragement, but there was no guarantee that I would get out. And there's no verse in the Bible that says, "Andrew will be released from prison." So, it was an encouragement, I could see that God was working. I know that there was a lot of grace, but it was an unfelt grace, so I didn't feel, "oh! All these prayers are pouring in, I have strength!" It was more I know objectively that people are standing with me in prayer. This is an encouragement, but I still feel weak.

Announcer: So just after two years you get on a plane and then you come down those steps and you see your wife and your kids. Tell me about that moment and what you were feeling.

Andrew: It was a rollercoaster that day because I was taken to my fourth trial session and I was actually convicted of being a terrorist and so they convict me, they sentenced me to prison, and there'd been all this pressure for me to be released and I thought well none of it worked, now I'm going back to prison. So, they convict me, they sentenced me, and then suddenly they say we're releasing you while you appeal the sentence. Then there's a rush to get me to the airport onto an Air Force plane and back to the states. So, we went from being convicted in a court to 24 hours later being in the White House.

Announcer: Tell me about that. I mean, here's a guy that thinks maybe you're gonna spend the rest of your life in prison and, "whatever God you're gonna do what you're gonna do." And then you're in the White House. I mean I can't even get my brain around that.

Andrew: It was a real whirlwind and it felt very surreal to me. It felt to me like it was happening to somebody else. If you can imagine the rollercoaster of emotions from conviction, thinking I'm going back to prison, to suddenly within a day, seeing my children and being free again. It was only God.

Announcer: We have less than 30 seconds left, but just tell me for someone watching right now who's going through a trial, who may be experiencing some of the same emotions you felt, what advice would you have for them?

Andrew: You have a choice. No matter how difficult your situation is, you have a choice to turn toward God or away from him. And it was my turning toward Him and determining that I was going to keep looking at Him that invited Him into my situation, and I began to cooperate with grace. So, everyone can turn to him.

(Andrew Brunson is an American pastor who moved to Turkey in the mid-1990's where he pastored the Izmir Resurrection Church. Brunson was falsely arrested in 2016, and spent two years in a Turkish prison. https://www.youtube.com/watch?v=15AyFGQG0V4&t=2s)

CHAPTER 24
GOD'S PLAN FOR IRAN

I will set My throne in Elam, And will destroy from there the king and the princes,' says the Lord. (Jeremiah 49:38)

Dr. Hormoz Shariat is the founder and president of Iran Alive Ministries (IAM), a Christian ministry that uses satellite broadcasting and the internet to reach Iranians with the gospel. He is an Iranian Muslim convert who has a Ph.D. in Artificial Intelligence from the University of Southern California and a BA in Bible and Theology from Jessup University.

He shared the following update on November 14, 2023:

When you look at the Bible, any prophecies about Persia and Elam relate to Iran today, because Elam is completely inside Iran, and Persia is the main part of Iran, the ethnic and historical background. What we see in this war is another step towards the fulfillment of the prophecies, but it's not the final fulfillment.

I don't see the imminent fulfillment of the prophecies in Ezekiel 38 and Jeremiah 49 at this time, but it's just another step in that direction.

In Ezekiel 38, we know that Persia with Russia and other nations will attack Israel. As this war started, you see that there's even more alignments, like Turkey taking sides more clearly and aligning itself with Iran and with Russia, which is part of the prophecies of nations in Ezekiel 38. In Ezekiel 38, there is a list of nations that will unite to attack Israel, and that list even during the last five or six years has been amazingly coming into alignment. The nations that are not part of these prophecies are getting taken off the list of the enemies of Israel, and those who will attack Israel are being added to that list.

At the same time in Jeremiah 49, Iran fights against Israel, and in Jeremiah 49:38, we see that Iran will be saved. God says, "I will set my throne in Elam." So, through this war you have good news and bad news. The war and the suffering, and all that you see, we know the Lord's heart, that He is not pleased even when an evil person is killed. So, a child dying in Israel is the same, and has the same pain for us as Christians as a child dying in a Palestine. From the Lord's perspective, there is suffering in war, and we have to have His heart, but going to prophecies, we see that both sets of prophecies are being fulfilled in Iran at the same time.

It's amazing! How could that happen, Iran attacking Israel, and Iran being a Christian nation according to Jeremiah 49:38? You see that picture even in this war. We see that the government of Iran has been supporting Hamas and Hezbollah and the Houthis in Yemen. We know that Iran has been a supporter of this war even giving money and weapons to Israel's enemies. The government of Iran is very much involved in this, and they're developing a nuclear bomb, and the moment they have it, they're going to use it, maybe not directly against Israel, but at least to show and bully itself over nations like the U.S., Israel, and the surrounding nations.

Some people say they are very close to it, and some people say they're not, but the moment they have it, they will use it, either directly or indirectly for this war. It's amazing what happened in the last few weeks! The government of Iran has celebrated the war, but at the same time when they felt that there might be an attack on Iran, they kind of verbally backed off. Practically, the government of Iran is supporting this war with money and with weapons. They're saying we're not doing it, but the Hezbollah and Hamas leaders have always said that they're being supported by Iran, by millions and millions of dollars every year. They have always said that, but now the Iranian government is a bit scared of being attacked by Israel and the U.S., so they are kind of verbally saying they don't have a part in this war, so please don't attack us.

It looks like the Iranian government is kind of scared, and rightfully so, because when Israel settles this war, which sooner or later it will settle this war, just like the other wars of the last century. Whenever Israel has been attacked, the Lord somehow, even miraculously, saves them and turns the tables around always with Israel ending up on top. So, I believe this is going to happen again, and Israel will benefit long-term from this war. They will settle it and destroy their enemies. It's a real danger for Iranians if Israel and the U.S. attack Iran's nuclear and missile sites. The Iranian government knows that, that's why they're backing off a little, and at least verbally saying, "We don't have a part in it."

Now, about the people of Iran, this is the good news. The Iranian people even after this war have showed support for Israel. I don't think most people know, but after the war started, there were rallies by Iranians outside Iraq, in Los Angeles, Washington D.C., Seattle, and many cities in Europe, Iranians came on the streets supporting Israel with the Israeli flag. Inside Iran there is a trending hashtag *@isupportisrael* during the last few months, so there is a disconnect between the Iranian government and the people. The government is so anti-Israel that the people are becoming pro-Israel. The people are saying to the government, "Why should we hate Israel? They have not done anything to us. It's you the clergy, you're the ones who have ruined our lives. You have destroyed our lives. You are our enemies not them. We hate you; we don't hate them."

This is trending, the people of Iran have come to a point of even loving Israel and supporting Israel. As we see that there is a spiritual result; the Iranian people becoming very open to the gospel. In the last few weeks, we see a surge in the number of viewers of our online postings by Iranians. We do satellite television in Iran. We broadcast 24x7 satellite into people's homes, and we also reach people online. In the last few weeks there has been 20 times more people watching our clips about the war, and about the spiritual aspect.

So, pray that the government of Iran, that spiritual Prince of Persia that hates Israel, be contained. Pray for the people of Iran, that they would continue to come to Christ. We also know that because of this war, there's a very real possibility that the U.S and Israel will attack Iran within the next few weeks or few months.

Can you believe this, that the people of Iran are saying to the U.S. and Israel, "Please attack us. Please attack us." They have this idea that if the U.S. and Israel attack and destroy the Islamic government, they will be free. What they don't understand is that war is suffering, and no matter what, they're going to suffer.

So, pray for the people of Iran and the imminent very possible attack of Iran by Israel on the nuclear sites in the next few months. Pray for the prophecies. Pray to contain the hatred towards Israel. By the way, the hatred towards Israel in Iran is not an Iranian hatred; it was imported by Islam. It's an Islamic, it's an Ishmael issue, it's not the Iranians. Iranians are not children of Ishmael, so, it's an imported hatred towards Israel, and the people of Iran do not accept that. Pray for the people of Iran. Pray that the anti-Israeli, anti-Jewish spirit imported into Iran will be contained and bound at this time.

(Note: The Persian people have historically been favorable to the Jewish people, dating back to Daniel who was a trusted advisor of King Darius (Daniel 6), King Cyrus (2 Chronicles 36:22-23) who authorized the Jewish people to rebuild the temple and return to the land of Israel, and King Ahasuerus, the husband of Queen Esther, who saved the Jewish people from destruction.

In modern times, Iran was a haven to the Jewish people up until the Islamic Revolution of 1979.)

CHAPTER 25
HATIKVAH

"To live without hope is to cease to live." - Fyodor Dostoevsky

The English translation of the Israeli national anthem Hatikvah (The Hope) is:

> As long as within our hearts
> The Jewish soul sings,
> As long as forward to the East
> To Zion, looks the eye –
> Our hope is not yet lost,
> It is two thousand years old,
> To be a free people in our land
> The land of Zion and Jerusalem.

According to Alexander Pope (1688-1744), "Hope springs eternal in the human breast: Man, never is, but always to be blest." Hope has been the anchor of the Jewish people that sustained them throughout their bitter struggles, and the hope for peace and security within Eretz Yisrael remains the hope of the nation today.

The Psalmist David found hope in the Lord through his many trials, and he encouraged his people to hope in the Lord.

> "O Israel, hope in the LORD from this time forth and forever. (Psalm 131:3)

As a Messianic believer, my hope is in Yeshua, who is our living hope. According to the writer of the Book of Hebrews:

> *You (God) have put all things in subjection under his feet. (Psalm 8:6)*

> *For in that He put all in subjection under him, He left nothing that is not put under him. But now we do not yet see all things put under him. But we see Jesus, who was made a little lower than the angels, for the suffering of death crowned with glory and honor, that He, by the grace of God, might taste death for everyone. (Hebrews 2:8-9)*

We see three things in this passage:

1. God has put all things in subjection to Messiah.
2. All things are not yet under Him.
3. We need to focus our attention on Messiah.

The hope of our salvation is perfectly sealed by the finished work of Messiah, and although we wait for its completion in this life, we look to Him to shepherd us to our final destination.

During this time when hopelessness prevails in the hearts of many people, Pastor Mark Spencer shared a message on

November 26, 2023 on the importance of hope. The following are excerpts from his message, which is relevant to the nation of Israel, as well us as individuals.

"I want to talk to you about hope. I know 99% of you were thinking he's going to talk about Thanksgiving, but we're talking about hope because it's such an incredibly important virtue right now. We live in such a turbulent world. It's very confusing. I don't think it's because I am 66 years old, and I'm not in my rocking chair just seeing what's happened to the world. I think all of us are rocking a little because of the amount of change and the amount of flux. It's created massive amounts of anxiety.

These are the latest stats on anxiety among various age groups in America. And I don't think these stats tell the whole story because there's lots of people that won't report or go see a doctor. But we're looking at 32% of all adults are reporting symptoms of anxiety and or depression. It's alarming to me that half of those in the 18 to 24 age group are reporting symptoms of anxiety and depression. It has to do with the flux we're feeling in the world. Like COVID was a crazy thing, but there's lots of crazy things right now, and so when we're confused, and we don't know what to do, we experience anxiety, and we find ourselves not knowing what to do. We don't like that feeling when we don't know what to do because we like the illusion that we have a little bit of control, and when we don't know what to do, we really feel lost. So, what we typically do when in doubt, we consult the big G; Google that is. When I talk to young people in the coffee shop, they say, "Wait, let me Google that; let me see if what you're saying is true, certainly Google will know." Google the Almighty!

In preparing this message, I thought okay I'm going to Google it, so I Googled "I don't know what to do," and I came up with 18 billion results in .35 seconds! I looked at that, and thought "That's hardly hopeful for me." So, the big question is, how do we have hope when we don't know what to do? We often wish for certain things to happen. However, when the Bible talks about hope. It isn't this kind of wishing, it's quite the opposite. When life has brought us into this unknown, into the frightening, into the horrible, into the I don't know what to do, wishing doesn't quite get the job done. What we crave in that moment is a deep anchored secure hope, not some 18 billion shaky possibilities about what Google says.

So, as I'm talking about hope, put this in the front pocket of your brain; biblical hope not only wishes for something, it expects it to happen! It not only expects it, is confident that it will. One reason that people get hope-sick, like the proverb says: Hope deferred makes the heart sick (Proverbs 13:12), is that their hope is misplaced. So, God often has to do a work in us and on us to redirect or replace our hope. It needs to be firmly placed on the truth of God, the unchangeable and shakeable and wavering constantly true truths, because those truths lead us to a God of hope, and that God is already working on it, and he's working on us. Here's the reality: God isn't just after a moment of hope; what he's ultimately crafting is a bunch of solid hopes because what He would love to see is that you, the solid hopers of God, would walk into a hopeless world and display for all to see that you can have real unshakable hope in a very confusing world.

That is our business! That is why Peter said: "Always be ready to give a defense to everyone who asks you a reason for the hope that is in you." (1 Peter 3:15) So, what I want to do is to pack your pockets with some truths about hope that will propel you to becoming the kind of Grade-A hopers that God desires us to be.

The first point is that hope doesn't come first. Paul writes, "And not only that, but we also glory in tribulations, knowing that tribulation produces perseverance; and perseverance, character; and character, hope. (Romans 5:3-4) We want to skip ahead in Romans, but we must first glory in our sufferings. Why? Because suffering produces perseverance and perseverance character, and character hope. I don't know about you, but that glory in your suffering stuff makes me go "Gulp."

Let me ask you this, "How many of you did your deepest, most enduring spiritual growth on the mountain top?" It happens down here in the valley in those low places, those hard spots where you didn't see that coming, where you didn't know what to do, where you felt lost, you were confused, where you're down in this spot, and God builds something into you. He crafts something into you, and He is making you a Grade-A hoper.

So today we're going to follow the hope story in a king's life. He has a funny name, but he also has really sincere faith. King Jehoshaphat in Second Chronicles chapter 20 is going to demonstrate to us how you and I can have hope when we don't know what to do. Here's how the story opens

> *Then some came and told Jehoshaphat, saying, "A great multitude is coming against you from beyond the sea, from Syria; and they are in Hazazon Tamar" (which is En Gedi). (2 Chronicles 20:2)*

Talk about being struck with a little bit of hopelessness, a vast army, this is not a small army, have built up in a massive force. The enemies of Israel were starting to hook arms. This is something akin to Russia and China saying, "Let's go after him together," and they're on the doorstep. It's a world war!

So, what happens:

And Jehoshaphat feared (2 Chronicles 20:3a)

Yeah, I get that. Do you get that? How are you feeling in the moment? Jehoshaphat's afraid, which leads us to note a very important truth: that even though you might be hoping, you may feel some other things. Having hope doesn't mean that's all you're gonna have. You're gonna have other emotions that are swirling around. There are other emotions that are challenging your head and your heart. We can think that if I was really hopeful, I wouldn't experience those. But that's not true. That's not Biblical. It's not realistic.

One of my war heroes, a guy that I've read and studied, is General George Patton. He was interviewed somewhere at the tail end of World War II, and as he is being interviewed, the guy said to him, "What is it like to be fearless?" General Patton said, "I don't know what you mean." The interviewer said, "Well you're certainly fearless." And Patton replied, "No I'm not fearless. In fact, I'm an utter coward. Every time I hear a gunshot, or a bomb go off, my palms sweat, my body starts to shake with fear. But here's what I've learned very early in my life, never take the council of my fears."

As spoken by one of the most extraordinary leaders in wartime, the fact that you're noted as courageous, or you need to muster courage, doesn't mean you're not gonna have to walk through fear. The fact that you're in a time where you don't know what to do, and you're trying to muster hope, doesn't mean you're not gonna encounter fear or confusion or sadness or sorrow. This truth begins to shift our focus in a way where we realize that hope is fostered; it's nurtured. It's nourished, and you and I grow hope just like you grow faith; just like you grow love; you grow it.

I wish at times that hope came first, but it doesn't. I wish that if trouble was coming, all of a sudden four UPS trucks would come and they'd be busy unloading massive boxes of hope. And then they would say, "Spenser, you're gonna need this. Hang on." At least I got a big stockpile full of hope. It's not how it works. You and I nurture, foster, and we grow hope.

And we see this with the king. Look at this the first thing the king does:

> *And Jehoshaphat ... set himself to seek the Lord. (2 Chronicles 20:3b)*

He resolves to seek God. He's not going after answers, he's going after God. That's what we need – God. We need the living God. We need the presence of God where there's fullness of joy. The presence of God where there's hope. An answer might provide temporary relief, but a deep anchored relationship with the Almighty - now we're talking! Jehosophat resolves to inquire of the Lord.

And look what he does:

> *And Jehoshaphat ... proclaimed a fast throughout all Judah. (2 Chronicles 20:3c)*

He proclaims a fast. I hate fasting; fasting is not fun. Sometimes if we're gonna nurture good hope, if we're gonna foster good hope, what we really have to do is clear the runway. Maybe it's not even food, maybe it's those phones, maybe it's no screen time. We're gonna push it aside. Jehosophat is serious. He says we're fasting so that we can clear the runway. We wanna make our hearts open. We want our minds to be ready. We want our eyes watching. We don't want to be distracted by anything. When you fast and you seek the Lord, you put away the distractions and the attractions that surround us. And we got a lot of them. It's like if I fast, it seems like brownies just come chasing me all the time. If we're gonna foster hope, we need to resolve, to determine in our heart that I'm seeking God. I'm gonna seek God in such a way as I'm gonna clear the runway. I'm gonna fast.

And then look what he does:

> *So Judah gathered together to ask help from the Lord; and from all the cities of Judah they came to seek the Lord. (2 Chronicles 20:4)*

The people of Judah come together, and they seek help from the Lord. We need others to help us see God. I don't see God well on my own. The reason that you have prophetic gatherings is that you trust that spiritual gift is gonna help you see something you can't see on your own. The reason we do this today is that you're together, is that you might see one another, that you might stop and ask, "How are you doing?" "Not so well," so you sit down, you talk, you listen, and you pray and there might be a word that God gives you. There might be an encouragement. Just the fact that you saw the person and listen to them could be huge. And so, Jehoshaphat knows this: we gotta get our people.

Who are the people in your life that help you see God? You should know that. You should be able to get on the horn. I've got a handful of these people that I'm current with, and they're current with, me and they help me see God because I can't see God sufficiently on my own. So, as Jehosophat gathers these people, look what he does:

> *Then Jehoshaphat stood in the assembly of Judah and Jerusalem, in the house of the Lord, before the new court, and said: "O Lord God of our fathers, are You not God in heaven, and do You not rule over all the*

> *kingdoms of the nations, and in Your hand is there not power and might, so that no one is able to withstand You? Are You not our God, who drove out the inhabitants of this land before Your people Israel, and gave it to the descendants of Abraham Your friend forever? (2 Chronicles 20:5-7)*

He begins to preach to the people, and he starts to declare the truths of God that are unchanging and unwavering. It doesn't matter how old they are. It doesn't matter what people say about them. They are the solid truths of God you can stand on! The saints of old stood on them. The prophets of old stood on them. The kings of Israel stood on them, and the people of God need to stand on them. He remembers as he's declaring this what God has done. Sometimes we need to preach to ourselves. Come on Spenser, quit looking at the problem, and put your trust in God.

I go into the woods and leave my problems in the back seat of the car, and I cry out, "Lord, I need to see You. I need Your truth to stand on." I remember all the things that God has done.

Do you have a Hall of Faith that you visit; a hallway in your memory where you walk down, and you remember all the God has done?

Parents once brought their young 16-year-old girl to come see. She had been traumatized, a terrible situation, and they couldn't find any place to go where there was a Christian who understood counseling. I watched God transform an immense trauma in a 16-year-old life. I remember what it looked like to see her go from being anxious to peaceful, hurt to healthy, weak to strong, unsure to determined faith. Remember that.

I hope you have storerooms jam packed with the things that God has done for you and for others that you could revisit, because that's what Jehoshaphat's doing. He's gone back over this; remembering this. I want you to remember this because when you don't know what to do, there's still plenty you can do. You can resolve to see God. You can get the people on the horn that know you well. You can fast. You can dig in.

That said, this next truth is important to take home with you. If you have hope, it doesn't mean you have the answer. Hope is future faith. Hope is down the road. I can see it, but I don't know how God's going to do it. I don't know when God's going to. I just know God will do it. King J still doesn't have an answer. but that's okay because King J's hope is not in an answer. The king says that we have no power to face this vast army that's attacking us. He's honest. He's realistic. I don't know. I don't know.

But how many of the stories that we draw courage and hope from in this book are places that lead to I don't know. Moses finally gets the people of God out of Egypt. They think they're heading home free, and what happens? All of a sudden, there's an army pursuing you, the world's strongest army, by the way, and you are staring at a gigantic sea in front of you.

It's an "I don't know what to do moment." There's a giant that pesters Israel day, and, taunting them; making fun of their armies. We don't know what to do. God sends the unlikely teenager. I mean it just doesn't make sense, but here's the reality for us to think on, there has to be a test before there's a testimony. That's the reality! The testimony is coming when you're in the test. There has to be a test. This is why Paul writes:

> *We are hard-pressed on every side, yet not crushed; we are perplexed, but not in despair. (2 Corinthians 4:8)*

Paul is talking about a hard time; he's talking about a perplexing time when you and I don't have answers. I remember digging into this scripture one time when I was perplexed. I didn't know what was happening. I was confused, and I landed in this section of 2nd Corinthians, and studied and studied and looked at all the translations. I mapped it out exegetically. I studied the original languages, and I want to offer to you a Mark Spencer paraphrase. Are you ready? This is not for sale yet, but this phrase "perplexed, but not in despair," if it were translated the Mark Spencer paraphrase; this is free of charge by the way.

"We don't have the immediate answer, but we know the one who is the answer."

That's what Paul is saying. In the Greek he's saying, "We don't know. We don't have the answer right now, but don't worry we know the One who says He's the Way, He's the Truth, He's the Life.

When you're lost and without answers, and you're feeling confused I ask you this, "Would you rather have someone hand you a map to follow or send a living guide to hold your hand and walk you through." What you see with King J is, "I'm not taking the map, I want the hand," and as he does, he locks eyes with the Almighty. You see King J looked at the odds; he's listened to the battle plans; he studied this situation. It looks humanly bleak. Now is the time to fix your gaze on the One who does the impossible.

So, the king says, "We don't know what to do, but our eyes are on You." This is it! We don't know what to do, but what does it take to save people - our eyes are on You. It's not the numbers; not the might; not how many weapons we have; not on ideas, planned schemes; not on answers, they're on You, You, You.

The New Testament writer would be shouting at this; shouting because this is what they said. He said:

> *Fixing your eyes on Jesus, the pioneer and perfecter of faith."*
> *(Hebrews 12:2)*

These poor Hebrews! They are being persecuted severely, threatened, jailed, beaten, some murdered for their faith. Talk about a confusing time! We don't know what to do. The author is beginning to land his plane of careful argument in the Book of Hebrews, that he says what King Jehosophat had said back in Second Chronicles: Fix your eyes on Jesus. Lock eyes with Him; that's where hope is. He's the living hope.

And while you're gazing at the Almighty, take a page out of King J's playbook. What King J offers to us is worship.

> *And when he had consulted with the people, he appointed those who should sing to the Lord, and who should praise the beauty of holiness, as they went out before the army and were saying:*
> *"Praise the Lord, For His mercy endures forever." (2 Chronicles 20:21)*

Hope worships. Worship is worth ship. W-O-R-T-H-Y, God is worthy! "You are worthy." "You are worthy." "You are worthy to be praised."

In these moments there's something very important that we the people of God are doing. We are declaring not just to the people on Earth, but to the heavenly realm we're declaring God's worth ship. I don't know what to do. I don't know the answer, but I do know God's worthy, so I'm going to worship.

There's two times to praise God, when things look good, and when things don't. Those are the two times to worship. Easy to worship when things are good, but when you're staring at something like a massive army knocking on the door of your neighborhood, it's time to worship. And so, they send the band out there.

But look at this, this is amazing!

> *Now when they began to sing and to praise, the Lord set ambushes against the people of Ammon, Moab, and Mount Seir, who had come against Judah; and they were defeated. (2 Chronicles 20:22)*

When they began to sing and praise the Lord, God sent an ambush against these armies and they were routed. The battle is the Lords! They begin to just praise the Lord, and they came out with a tremendous victory.

I love this because they didn't have U-hauls back then, but they sure needed them.

> *When Jehoshaphat and his people came to take away their spoil, they found among them an abundance of valuables on the dead bodies, and precious jewelry, which they stripped off for themselves, more than they could carry away; and they were three days gathering the spoil because there was so much. (2 Chronicles 20:25)*

They found more loot than they could carry off! This is Captain Jack Sparrow territory! They're just loving this equipment and clothing. It took three days to make off with the goods. That's a big victory people!

Think with me, this is an important turn. King Jehoshaphat's work brought them to a place of trust and hope in the Lord. But how do you think they would have responded had they not walked through that process of fixing their hope on truth? If they would have started with "Let's send Eric and the worship band out there?" That would sound a little crazy. Wouldn't it? You see, sometimes when we're looking for an answer, the answer that the Almighty gives sounds crazy.

Like we talked about. Send a teenager to fight a 9-foot trained professional MMA butcher. That doesn't make sense. Pick Peter. Peter? Sweaty guy. Select Saul who will become Paul. That doesn't make sense. Does it? Select Spencer to be a pastor and a counselor? Do you know this guy? You see the process of hope was shifting, so they could be resting on God. The exercise was shifting the people of God and their hope, to hope in God. The battle is His. Our hope is in Him."

> *If it had not been the Lord who was on our side,"*
> *Let Israel now say —*
> *"If it had not been the Lord who was on our side,*
> *When men rose up against us,*
> *Then they would have swallowed us alive,*
> *When their wrath was kindled against us;*
> *Then the waters would have overwhelmed us,*
> *The stream would have gone over our soul;*
> *Then the swollen waters*
> *Would have gone over our soul."*
>
> *Blessed be the Lord,*
> *Who has not given us as prey to their teeth.*
> *Our soul has escaped as a bird from the snare of the fowlers;*
> *The snare is broken, and we have escaped.*
> *Our help is in the name of the Lord,*
> *Who made heaven and earth. (Psalm 124)*
>
> *O Israel, hope in the Lord; For with the Lord there is mercy,*
> *And with Him is abundant redemption. (Psalm 130:7)*

(Mark Spencer is a Teaching Pastor at Bridgewood Community Church in Blaine. MN. He is also the founder and Chief Social Engineer of Clarity Coaching and Consulting. Mark has planted two churches and coached the launch of 3 others. He holds a BA in Sports Medicine (Ripon College), MA in Theology, and MA in Marriage and Family Therapy (both from Bethel Seminary). Mark embodies the pastoral gifting.

CHAPTER 26
HEBREW VERB TENSES

When the enemy comes in like a flood, The Spirit of the Lord will lift up a standard against him. (Isaiah 59:19)

The English language has 12 verb tenses:

- Past Simple I lifted up
- Past Continuous I was lifting up
- Past Perfect I had lifted up
- Past Perfect Continuous I had been lifting up
- Present Simple I lift up
- Present Continuous I am lifting up
- Present Perfect I have lifted up
- Present Perfect Continuous I have been lifting up
- Future Simple I will lift up
- Future Continuous I will be lifting up
- Future Perfect I will have lifted up
- Future Perfect Continuous I will have been lifting up

The Hebrew language only has two verb tenses:

- Perfect (Completed action) I lifted up
- Imperfect (In progress or future action I will lift up)

Israel can look back at times when God lifted up a standard against the attack of the enemy in Biblical times, in 1948, in 1967 and in 1973. This gives us hope for the future.

In the present time, Israel can have faith that God will lift up a standard any and every time the enemy attacks them.

During Chanukah, Jewish people sing the song "Nes Gadol" to commemorate God's miraculous workings on their behalf in the past. The chorus goes:

"Nes gadol haya sham." (נס גדול היה שם) translated: A great miracle **happened there.** (perfect tense)

Let's change that to:

"Nes gadol yiheyeh po." (נס גדול יהיה פה) translated: A great miracle **will happen here.** (imperfect tense).

CHAPTER 27
IF ISRAEL JUST ALLOWED THE PALESTINIANS TO HAVE THEIR OWN STATE

If Israel just allowed the Palestinians to have a state of their own there would be peace in the Middle East, right? That's what you hear from UN ambassadors, European diplomats, and most college professors. But what if I told you that Israel has already offered the Palestinians a state of their own, and not just once but on five separate occasions. Don't believe me, let's review the record.

After the breakup of the Ottoman Empire following World War I, Britain took control of most of the Middle East including the area that constitutes modern Israel. Seventeen years later in 1936, the Arabs rebelled against the British and against their Jewish neighbors. The British formed a task force, the Peel Commission, to study the cause of the rebellion. The commission concluded that the reason for the violence was that two peoples, Jews and Arabs, wanted to govern the same land. The answer, the Peel Commission concluded, would be to create two independent states; one for the Jews and one for the Arabs, a two-state solution.

The suggested split was heavily in favor of the Arabs. The British offered them 80% of the disputed territory, the Jews the remaining 20%. Yet despite the tiny size of their proposed state, the Jews voted to accept this offer, but the Arabs rejected it, and resumed their violent rebellion. <u>Rejection number one.</u>

Ten years later in 1947, the British asked the United Nations to find a new solution to the continuing tensions. The U.N. decided that the best way to resolve the conflict was to divide the land. In November 1947, the U.N. voted to create two states again. The Jews accepted the offer, and again the Arabs rejected it. Only this time they did so by launching an all-out war. <u>Rejection number two.</u>

Jordan, Egypt, Iraq, Lebanon, and Syria joined the conflict, but they failed. Israel emerged victorious from the war and swiftly transitioned to the task of constructing a new nation. The majority of the land allocated by the UN for an Arab State—specifically the West Bank and East Jerusalem—became occupied territory, not by Israel, but by Jordan.

Twenty years later in 1967, the Arabs led this time by Egypt, and joined by Syria and Jordan, once again sought to destroy the Jewish State. The 1967 conflict, known as the Six Day War, ended in a stunning victory for Israel. Jerusalem and the West Bank as well as the area known as the Gaza Strip fell into Israel's hands.

The government split over what to do with this new territory; half wanted to return the West Bank to Jordan and Gaza to Egypt in exchange for peace, the other half wanted to give it to the region's Arabs who had begun referring to themselves as the Palestinians, in the hope that they would ultimately build their own state there. Neither initiative got very far, a few months later the Arab League met in Sudan, and issued its infamous three no's: no peace with Israel, no recognition of Israel, no negotiations with Israel. Again, a two-state solution was dismissed by the Arabs making this rejection number three.

In 2000, Israeli Prime Minister Ehud Barack met at Camp David with Palestinian Liberation Organization chairman Yasser Arafat to conclude a new two-state plan. Barack offered Arafat a Palestinian state in all of Gaza and 94% of the West Bank with East Jerusalem as its capital, but the Palestinian leader rejected the offer. In the words of U.S. President Bill Clinton, "Arafat was here 14 days, and said "No" to everything. Instead, the Palestinians launched a bloody wave of suicide bombings that killed over 1,000 Israelis, and maimed thousands more on buses, in wedding halls, and in pizza parlors. Rejection number four.

In 2008, Israel tried yet again. Prime Minister Ehud Olmert went even further than Ehud Barack had, expanding the peace offer to include additional land to sweeten the deal. Like his predecessor, the new Palestinian leader Mahmud Abbas turn the deal down. Rejection number five.

In between these last two Israeli offers, Israel unilaterally left Gaza giving the Palestinians complete control there. Instead of developing this territory for the good of its citizens, the Palestinians turned Gaza into a terrorist base from which they have fired thousands of rockets into Israel. Each time Israel has agreed to a Palestinian state, the Palestinians have rejected the offer, often violently.

So, if you're interested in peace in the Middle East, maybe the answer is not to pressure Israel to make yet another offer of a state to the Palestinians. Maybe the answer is to pressure the Palestinians to finally accept the existence of a Jewish state.

"Jerusalem, Judea and Samaria – they are all Israel. The homeland of the Palestinian people is the Kingdom of Jordan." (Geert Wilders, Netherlands Prime Minister)

(By David Brog, Executive Director of the Macabee Task Force for Prager University https://www.youtube.com/watch?v=hcp_aq51iIU)

CHAPTER 28
IMA'S GOODIES

Renee Shmuel has a very unique ministry called Ima's Goodies. She is an incredible cook, and what she has done for years is, she bakes these amazing things, loads up her car with them, and takes them around to different IDF bases, and gives the goodies to the troops, and then she is usually able to say a prayer, and talk about how good God is. And she has won over the hearts of many IDF soldiers and their commanders. God has called Renee into this ministry for such a time as this because she already has favor and is already well known in the land.

It all started on June 12th 2014 when three teenage Jewish boys were kidnapped and murdered in the city of Hebron. During this time there were constant missile attacks on residents in the south of Israel, and as a result IDF forces searching for these three young men, found many underground tunnel systems leading from Gaza to within Israel's border. The government and IDF forces went on full alert to try and stop the barrage of rockets. Over 75,000 reservists were called up for duty. It was during this time frame of "Operation Protective Edge" that Ima's Goodies was started, as they wanted to do their part as well. They thought it was so important for the soldiers to know that believers living here in the land, as well as Christians from around the world, love and support them. So that's when Renee picked up her mixing bowl and her supplies, and went to work.

Renee shared the following update on November 15, 2023:

I will just share what I know from being boots on the ground, or sometimes sandals on the ground; I mean basic. I'll start off by sharing a quick scripture from Psalms 83. This whole chapter is a chapter that is usually said at memorial services for our IDF soldiers, and also over memorial services for our Holocaust people. They know the scripture, and it says:

> *Do not keep silent, O God!*
> *Do not hold Your peace,*
> *And do not be still, O God!*
> *For behold, Your enemies make a tumult;*
> *And those who hate You have lifted up their head.*
> *They have taken crafty counsel against Your people,*
> *And consulted together against Your sheltered ones.*
> *They have said, "Come, and let us cut them off from being a*
>   *nation,*
> *That the name of Israel may be remembered no more."*

Then at the very end of the chapter it says:

> *Let them be confounded and dismayed forever;*
> *Yes, let them be put to shame and perish,*
> *That they may know that You, whose name alone is the Lord,*
>   *Are the Most High over all the earth.*

Thank you for your prayers for Israel, because this has been a very trying time. This is a hard time. It's really been crazy in Israel, because it's hard to know what's going to happen from one moment to the next. And I think we all in Israel are awaiting with anticipation, what's going to happen with Gaza, or what's going to happen with our hostages? I am busily involved with the soldiers. However, being engaged with the soldiers inevitably entails praying for the hostages, Israel, and the safety of the borders. They're all wrapped up together like a wonderfully made cake.

There are things happening on the northern border that I think we're just hitting the tip of the iceberg on. It seems like people are saying, "Well, it's kind of heating up." And that's for sure what's happening. It's every day now, like what used to be in Gaza for years, is now happening on the northern border. They're constantly throwing rockets and RPGs over, and people are getting killed. The northern border communities have all been evacuated from that area. So, we have the southern communities evacuated from about 40 kilometers from the fence, and then we have all those being evacuated on the northern border. We're all kind of now in this middle of the country together.

But one of the things that I think that's necessary to pray for is extra supernatural strength for our soldiers. The soldiers are on my heart. Israel is on my heart. That's why I came to Israel years ago, Israel at my heart. It's a supernatural strength, and ability to keep on going, when we're not having any answers, when we're not seeing any provision, when we're not seeing anything happening, when we're kind of running into the dark again, and again, and again. And the same thing, especially for our soldiers; our soldiers are out there. We know the scripture that we can run and not grow weary or be faint or be tired. But our soldiers don't know that all the time.

We live in the Holy Land, but we are not a holy people. And so, our soldiers don't know this. Pray for supernatural strength, when they lay down to rest, whether it's two in the afternoon when they when they finish a shift, or it's eleven at night. Pray that whether they lie down for three or four hours, the rest they get would be doubled or tripled.

All the soldiers I meet, say, "Yeah, we're good, we're good," but we also know that when you talk to them one on one, they're like, "Man, this is wearing on, and this is tiring." So, these are just some really quick prayer points. I've been with soldiers from all sorts of different units and groups, some that I don't even remember or understand what they're doing. But God has opened the door to certain groups who have called me and contacted me. And so, I've gone to those groups. And we've been able to help so many people. We've been able to bless a lot of soldiers.

I'm talking in the hundreds of soldiers that we've been able to bless. So, they are very open to receiving. They're very open to love. They're very open to the hugs that we give. But we know that they're very, very tired.

One of the things that we've done lately is to be able to bless them with some toasters, sandwich makers that you press, and you put your meat or your cheese inside bread and make it a toasty. So, little things like this, that's helping them as they continue through the day, as they continue pressing on.

It's not just for us, it's not just cakes, or cookies, or goodies, it's to find out what certain groups need. We had an undercover unit the other day that we blessed with some amazing special sunglasses that they needed, because they're out in the sun all the time. And these sunglasses are not just sunglasses like you'd buy at the normal store, these are like Navy Seal undercover glasses, all these special sunglasses, and we were able to bless them. They also needed toiletries, so, we blessed them also with toiletries.

The soldiers are getting blessed with a variety of things. And there's a variety of groups and people that are blessing them. We're very thankful for the generosity. The biggest need right now though, is to pray for the continuing fighting spirit, to continue to go forward at the same pace and at the same speed. We all know that. Even as I drive sometimes, suddenly, I feel like my foot goes off the gas, and I realize I'm in a slower position than I was when I first started the trip. A continuing strong spirit, emotional strength, physical strength, mental strength, and spiritual strength are needed now for our soldiers more than ever.

Thank you to everyone who's praying. Also, remember to pray for those of us living in this land who are actively involved because the needs are plentiful. There are countless individuals in dire need, and numerous units seek guidance and support. I'm navigating these challenges, seeking clarity on where to focus and how to address the needs within our financial means. What day can we go? When can we get this done? One of my biggest prayers that I always pray is, "God today, I want You to make two plus two equal five." I know in the natural, two plus two equals four; we know that's a given. "But today, I need you to make two plus two to equal five." And I'm always amazed at how He does it. So, thank you so much for your prayers. Amen.

For more information on Ima's Goodies, check out:

Website: https://www.imasgoodies.com

Email: imasgoodies@gmail.com

Twitter: ImasGoodies

Facebook: ImasGoodiesIsrael

Instagram: imasgoodies

Paypal: paypal.me/ImasGoodies

CHAPTER 29
IN MEMORIAM

Another Israeli Messianic Jewish hero from the Shavei Tzion-congregation fell at the hands of Hamas. Lieutenant Alina Pravosudova, 23, bravely shielded fellow soldiers during the terrorist attack on October 7, 2023.

Pravosudova, a 23-year-old affectionately known as "Redhead" by her friends, was born in Israel to Russian-Ukrainian immigrants, Olga and Michael. She embodied their dreams for a better future in Israel and excelled in every endeavor: her studies, her passions like ballet dancing, and her dedication to martial arts at her grandparents' Aikido school in Haifa.

"She was gentle but incredibly strong," her mother, Olga Pravosudova, said.

Pravosudova grew up on Hachashmal Street in the Neve Yosef neighborhood. A few years ago, after the family's move to their current apartment, she began volunteering at the nearby MDA branch, located within walking distance from their home. She left behind her parents, grandparents, and a 15-year-old brother.

Her childhood friends remember her as "the redhead who caught everyone's attention."

During her service in the IDF, Pravosudova ascended from a soldier-fighter in the Home Command to a commander in the Southern Command, an area officer, and an authority tasked with preparing the Bedouin community for emergencies. She relocated to Be'er Sheva to be closer to the Negev residents she served and the base.

Her friends can recount how Pravosudova spent Shabbat at her base near Kibbutz Re'im.

"She was the officer on duty, overseeing the close of Shabbat. Terrorists infiltrated the base, and she engaged in a fierce confrontation with them, ultimately losing her life while shielding her fellow female soldiers. Her courageous actions saved lives, with some still in serious condition and hospitalized," her friends said.

Back at home, her parents and friends anxiously tried to contact her.

"We haven't heard from her since then," two friends, Emily and Karina explained, "but she wasn't reachable. Her boyfriend, who also serves there and was involved in the incident, only mentioned there was an encounter at the base. He was in touch with her when the order came for all base soldiers to return to camp after the initial rocket attack."

Another one of their friends sustained a gunshot wound and was hospitalized at Barzilai Hospital and later Sourasky Medical Center. He has already undergone three surgeries. Unfortunately, his injuries prevented him from attending Pravosudova's funeral, which took place on Tuesday in Haifa, though his parents paid their respects.

This tragic event also brought a halt to Pravosudova's military career, which she had planned for herself after enlisting in 2019 and signing up for service until 2027.

"We will remember her for her radiant smile, her unwavering dedication to volunteering at MDA Carmel," her friends shared. "We'll cherish the memory of her as the 'orange heart' because she was a typical redhead, and we'd joke that her beret even matched her hair color."

(https://www.jpost.com/middle-east/article-767728)

CHAPTER 30
INDIGO GIRLS
BY RABBI FELICIA SOL

When I was in high school my brother was in college, and he took me to the Yale green to watch a concert of some new bands, one of which was called the Indigo Girls. They were young, I was younger. Who knew where they would be many years later?

The next time I saw them, they were opening for R.E.M. in Providence.

Two weeks ago, on *Motse* Shabbat, on Saturday night, I got last minute tickets to bring my daughter to go see the Indigo Girls in Westchester. While I was seated, they performed one of their recent songs, titled "Look Far" by Emily. As I was thinking and listening to the song, I was thinking that high school girl could have never looked that far ahead. I could have never imagined that I would be 30 years, less than 30 years, later where they had become very famous, sitting with my daughter and watching an Indigo Girls concert.

Now, obviously, the demographic and the audience were my age or above, for the most part. It was the first night that I did something since October 7th that was different or "normal." I finally got out in the world again. It was the first time that I felt like a different kind of human being. I actually was transported out of the fog, the trauma, the heartbreak, the fear of what October 7th delivered to Israel and us in so many different and profound ways. I was thinking how hard it is to look far when you're traumatized.

Actually, we see a little bit of that in this week's *parashah*, in Genesis chapter 27, it says, "When Isaac was old, and his eyes were too dim to see." The dimming of Isaac's eyes is attributed in one Midrash to when he's bound upon the altar, the tears of Abraham actually make him blind. The Meir Soloveichik, a Hassidic commentator, contrasts Yitzchak's inability to see to Moshe. When Moshe dies, it says that his eyes were not dimmed, and his strength did not abate.

The Meir Soloveichik say Isaac never leaves Eretz Ysrael, but Moshe never gets to Eretz Yisrael. And here, obviously, the vision is not a literal vision. This is not about true blindness, the ability to see as is. But what I think the Meir Soloveichik is pointing to is when we're in limited space, some would say *daled amot*, when we're in our four cubits of space, it's very hard to see beyond.

When we're living in trauma, or even in our own isolated existence, it's very hard to see past, to have a vision, to imagine something different, when we're kind of locked up in one story. And Moshe spent his life longing for the Promised Land, looking for something that he could not see. And of course, the tradition attributes his prophet status, that there was never another prophet like Moshe. [1]

Yitzchak's is an ancestor; Moshe was a prophet. And I've been thinking a lot about how we maintain that kind of longing in traumatizing times. We can't expect a prophet to arise to deliver everyone out of this madness. It's not one person's responsibility to present that vision. However, our tradition venerates Moshe's vision and yearning, recognizing that it's the sole means to transcend our limited spheres and expand beyond our confined four cubits of space.

In this time when our inclination may be to withdraw and focus inward, solely delving into our own narrative and affirming our truths, I encourage us to expand beyond these boundaries. Our story holds power and provides comfort, fostering closeness, security, and unity. But part of our responsibility also is to yearn, to look far, and to imagine that something could be different, and know that there are people who are putting out that kind of vision.

Just a week and a half ago, two individuals, featured in the New York Times, were witnessed in the sanctuary. They spoke about "omdim beyachad," the concept of standing together. Individuals—both Jews and Palestinians—are not confined to a singular narrative, nor do they exclusively acknowledge one form of suffering. Their lives extend beyond a single side of the green line or the Gaza Strip; they transcend these boundaries, even in college settings where typically only one narrative is permitted. There are those that are looking far because the only way to get to a promised land is to look far. We will never get there if we just stay in our own story.

So, I invite us on this Shabbat of *parashah Toldot* (Generations); we don't know what we'll be, and today looks very hard. These are hard days, but as a religious person, as someone who is thinking about not only Yitzchak, but Moshe too, about my 15 or 16-year-old self and my 52-year-old self. Some of those dreams we have to cultivate today, and some of the stories we could have never imagined, but the worst thing that we could do is to lose our longing. And that is what Shabbat is for. It's a day of longing, *yedid nefesh* is a search for longing to find God. It's a taste of the world to come, which is not yet here, but we want to taste it to awaken our longing.

And so, I invite us on the Shabbat, in all our sorrow, in all our pain to find something that reminds us of what we must long for, of people in our lives or that we've heard, or that we've read that remind us that there's a promised land out there. A vision of what we know to be true. Its people who are different and have different narratives can come together and listen and be heard. And even when we feel like we just want to crawl up in our beds or in our homes or in our own story, that sometimes we have to step out to another land and look for something new and different.

So, may it be!

(Rabbi Felicia Sol serves as a Senior Rabbi at B'nai Jeshuran Congregation in New York City. This is the Kabbalat Shabbat *derasha* (sermon) that she shared on November 17, 2023.

1. Authors note: Moses also spoke about another Prophet (Messiah) who would come:

The Lord your God will raise up for you a Prophet like me from your midst, from your brethren. Him you shall hear. (Deuteronomy 18:15)

CHAPTER 31
IRON SWORDS
BY REUVEN DORON, DECEMBER 13 2023

Wouldn't it be great If we could get a sign from God that He is in full control and that everything 'will be ok?' If only He could reassure us that "Iron Swords," the name Israel named this war, is His war as well.

National Geographic recently announced their "number one archaeological discovery of 2023." What was that discovery? Ancient iron swords which were found in a remote cave in the Judean Desert. These four swords were hidden by Jewish fighters during the great revolt against the Roman Empire, and the official report says: "Four ancient but well-preserved iron swords ... found by an Ariel University archaeologist who slipped his hand into a hole in a hidden chamber of a Judean Desert Cave ... have been named the 'Number-One Find for 2023' of National Geographic Magazine."

Four ancient, well preserved, iron swords. Can these swords be pointing to the war on Israel's four fronts? Right now, the IDF fights back against hostilities from Hamas, Hezbollah, the West

Bank, and the Red Sea (Yemen). A sign for those who have eyes to see and ears to hear.

(Reuven and Mary Lou Doron serve God and His people in Israel. reuven.doron@gmail.com)

CHAPTER 32
JEWISH HUMOR
BY TONYA ZUCKERBROT

Jews are known for their humor. The late comedian Robin Williams was on tour in Germany, and an interviewer asked him, "Mr. Williams, why do you think there's not much comedy in Germany?" He answered, "Perhaps it's because you killed all the funny people?"

They say to make another person laugh is a mitzvah. Jewish humor was out in full display at yesterday's Pro-Israel Rally. Leave it to the Jewish people to find humor during their darkest hours.

Below are some of my favorite posters from the rally:

1. Spread Cream Cheese not Hate
2. Turn Hamas into Hummus
3. Will trade Ivy-League Antisemites for Hostages
4. I live between the river and the sea and I am not going anywhere
5. When they go LOW we go CHAI

6. Did you dance on the streets on 9/11?

7. 50 Muslim Nations. 1 tiny Jewish Nation. Rejecting only Israel ("anti Zionism") IS ANTISEMITISM, duh.

(https://www.facebook.com/story.php?story_fbid=10159763373246381&id=738961380)

CHAPTER 33
JEWS FROM ARAB LANDS: THE MIDDLE EAST'S FORGOTTEN REFUGEES
BY WILL BARCLAY, NOVEMBER 23 2023

By the end of the 1970's, 900,000 Jews were expelled from Islamic states and Muslim nations around the world.

In 1947, the United Nations (UN) adopted UN Resolution 181 and, thereby, resolved to subsequently divide Great Britain's former Mandate into Palestinian and Jewish states. [1]

Although the international community and the Jewish People eagerly embraced UN Resolution 181, all of the Arab nations that surrounded the nascent state of Israel immediately vowed to exterminate the newborn Jewish state.[2]

Numerous Arab and Muslim leaders also explicitly declared that they would severely punish and expel any Jews who elected to remained within their territories.

For example, in 1947, Syria's Permanent Representative to the United Nations, Faris el-Khouri, stated that, "Unless the Palestine problem is settled, we shall have difficulty in protecting and safeguarding the Jews in the Arab world." [3]In addition, the Prime Minister of Iraq, Nuri al-Said, proudly declared that "...if a satisfactory resolution to the Palestine case was not reached, severe measures should be taken against all Jews in Arab countries."[4]

Consequently, when the state of Israel was ultimately founded in 1948, swathes of Jews from Arab and Muslim countries were slaughtered and violently expelled from their ancestral homes and communities. In fact, over 90% of the Jewish population in Iraq and Yemen was forced to escape with only their lives in tow.[5]

Yemen, for instance, boasted a Jewish population of 55,000 in 1948. [6]Due to the rampant antisemitism that plagued Yemeni Jews after the advent of the state of Israel, 50,000 Jewish people were quickly forced to evacuate from Yemen between 1949 and 1950. [7]By 2016, only 50 Jews remained in all of Yemen.[8]

Moreover, approximately 160,000 Jewish people inhabited Iraq in 1948.[9] However, after the state of Israel was founded, Iraq was placed under martial law and the state of Iraq actually amended its own respective Criminal Code, in order to render Zionism a criminal activity and punishable by death.[10] In fact, Shafiq Adas, a famous Jewish magnate and "the richest Jew in Iraq", was arrested and publicly hanged, due to the fact that he allegedly sold goods to the state of Israel.[11]

Furthermore, Iraq's Prime Minister, Nuri al-Said, personally campaigned to violently excise and eliminate Iraq's Jewish population. According to Britain's Ambassador, Sir Alec Kirkbride, "Nuri Said...came out with the astounding proposition that a convoy of Iraqi Jews should be brought over [to Israel] in army lorries escorted by armored cars... Either the Iraqi Jews would have been massacred or their Iraqi guards would have had to shoot other Arabs to protect the lives of their charges." [12]

By the end of 1952, nearly 130,000 Jews had fled Iraq, and, by 2004, Iraq's vibrant Jewish community was reduced to a paltry 35 Jews in Baghdad.[13]

Ultimately, 900,000 Jews were violently expelled from Islamic states and Muslim nations around the world by the end of the 1970's.[14] However, throughout the modern era, the international community and human rights activists have focused their efforts overwhelmingly on the 360,000 Palestinians that were displaced as a result of the outbreak of the Israel-Palestine Conflict.[15]

The reality that countless Jews were murdered and savagely displaced from their ancestral homes and communities that they lovingly inhabited for well over 2500 years has become forgotten, and is, in fact, often unabashedly ignored by modern political actors because the international community is unwilling to confront the intergenerational antisemitism that has permeated throughout the Middle East for millennia.

Works Consulted

Basri, Carole. "The Jewish Refugees from Arab Countries: An Examination of Legal Rights-A Case Study of the Human Rights Violations of Iraqi Jews". in Fordham International Law Journal. 2002.

"Jews in Islamic Countries: Iraq". Jewish Virtual Library. [8 November 2023].

"Jews in Islamic Countries: Yemen". Jewish Virtual Library. [8 November 2023].

Ministry of Aliyah and Integration. "On Eagles' Wings"–Aliyah from Yemen (1949). 2022. [8 November 2023].

Morris, Benny. 1948: A History of the First Arab-Israeli War. Yale University Press, 2008.

"Quotes from Arab and Islamic Leaders Regarding Jews and Israel". Jewish Virtual Library. [8 November 2023].

United Nations. Progress Report of the United Nations Mediator on Palestine: In pursuance of paragraph 2, part II, of resolution 186 (S-2) of the General Assembly of 14 May 1948. 1948.

United States Department of State: Office of the Historian. Milestones: Creation of Israel, 1948. [8 November 2023].

United States Department of State: Office of the Historian. Milestones: The Arab-Israeli War of 1948. [9 March 2023].

---

1. United States Department of State: Office of the Historian, Milestones: Creation of Israel, 1948. <https://history.state.gov/milestones/1945-1952/creation-israel> [8 November 2023].
2. United States Department of State: Office of the Historian, Milestones: The Arab-Israeli War of 1948. <https://history.state.gov/milestones/1945-1952/arab-israeli-war> [9 March 2023].
3. "Quotes from Arab and Islamic Leaders Regarding Jews and Israel", Jewish Virtual Library. <https://www.jewishvirtuallibrary.org/myths-and-facts-quotes> [8 November 2023].
4. Benny Morris, 1948: A History of the First Arab-Israeli War, (Yale University Press, 2008).
5. Carole Basri, "The Jewish Refugees from Arab Countries: An Examination of Legal Rights-A Case Study of the Human Rights Violations of Iraqi Jews", in Fordham International Law Journal, (2002).
6. "Jews in Islamic Countries: Yemen", Jewish Virtual Library. <https://www.jewishvirtuallibrary.org/jews-of-yemen> [8 November 2023].
7. Ministry of Aliyah and Integration, "On Eagles' Wings"–Aliyah from Yemen (1949). (2022). <https://www.gov.il/en/Departments/Guides/the-aliya-story?chapterIndex=7> [8 November 2023].
8. "Jews in Islamic Countries: Yemen", Jewish Virtual Library. <https://www.jewishvirtuallibrary.org/jews-of-yemen> [8 November 2023].
9. Carole Basri, "The Jewish Refugees from Arab Countries: An Examination of Legal Rights-A Case Study of the Human Rights Violations of Iraqi Jews", in Fordham International Law Journal, (2002).
10. ibid.
11. ibid.
12. ibid.

13. "Jews in Islamic Countries: Iraq", Jewish Virtual Library. <https://www.jewishvirtuallibrary.org/jews-of-iraq>
14. Carole Basri, "The Jewish Refugees from Arab Countries: An Examination of Legal Rights-A Case Study of the Human Rights Violations of Iraqi Jews", in Fordham International Law Journal, (2002).
15. United Nations, Progress Report of the United Nations Mediator on Palestine: In pursuance of paragraph 2, part II, of resolution 186 (S-2) of the General Assembly of 14 May 1948, (1948).

(https://aish.com/jews-from-arab-lands-the-middle-easts-forgotten-refugees/?src=ac)

CHAPTER 34
JUSTICE AND FORGIVENESS
PETER TSUKAHIRA, DECEMBER 3, 2023

Well good morning to everybody, it's so wonderful to be here in the House of the Lord and in the presence of his Spirit. We thank God that in the past week more than 100 hostages have been released by their kidnappers in Gaza. This is the answer to many prayers that have been offered. we are still praying for almost 140 others that are still held captive. They need our prayers more than ever before. Their condition is not known to us.

Yesterday, the bitter struggle of warfare began again. It is a war that must be fought, and must be won, but as the people of God, we should never allow the struggle to consume us. It's such a refreshment to come in the midst of war to a house where God is being worshiped, and there is rejoicing in the midst of it. As the Lord's people, we need to look beyond war, because there's a future and a hope for Israel. Even in the midst of the fury and fire of war, we as God's people must never abandon or ignore our values and our beliefs. Our values, our believes from the word of God, that's the light within us, and our responsibility is to keep the light burning and shining.

Turn with me to the second chapter of the letter of James in the Brit Hadassah. These two verses are the theme of today's message.

> *So speak, and so act, as those who are to be judged by the law of freedom. For judgment will be merciless to one who has shown no mercy; mercy triumphs over judgment. (James 2:12-13 NASB)*

Justice and mercy are both parts of God's righteous and eternal nature. God's laws and His judgment are foundations for His mercy and forgiveness. Let's be clear, there is no favoritism with God. Justice means equality before the law. Let's take a look at how important justice is to God.

> *Eye for eye, tooth for tooth, hand for hand, foot for foot, 25 burn for burn, wound for wound, bruise for bruise. (Exodus 21:24-25 NASB)*

> *If someone injures his neighbor, just as he has done, so shall it be done to him: fracture for fracture, eye for eye, tooth for tooth; just as he has injured a person, so shall it be inflicted on him. (Leviticus 24:19–20 NASB)*

This is God's standard of justice. We understand that justice of God is a law of God. Justice produces liberty, because good law protects citizens from injustice. We love the laws of God. We love His protection. We love His justice. We want a society that has justice in it. Of course, these are laws of Torah.

Who gave the laws of God to Moses? When God wrote these laws with His finger on the tablets of stone, do you think Yeshua was there? Well, of course He was there! He is the eternal only begotten Son of God. When Yeshua says, "I and the Father are

One," He doesn't mean we are One at that particular moment, that we happen to agree at this particular point in time. He means, "We have always been One. We always will be One." It's an eternal bond that They share as God. So, those laws are Yeshua's laws too. God's law of justice is a law that guarantees freedom for those who live in the framework of His law. And this justice is a light for Israel and for the world.

Turn with me to Isaiah chapter 51.

> *"Pay attention to Me, My people,*
> *And listen to Me, My nation;*
> *For a law will go out from Me,*
> *And I will bring My justice as a light of the peoples.*
> *My righteousness is near, My salvation has gone forth,*
> *And My arms will judge the peoples;*
> *The coastlands will wait for Me,*
> *And they will wait expectantly for My arm." (Isaiah 51:4–5 NASB)*

We want God, the Righteous Judge to rule the nations. We want to live in a world that is defined by His justice.

Let me tell you a story that has come to our attention during these last weeks of war. This is part of a story of Mosab Hassan Yousef. He has also been called "The Son of Hamas." Here in Israel, he was known for a while as "The Green Prince." This young man is 45-years-old now. He was born in Ramallah on The West Bank, and he is the son of one of the seven founders of Hamas. His whole life growing up was being part of Hamas, his family, his society, his whole life. He was arrested as a teenager and imprisoned in Israel for participating in terrorism. He spent about a year in Megiddo prison. He witnessed the brutality and the injustice of the Hamas leaders in prison, as they enforced their brutality over the

Palestinian prisoners. And he couldn't deal with that in his heart as a young man.

He went through a period of crisis and really questioning his values, and during that period, he was recruited to work with the Israeli Intelligence Shin Bet. He became an informant for Israeli Intelligence to stop the suicide attacks that were going in that period of time. Part of what was motivating him, according to his story, is that he wanted to save his father's life, because he knew that if his father was implicated in suicide bombings, that he would be killed by the Israeli authorities. So, for several years, he informed on groups that were going out to commit suicide bombings, and he is credited with saving dozens and dozens of lives.

Eventually, he moved to the United States, and for years he dropped out of sight. We knew about his story about 15 years ago, then we didn't hear anything for a number of years. Many of us became interested in the story of Mosab Hassan Yousef because he published a book *Son of Hamas* in 2010, but then it seemed he dropped out of sight for years.

However, since October 7, he has reemerged as a very outspoken critic of Hamas. I mean, really outspoken, harsh, and bold. He speaks as a son of Hamas, and he speaks as a defender of Israel's right to punish Hamas. He is out there on network news. He is being interviewed by world famous interviewers. He is speaking in churches. He is speaking in synagogues, and he is speaking out on social media. All you have to do is google him. And as someone who grew up in Hamas, he is calling for the complete destruction of Hamas as an organization. And he is calling for freedom for the Palestinian people from the brutality of Hamas rule. He argues that people of faith, Christians everywhere need to call out for God's justice and righteousness to be done.

Clearly, this man is now putting his life on the line. We understood when he disappeared from public view years ago because there was a stack of fatwahs and death threats against him. Now, it would appear that he doesn't care, and that he feels compelled to speak out.

I was looking at his book from 2010, and he tells what changed him. According to his testimony, at a certain point, he became a born-again Christian. I just want to read for you a couple of sentences from his book. He was questioning Christian faith, and reading the Bible.

"Then I read this: "You have heard that it was said, 'Love your neighbor and hate your enemy.' But I tell you: Love your enemies and pray for those who persecute you, that you may be sons of your Father in heaven" (Matthew 5: 43-45). That's it! I was amazed by these words. Never before had I heard anything like this, but I knew that this was the message I had been searching for all my life."

I've heard him say that when he read these words, it changed his world, because he realized deep down that only God could say something like this. Remember the Scripture we read earlier, "Mercy rejoices over judgement." He lived in a dark, dark world all of his life, and then light began to shine. This was the light of God's truth shining into the darkness of Hamas. It's a spiritual light that goes even beyond justice, judgment and God's punishment of evil. It's the light of God's mercy, and that's why we are sitting here today. It is one of the core values of our belief. If we want to be a light that shines, we must never sacrifice or ignore our values.

What better time to talk about divine light shining into darkness than the Hannukah season. The Festival of Lights is coming to Israel, and soon it will be time to light the Hannukiyot, and to celebrate God's miraculous deliverance of Israel. Christmas is also coming this month and much of the world will be celebrating the coming of Yeshua, the Prince of Peace, into our dark and troubled world.

Turn with me to Second Corinthians chapter 4.

> *For God, who said, "Light shall shine out of darkness," is the One who has shone in our hearts to give the Light of the knowledge of the glory of God in the face of Christ. (2 Corinthians 4:6 NASB)*

For God, who said, "Light shall shine out of darkness," is the One who has shone in our hearts to give the Light of the knowledge of the glory of God in the face of Messiah. Yeshua, the Light of the World, is coming to judge the world, but He also offers God's mercy to all who call upon Him for forgiveness!

I would like to circle back and read the theme verses of this message to you once again:

> *So speak, and so act, as those who are to be judged by the law of freedom. For judgment will be merciless to one who has shown no mercy; mercy triumphs over judgment. (James 2:12-13 NASB)*

We love the laws of God. We want to live a life in a society that honors God's law. We want to live in a society where those who murder are punished. But we want a place that by faith we can enter into the mercy of God. These verses we just read say that mercy triumphs over judgement, but it doesn't say that mercy replaces judgement. These are two deep values for the kingdom of God. How does that work?

Let me tell you a story. This is a true story. It's a story about a young Australian man named Andrew. Andrew became a convicted drug smuggler. This young man was convicted of smuggling 8 kilograms of heroin out of Indonesia in 2005. He went to trial in Indonesia, and he was sentenced to death when he was 22 years old. Many people know that the penalty for drug smuggling in Indonesia and other Southeast Asia countries is death, and they mean it! So, at 22, Andrew was sentenced to death by a firing squad.

But, of course, there was a long legal struggle, and there were appeals, and governments got involved and human rights organizations got involved. There was a long legal battle. And during those years that Andrew was a prisoner near Jakarta, under a death sentence, he became a believer. Someone led him to the Lord, and he began to lead everyone around him in the prison to the Lord. Here's what Andrew said after he received his death sentence.

"When I got back to my cell, I said, 'God, I asked you to set me free, not kill me.' God spoke to me and said, 'Andrew, I have set you free from the inside out, I have given you life!' From that moment on I haven't stopped worshipping Him. I had never sung before, never led worship, until Yeshua set me free."

Andrew was executed in 2015. He was executed along with six other convicts, not involved in his crime, but involved in other crimes. It says that they refused to wear blindfolds on their face. They wanted to show that they weren't afraid. Before they died, they sang together "Amazing Grace" and that Matt Redmond song "Ten Thousand Reasons." You know the song," Bless the Lord, Oh my soul." They sang these two songs before they were killed by the 12-member firing squad. When Andrew was executed, most of the Indonesian legal system and members of their government, right up to the Prime Minister, said that justice was done.

But I want to tell you that mercy triumphed. One of the men Andrew led to the Lord was an Indonesian man who had been a religious leader in that country. His life was radically transformed by Yeshua, and when he was released from prison, he became a radical, outspoken disciple of the Lord, and a defender of Israel in the most populated Muslim country in the world. That young man came here to this congregation for one of our Schools of Ministry. He has a great heart for Israel. He is preaching now not just in his region, but he is preaching all over now. We are friends to this day.

Andrew's life ended when he was just 31 years old. He was convicted and executed as a criminal. But I want to tell you, this young man found mercy, and if it is only for that he led this one man to the Lord in prison, but there were many, I know he will hear the Lord say, "Well done, good and faithful servant!" You see, mercy triumphs over judgement!

I hope you understand, mercy doesn't replace judgement. We have to fight this war. People have to die. We have to win this war. In this place, we will celebrate when victory is won. Let's not forget, there is a triumph that goes beyond that victory. That's what makes us different. That's the light that shines from us.

Let's look for a moment in the life of Yeshua. Turn with me to Luke chapter 23. These are about the last hours of Yeshua's life on earth.

> *And when they came to the place called The Skull, there they crucified Him and the criminals, one on the right and the other on the left. [But Jesus was saying, "Father, forgive them; for they do not know what they are doing."] And they cast lots, dividing His garments among themselves. (Luke 23:33–34 NASB)*

We know in those days that the Romans were strong and they were organized, and at that time they ruled the whole world, but they lived in spiritual darkness. Imagine, those soldiers mocked and tortured the Son of God even though He was innocent, and they knew it. They didn't care. They drove long nails into His hands and feet. They executed Yeshua in a deliberately painful and humiliating way. They mocked Him. They laughed at His suffering. They were in moral darkness. And yet, how did Yeshua pray to His Father about them?

This is the light of God that shines into our terrible world. This is the light that only comes from God. This is the mercy that triumphs over judgement. Yeshua is The Light that shines into our terrible world. When torture and bloodshed come to our own doorsteps, we get to feel some of the injustice that was given to Him, the darkness, the injustice of His crucifixion. We have an opportunity to understand what a great truth He has given to us!

Should we condemn the people of Hamas and their supporters in Gaza? Condemn them to hell because they live lives in deep darkness? This is a question we should ask; I believe. Can we ever forgive them for what they have done? Ultimately, this power of forgiveness is the only truth that will really change our world. It was the only truth that changed us. It's the only power that can come from God that will change your enemies into friends. This truth has power, the power of God. It has potential to change the killers of our people into brothers and sisters in the Lord. Do you believe this? Is this one of our core values? Can we remember when we lived in complete darkness?

This has been called "the scandal of grace." For centuries, people have asked, "How can you forgive people who do terrible, inhuman things? How can you forgive them?" But, can we really sit here in the grace of God and blame those people because of the darkness that their lives are? Are we going to ask God to serve us by destroying our enemies, or are we going to come before God to serve Him and His purpose for saving the world?

We should never think that our lives are devoid of darkness? We have come to the light out of darkness. But even though we are walking in the light, there are things called "blind spots." There are points of darkness that need the light of God to be destroyed.

A number of years ago, I started to lose my vision in one of my eyes. I began to notice that there was a place in the vision of one of my eyes that was just dark. During those years, I went to a lot of doctors, and they all said the same thing, "There's no cure for this. There's nothing we can do." So, I went through a period of wondering whether I was going to go blind. And I'm telling you just the thought of that filled me with terror. I would test myself. I'd say, "Peter, what would it be like? Would you be able to handle it if you couldn't see anymore?"

Here's how I tested myself: I just shut my eyes, I said, "That's what it would be like, but you won't be able to open them again." I am not advising you to try this, but you might want to if you are interested. I just closed my eyes and tried to deal with a world that was just black. I couldn't make it 30 seconds. The only way I could get through 30 seconds of that was by telling myself after 30 seconds, I would open my eyes again. The idea of being in darkness permanently was terrifying!

So, we prayed, we prayed here in the congregation, and it stopped getting worse. Thank God! I'm so grateful that I can still see. They still let me drive. Light is beautiful! Colors are beautiful! People's faces are beautiful! But I have a permanently dark spot in one of my eyes.

There are other blind spots that I know I have, and everybody has them. Areas of your life that are dark, but you can't see them. Sometimes bad behavior, hurtful words, evil thoughts arise from these dark areas. It can be a surprise sometimes. But we are aware of other people that have blind spots in their eyes. It's easy to spot other people's blind spots, and it's easy to criticize other people for the things they can't see about themselves. The point is that everybody needs God's mercy. Everybody needs God's light; especially in these dark days. So, we love justice, but we also love mercy. Mercy is not going to take the place of justice. We want justice to be done in God's time. We know the cost of justice; there will be a high price for this. But I think I speak for most of the people of Israel, in saying that it is worth the price. But we as the people of God, we have to stand for a greater triumph than just victory on the ground.

Can we stand with Yeshua when he looked at those brutal darkened men who were killing Him, and say, "Lord, forgive them because they are in darkness. They don't know what they're doing." So, I would ask you to pray with me. Before we pray, I would like to read from Isaiah chapter 9.

> *The people who walk in darkness*
> *Will see a great light;*
> *Those who live in a dark land,*
> *The light will shine on them. (Isaiah 9:2 NASB)*

Let's ask the Lord to cleanse our hearts of hatred, fear, desire for revenge, hatred of our enemies. Let's ask the Lord to renew the godly values that bring His light into our lives. Let's ask God for a vision of triumph that goes beyond freeing hostages and eliminating Hamas. And, can we pray that Yeshua's light will be ever brighter in our personal lives. That for us, this season can be a turning point for each of us, and also as a community, that we would walk in a greater light, a greater grace, and we stretch out to grab hold of a greater triumph.

Let's pray. Lord, we want to thank you that Yeshua, you are the Light of the World. We honor You in this season. We lift up Yeshua. You who called us out of our darkness. Without You, we would have been lost. We could have been those prisoners in the Indonesian jail. We could have been those radicals in Ramallah. But You called us, and by the grace of God, we said," Yes." And now Your light is shining on us. I'll pray that we will step up, and we will be the light that shines, a light of justice, real justice. And a light of mercy that triumphs even over the judgement of God.

So, Lord, fill us with light in this season. Let Your light shine on Israel. I want to thank you for our nation. Thank you for Jews and Arabs, and people of all kinds who have come to be a part of this land. I want to pray, let Your light shine on Israel. Let this nation be a light to the others. That's what You wanted from the start. Let us step up into that place. Let Your light shine on us today. Let Your light shine into Gaza today. And we pray this in the name of Yeshua. Amen.

(From a message given by Peter Tsukahira, Co-Founding Pastor, Kehilat HaCarmel given December 2 2023)

CHAPTER 35
MIRACLE AT GOLAN HEIGHTS

Something miraculous happened to an Israeli army unit during the 1973 Yom Kippur War between Israel and their Muslim Arab neighbor Syria on the Golan Heights. Commander David Yinni was in the process of pulling his troops out of a confrontation with the Syrian army, when he realized that they were trapped in a minefield. Knowing it would take a miracle for them to make it out alive, the troops began crawling on their bellies while using their bayonets to try and find the mines without setting them off.

"Stop!"

"Stop We're in a mine field."

"What do we do now?"

"Quiet Ilan … Do you want to lead the Syrian army toward us"

"We can't go back."

"But there is no chance we can get out of this minefield alive."

"Well … at least we all die together."

"It's not funny Rafi!"

"There could be 100,000 mines out there."

"We'll have to crawl our way across."

"Use your field knife and do what we're trained to do."

"If you feel a mine, dig it out and disarm it."

"There's no other way to do this."

"Let's do it!"

"If we don't get across by daybreak …"

We'll get across. Just start digging."

"Do it carefully."

At some point, one of the soldiers uttered a heartfelt prayer. Suddenly a gust of wind comes out of nowhere. The soldiers hunkered down until the storm subsided, and when it did, they saw that the storm had blown away so much of the dirt that the mines were exposed. So, the entire platoon walked out of the minefield safely, and they all survive!

In the end, due to a number of similar occurrences of Divine Providence – not unlike those of previous wars – Israel managed to emerge victorious in the face of seemingly insurmountable odds.

(https://www.youtube.com/watch?v=HNXwhv8Mooo)

CHAPTER 36
MIRACLES AND MARTYRS

HEROD'S VIOLENCE TO THE CHURCH (MARTYRS)

Now about that time Herod the king stretched out his hand to harass some from the church. Then he killed James the brother of John with the sword. And because he saw that it pleased the Jews, he proceeded further to seize Peter also. Now it was during the Days of Unleavened Bread. So when he had arrested him, he put him in prison, and delivered him to four squads of soldiers to keep him, intending to bring him before the people after Passover.

PETER FREED FROM PRISON (MIRACLES)

Peter was therefore kept in prison, but] constant prayer was offered to God for him by the church. And when Herod was about to bring him out, that night Peter was sleeping, bound with two chains between two soldiers; and the guards before the door were keeping the prison. Now behold, an angel of the Lord stood by him, and a light shone in the prison; and he struck Peter on the side and raised him up, saying,

"Arise quickly!" And his chains fell off his hands. Then the angel said to him, "Gird yourself and tie on your sandals"; and so he did. And he said to him, "Put on your garment and follow me." So he went out and followed him, and did not know that what was done by the angel was real, but thought he was seeing a vision. When they were past the first and the second guard posts, they came to the iron gate that leads to the city, which opened to them of its own accord; and they went out and went down one street, and immediately the angel departed from him.

Miracle: A surprising and welcome event that is not explicable by natural or scientific laws and is therefore considered to be the work of a divine agency. "The miracle of rising from the grave"

Martyr: A person who is killed because of their religious or other beliefs. "Saints, martyrs, and witnesses to the faith"

> *Rejoice with those who rejoice, and weep with those who weep.*
> *(Romans 12:15)*

Lord, we thank you for the lives you spared and delivered, and we thank you for those who sacrificed their lives that Israel might live before You. I pray that you will comfort all those who mourn today.

> *"The Spirit of the Lord God is upon Me,*
> *Because the Lord has anointed Me*
> *To preach good tidings to the poor;*
> *He has sent Me to heal the brokenhearted,*
> *To proclaim liberty to the captives,*
> *And the opening of the prison to those who are bound;*
> *To proclaim the acceptable year of the Lord,*
> *And the day of vengeance of our God;*
> *To comfort all who mourn,*
> *To console those who mourn in Zion,*
> *To give them beauty for ashes,*

The oil of joy for mourning,
The garment of praise for the spirit of heaviness;
That they may be called trees of righteousness,
The planting of the Lord, that He may be glorified." (Isaiah 61:1-3)

(https://languages.oup.com/google-dictionary-en/)

CHAPTER 37
MIRACLES IN GAZA

In the war-torn region of Gaza, remarkable stories are unfolding, echoing the biblical prophecies of the end times. According to Christian professor Michael Licona, a New Testament Studies professor at Houston Christian University, more than 200 Muslim men have experienced life-altering visions of Jesus in their dreams, leading them to embrace Christ. Licona, shared this extraordinary account through a Facebook post.

The Lord is working unbelievable miracles in the Israel-Hamas war! Hundreds of Muslims all dreamed of Christ on the same night. He then quoted the report from the ministries. "Over the past two days, we have ministered to hundreds of fathers who have lost most, if not all, of their children in the war. As we moved these men to safety, we fed them, washed their clothes, and began to read the Bible to them sharing the way of peace through Jesus. "Then, a big miracle happened. Last night, Jesus appeared to more than 200 of them in their dreams! They have come back to us to learn more from God's Word and are asking how to follow Jesus."

This isn't the first report of such dreams affecting Muslims.

About a month before the October 7th Hamas terrorist attack, Assemblies of God News reported that Muslims around the world were dreaming of Jesus and converting to Christianity at an unprecedented rate. Jesus is revealing Himself to Muslims in dreams as the Man in White.

Here is another miracle. The Lord flooded Hamas underground tunnels with water. As the fighting in the Gaza Strip continued, the biggest advancement that the IDF made in recent days was due to the rain. The skies opened up and poured down on Israel and the Gaza Strip. In the beginning it was believed that this rain would harm the Israeli maneuvers inside Gaza, because it makes it harder for the tanks and other armored vehicles to drive in muddy soil, but what actually happened was that due to the large amounts of water that poured down and entered the terror tunnels of Hamas, multiple Hamas terrorists drowned while hiding inside underground bunkers.

While other terrorists escaped the flooding in the tunnels to seek shelter inside Hamas buildings, they revealed their locations to the IDF that was monitoring from the sky. After multiple Hamas buildings were identified, the IDF easily destroyed these particular locations and neutralized multiple Hamas terrorists in the northern part of the Gaza Strip. During operations that were conducted by IDF, special forces created a long-term base of operations that will support the IDF forces that are maneuvering inside Gaza.

In their attempts to destroy Hamas, the IDF uncovered an underground terror tunnel 20 miles below the street level. In order to neutralize the threat of the tunnel, the IDF sent two drones. The first one exploded on the blast door that was defending the terrorist within, while the second one entered deep into the tunnel and exploded on the terrorists neutralizing them.

IDF forces conducted an operation to capture a military base belonging to the Palestinian Islamic Jihad, which is a terror organization that operates alongside Hamas inside the Gaza Strip, and is supported directly from Iran. In this location, IDF forces uncovered a weapons manufacturing facility that created weapons, missiles and other training capabilities in order to equip the terrorists of Hamas and the Islamic Jihad in their attempts against Israel.

A tank was found inside this facility that was used in order to train the terrorists on how to capture Israeli tanks. During the fight, an RPG rocket was fired towards the IDF forces that were capturing the command position of the Palestinian Islamic Jihad. This rocket was fired towards the troops from a nearby courtroom that is located very close to another hospital inside the Gaza Strip.

It became very easy for IDF forces to locate the areas from which Hamas is operating inside the Gaza Strip, and where it is holding its weapons and other ammunitions and military capabilities. All the IDF needs to do is look in hospitals, mosques, schools, and any other civilian buildings that are recognized by the International Community as areas that you are not allowed to attack during the war. That's how Hamas is operating in the attacks that were conducted against IDF troops. From the courtroom, the IDF was able to identify and neutralize the threat using a helicopter that destroyed the terrorists in that location. After 12 hours of fighting, the IDF was able to capture that Hamas base of operation and weapons factory.

In the northern front with Lebanon, the fighting still continues as IDF forces are striking down Hezbollah locations from which its operatives are carrying out attacks against Israeli territory, civilians, and IDF forces.

This fighting is long, and I call on all of you to join Israel in prayers. Please pray for the families that are staying home and are waiting for their loved ones to come home to them. If it's a son that is serving in the IDF, if it's a husband, or a father that was called to IDF reserve duty, family members do not know when and if he will come home safely. This is a very hard situation to live in, and the entire country of Israel is dealing with this uncertainty.

None of us want to go back to our normal life before we know that the IDF restored the security to Israel by destroying the threat of Hamas, so please join us in prayer for the situation. Pray that the IDF can keep fighting in order to destroy Hamas and release the hostages, and pray for the peace of Jerusalem.

(From Intercessors for America. The Informer November 21 2023)

CHAPTER 38
MIRACULOUSLY DELIVERED FROM HAMAS AND ABORTION
BY ARIEL HYDE DECEMBER 8, 2023

In Israel, we say that whoever saves a life, it is as though he had saved the entire world. And we're delighted to share that even in this time of war, God has been working powerfully through our Pro-Life and Gospel Campaign and saved many lives!

By God's grace, 11 children that were saved from abortion were born during November alone!

Also, for many, this period has put things in life into perspective, and helped people see the value and beauty of the gift of life itself and to choose life.

We were moved to be a part of these stories. And one family we've been helping experienced God's miraculous deliverance from death in more than one way.

STAGGERING STORY OF LIVES SAVED TWICE IN ISRAEL

On October 7th, during the brutal massacre perpetrated by Hamas terrorists, Koral* had to flee to save the life of her two toddlers and the life of the baby in her womb – the same one she wanted to abort just two months earlier.

Koral called our hotline in August looking for a private abortion. She was single with two small children and now she was pregnant again. She was very concerned about how she could raise another baby and said, "I simply can't have another baby – I won't make it." Our counselor Rachel encouraged her that she just spoke to a woman in a very similar situation who decided to keep her baby, and now says that she can't imagine life without her three little babies.

Rachel told Koral that her third baby's life was in her hands and that it was possible, although not easy, to raise three children close in age and promised that we would also help her financially. But Koral was flooded with memories of her own childhood, when her father couldn't work as he had epileptic seizures. The images of her mother looking through trash when she was a child haunt her like a dark shadow to this day.

She said, "My biggest fear is that I will fail to be a good mother and will not be able to raise my children well. These fears and doubts don't leave me and now I'm pregnant again."

Rachel asked the team for prayer and sent Koral the video showing the miracle of how a baby develops in the womb. Rachel urged her, "Before you have an abortion, please watch this video which has real footage of a baby like the one you have in your womb." Rachel also sent her a gift card to help in her difficult situation. And ultimately, Koral decided she would not abort the baby!

Rachel was so delighted to hear this! But none of us knew the nightmare that Koral was about to experience.

A PICKUP TRUCK LOADED WITH ARMED TERRORISTS

Shortly after the massacre, Rachel contacted her to see how she was doing, especially since Koral lived very close to the Gaza border. Rachel was concerned that Koral and her children were either killed or taken hostage.

"You won't believe what happened to me and my little ones," Koral confided in Rachel, "I had spent the night at a friend's house near my city the night before the massacre, and at 7:00 am on October 7th, I was making my way back home. I stopped at a red light at an intersection which usually changes quickly, but not this time. Suddenly, I noticed a pickup truck loaded with armed terrorists, chasing another car.

"In the car they were chasing and shooting at, there was a woman trying to escape. As they turned the corner, they shot at my car. Then they kept chasing the other car. Later on, I was told they murdered the woman who drove it. I was so scared that I put my car in reverse, but the car malfunctioned!

"So, I spread toys all around the car to make it look like it had been attacked and raided. Then I called the father of my girls to come get us – I hadn't spoken to him until then – and he told me to hide somewhere and he'd come quickly. The only place I could think of hiding safely with the two little girls was in the trunk of the car, so we hid there until he came to get us.

"As soon as he came and got us out, we drove insanely fast to my mother's house where we have a bomb shelter, passing straight through the red light. On the way, my life and my children's lives passed before my eyes as our car got shot at again.

We saw horrific sights such as a car where all five passengers were shot dead."

WHAT SHE SAW CHANGED EVERYTHING

After they had been cooped up in the bomb shelter for four days, the government evacuated Koral and her girls to a hotel by the Dead Sea. She and her children are all suffering from PTSD, but haven't yet received treatment. Every night she's tossing and turning, still reliving this nightmare in her dreams, even though she had returned home.

Rachel contacted her prayer partners asking for prayer for Koral and her children. Rachel has stayed in touch with her throughout this period of uncertainty, and even though she promised to keep her baby, she still had questions about how she can have another one when she and her children are experiencing fits of uncontrolled anger.

Rachel consoled her, "I know it's hard for you. But you saw for yourself how precious life is. Think about how those terrorists wanted to kill you and your baby – please don't kill your own baby! He's got hands and feet and his brain is already functioning."

Recently, Koral was finally able to go to an ultrasound and saw her developing baby with her own eyes. She found out she's carrying a boy! Her fears were relieved, and she's now looking forward to having her first son!

Please pray for Koral and her children – that they would be completely healed from all effects of trauma, and that they would have an open heart to the Gospel as we reach out to her with God's love and the message of the Messiah who heals the brokenhearted.

MIRACULOUSLY DELIVERED FROM HAMAS AND ABORTION

BABIES SAVED IN THE MIDST OF WAR

Elena, an ultra-Orthodox Jewess, called our hotline looking for an abortion. She told our counselor Rene that she was married off at age 17 and then divorced at 18. And now, as a pregnant 19-year-old, she didn't want to keep this child.

But as our team prayed for her and Rene stayed in touch, she was excited to see a sudden change of heart. It turned out that the war caused Elena to think about issues of life and death, and she realized she should keep this precious life inside of her!

———

Liraz, a 37-year-old from a kibbutz near the border with Lebanon, called the hotline a few days after the war broke out. "I'm already a single mother of a 4-year-old and I don't want another child," she told Rene. She felt overwhelmed being pregnant during a scary war.

She had to flee her kibbutz because of the war, and decided to go to Portugal for a while. While abroad, she couldn't go to a doctor or have an abortion in the first trimester when she wanted to. But now that she's returned to Israel, Rene contacted her again and was delighted to hear that Liraz now had a clear decision: She would keep her baby!

———

Shula is married with a 2-year-old child. Her marriage was on the rocks and they wanted to divorce each other. She told us, "I'm 15+ weeks pregnant, considering an abortion, and would like information about what kind of abortion procedure I would have."

After Rene shared with her the truth about abortion and encouraged her to choose life, she stayed in touch with her and asked how they were doing. Shula told Rene that they had quite a few war sirens because of bombardments, but they were OK. Her husband was also drafted into the reserves.

The whole situation caused them to rethink their life, their marriage, and her pregnancy. She said, "I decided to keep my pregnancy. We will try to go to couples' counseling." They are expecting a boy!

(https://www.treeoflifeisrael.org/en-c/miraculously-delivered-from-hamas-and-abortion?utm_source=Main+-+Tree+of+Life+Ministries&utm_campaign=fde0da7a3d-WN23.06&utm_medium=email&utm_term=0_-fde0da7a3d-%5BLIST_EMAIL_ID%5D)

CHAPTER 39
MOMENTS IN HISTORY
BY SHADI

"There are moments in history that are assigned by God to shift nations and to advance His eternal purposes. He moves His purposes forward through men and women who choose to submit to His leadership, responding accordingly to His perfect wisdom and timing. The first year that Cyrus became king of Persia was a key moment that shifted history, a convergence of God's appointed time with willing hearts on earth. Cyrus, his vassal Darius, and Daniel were anointed by God to see heaven's plans connect to reality on earth in their generation. The book of Daniel records several key events that occurred in the first year of the reign of Cyrus/Darius.

1. The fulfilment of Jeremiah's prophecy ending seventy years of exile. (Daniel 9:1-2)
2. The Medo-Persian Empire overtakes the Babylonian Empire. (Daniel 5:30-31)
3. The archangels Gariel and Michael fight against the prince of Persia. (Daniel 11:1)
4. Daniel is thrown in the lions' den. (Daniel 5:30-6:16)

5. Cyrus issues a decree freeing the Jewish exiles. (Ezra 1:1-4; 2 Chronicles 36:22,23)
6. The fulfilment of Isaiah's prophecy concerning Cyrus. (Isaiah 44-45)

It is important to ask some questions here: Were these simply random and unrelated events that happened to occur in the same year? Or were they somehow connected and perhaps even consequential? If so, what was the main event that set everything in motion?

I would like to suggest that the first event that had a dynamic domino effect was Daniel's prayer, recorded in Daniel 9: "In the first year of Darius, the son of Ahasuerus, of the lineage of the Medes who was made king over the realm of the Chaldeans, in the first year of his reign, I Daniel understood by books, the number of years specified by the word of the Lord through Jeremiah the prophet, (Jeremiah 25:9-14; 29:10-14) that He would accomplish seventy years in the desolation of Jerusalem." (Daniel 9:1-2 NIV)

He is referring to the writing of Jeremiah: After seventy years are completed at Babylon, I (the Lord) will visit you and perform My good word toward you and cause you to return to this place. For I know the thoughts that I think toward you, says the Lord, thoughts of peace and not of evil, to give you a future and a hope ... I will be found by you; says the Lord and I will bring you back from your captivity." (Jeremiah 29:10-14)

Undoubtedly, Daniel was also familiar with Isaiah's prophecy about Cyrus uttered two hundred years before. While the exact dates are not clear, Cyrus suddenly becomes the new king around the time of the seventieth year of the exile.

The convergence of the prophetic words of Isaiah and Jeremiah, in time and space, caused Daniel to recognize the diving and historic moment in which he was living. When Daniel realizes that the time has come for the fulfillment of these prophecies, his response (to God and to His word) is to set his face toward Jerusalem and toward the Lord in prayer, fasting and repentance: "Cause Your face to shine on Your sanctuary, which is desolate. Oh my God, incline your ear and hear, hear! Oh Lord, forgive! Oh Lord, listen and act! Do not delay for Your own sake, my God, for Your city and Your people are called by Your name." (Daniel 9:17b-19 NIV) Daniel's prayer was catalytic; it triggered a reaction in the spirit-realm that had a ripple effect provoking a response from the heavenly and earthly realms."

(Shadi. *Israel Born in Egypt Raised in Iran*. London, UK.: PublishU, 2023. Pages 143-145.)

CHAPTER 40
NEW YORK STANDS WITH ISRAEL

"I am not going to be long. I'm going to give you four words. This morning on my briefing, my special counsel Lisa Zornberg said something that I want us all to acknowledge. We've been through some tough times, New Yorkers. We have tough people. We saw the center of our trade collapse. We saw some of the horrific actions that played out on the stage of our city and our country, but she said something that hits me to my soul.

She stated to our team, "We are not alright. We are not alright when we see young girls pulled from their home and dragged through the streets. We are not alright when we see grandmothers being pulled away from their homes, and children shot in front of their families. We are not alright when right here in the city of New York, we have those who celebrate at the same time when the devastation is taking place in our city. We are not alright when Hamas believes that they are fighting on behalf of something in their destructive, despicable action that's carried out. We are not alright when we still have hostages who have not come home to their family. We are not alright."

And we're not going to say we have a stiff upper lip and act like everything is fine. Everything is not fine. Israel has a right to defend itself, and that's the right that we know. Your fight is our fight. Your fight is our fight. Right here in New York, we have the largest Jewish population outside of Israel. This is the place that our voices must raise and cascade throughout the entire country. We will not be alright until every person responsible for this act is held accountable.

We don't have to pretend. And I want to thank my religious leaders throughout the city, of all religious groups, who reached out to us, and clearly stated that they denounce the hatred and the anti-Semitism that was displayed on one of their holiest days of the year. This was intentional, this was bitter, this was nasty. This was something that shows Hamas must be disbanded and destroyed immediately.

So, I say to you, I'm not here because I'm your mayor. I've been in Israel as the state senator, I've protected the community of the city in general, but specifically, the Jewish community as a police officer. I stood with you as borough president, and now I'm here this day to say, not only am I the chief executive of this city, but I'm your brother. I'm your brother. Your fight is my fight. That swastika not only displays the pain of anti-Semitism; it displays the pain of racism among African Americans.

You marched with us with Dr. King, you stood with us with all the fights we had, and I'm saying we're going to stand with you and stay united together. And we don't have to be alright. We should be angry about what we saw. Thank you, Israel."

(Speech by New York City Mayor Eric Adams on October 12, 2023 https://www.instagram.com/reel/CyS8Jf7KI2M/)

CHAPTER 41
OUR COVENANT DECLARATION WITH THE GOD OF ISRAEL
BY REUVEN BERGER

We stand here this day, the 11th of October 2023, in Jerusalem, the city of the Great King, the city where God has placed His Name forever. As representatives of the first fruit, holy messianic remnant of Israel, we stand before the God of our fathers, the God of Abraham, Isaac and Jacob, the God and Father of our Lord Yeshua ha'Mashiach, to affirm God's faithfulness to His covenantal promises to His first-born-son nation, Israel. (Ex 4:22)

We affirm that the same God who made covenant with Abraham, Isaac and Jacob and their physical offspring forever, the same God who made covenant with Moses and Israel on Mount Sinai, the same God who made an everlasting covenant with David and his offspring forever, has fulfilled His covenantal promises to His people Israel, when He made the new and everlasting covenant with the House of Israel and the House of Judah according to the Word spoken through the prophet Jeremiah. (Jer 31:31-34)

This New Covenant was initiated and sealed at the last supper Passover meal of Yeshua and was ratified through His death, resurrection and ascension to the right hand of the Father. Those believers among the early, apostolic, Messianic Jewish Kehilah in Jerusalem and Israel, were the first heirs of this New Covenant inheritance promised to Israel. We acknowledge that this New Covenant, secured by the shed blood of Messiah, is the only way God has given to Israel to be redeemed and to receive the promise of final adoption as His first-born-son-nation.

We acknowledge also, that according to the scriptures, Yeshua, God's only Begotten Son, is the first and only legitimate heir to the Father's Vineyard, Israel. This inheritance belongs to Him, the firstborn Son; yet by faith in Yeshua we also understand that by receiving Yeshua as our King and Lord, we have become his brothers and heirs together with Him. (Galatians 4:1-5) By turning to Him in faith, we, the Jewish remnant in this land of Israel, who have been justified and sanctified by His blood and Word, joyfully participate with Him, in this inheritance of the firstborn. This "Vineyard Inheritance" given by God specifically to Israel—the Jewish people-- includes the adoption, the glory, the covenants and all the promises made to Israel; it also guarantees the right of inheritance to the land of Israel. (Rom 9:1-5; 2 Cor 1:20) Our repentance and restoration to the Father through Messiah Yeshua grafts us back into our *own* Cultivated Olive Tree, the Israel of God. (Rom 11:16-24; Gal 6:16) As the natural branches of this tree, we rejoice to be grafted together with all of the "wild," gentile branches, our brothers in Messiah from among the nations.

Once again, we acknowledge before heaven the great sin and guilt of our people Israel, in both demanding the death of God's beloved Son and of casting Him out of the Vineyard of which He alone is the rightful Heir. As a people and nation, we have greatly sinned, by presuming that as God's chosen people and first-born- son-nation, we could seize the covenantal inheritance for ourselves while rejecting and disinheriting the true Heir, Yeshua our King. We acknowledge before heaven that only as our people bow before our crucified and glorified King and receive Him back as Redeemer and Lord, can we inherit God's promises to us as a nation through His new and eternal covenant. For these and for many other sins of our people, we bend our knees before the God of Heaven and ask His forgiveness. Not only have we rejected our King, but we have also rejected and despised the ambassadors He has sent us, those who have borne His name in faithfulness to Him.

In addition, since the rebirth of our nation in 1948, we have killed and encouraged the killing of the unborn and have spilled much innocent blood. We have defiled this holy land by our corrupt, immoral, idolatrous and abominable ways. We have prided ourselves in wanting to make Tel Aviv the homosexual capital of the world; we have rejected and disdained the commandments of God as handed down to us in the Scriptures by our fathers. We have hated one another and the non-Jew in our land without cause and we are worthy only of God's righteous judgments. We have taken all the glory for ourselves in all that concerns the restoration and defense of our nation and land. We have worshiped the *golden calf* of mammon and made him our god. We thus bend our knees before our Father in the name of our Messiah Redeemer, Yeshua ha'Mashiach, and ask forgiveness for these sins and for a multitude of other sins that we have committed against Him and others.

We ask God's forgiveness for our sins as the Body of Messiah in the Land. As our people are divided and splintered amongst themselves, so have we not honored one another and have been divided and splintered amongst ourselves as Yeshua's disciples. We have often failed in our priesthood for our people by not living lives worthy of our calling and of not reflecting the true

Image of our King before our people. We have occupied ourselves more with the cares of the world than with the concerns of His Kingdom and the spread of the Gospel.

Despite our sins and in everlasting praise to our God for His grace, and as a first-fruit, priestly remnant of the nation of Israel, we believe that we are a sign and guarantee of all that which God has still promised to fulfill for our people, in faithfulness to His Word and covenants. (Rom 11:25-29) The existence and presence of a Messianic Jewish remnant in the land of Israel in these end-times is the sure evidence and seal that God is again turning His Face back to Israel and bringing a final close to the long period in which He has hid His Face *(hester panim)* from our people. (Rom 11:30-32) This remnant is the assurance and guarantee of the fulfillment of all that God has committed Himself to fulfill by His Spirit concerning Israel's final repentance, restoration and submission to the Lordship and Kingship of our Messiah Yeshua. When Israel will be saved as a nation, it will be "life from the dead" for all the Ecclesia and for all nations. (Rom 11:15)

When God's sons from Israel and from all nations are joined together in holy, covenantal love and are brought to glory (Hebrews 2:10) as mature sons, what Paul foresaw will become a great reality: the deliverance of all creation from its bondage to corruption into the glorious liberty of the sons of God. (Eph 2:11-16; Rom 8:20-22) When Israel acknowledges her sin and comes under the Lordship of Messiah, she will then be given her God-given position amongst the nations as the firstborn son nation to become a Kingdom of Priests for all nations, and the world will witness the final *restoration of all things* as was promised by the prophets and the apostles. (Acts 3:21)

In light of this mystery of God in which all believers in Messiah have their part, we, today, as representatives of the Messianic remnant of Jews who dwell in Israel, and as a prophetic priesthood established and rooted in Jerusalem and in the entire land of Israel, choose to take a new step. Our earnest heart is to further the healing and the restoration of the broken altar of Jerusalem, the foundational altar of God's ultimate reconciliation for the healing of the ancient breach between Israel and her God, the Jewish people and the King of the Jews, Yeshua ha'Mashiach, and the breach which has long existed between Jew and Gentile in Messiah. As Isaiah the prophet prophesied, a remnant of Israel would "raise up the former desolations and the ancient foundations of many generations; they would be repairers of the breach, the restorers of streets to dwell in and would be called 'Priests of the Lord.'" (Isaiah 61:4,6; 58:12). Together, as believers from Israel, Jews and Arabs alike, and believers from the nations, we commit ourselves to continue to repair the breach that has existed for centuries between the Jewish and Gentile believers, and ultimately between Israel and the nations.

On this day, **the 11th of October 2023**, as repentant and reconciled Israelites who have entered into the promised New Covenant inheritance made by the God of Israel with our people through the shed blood of Yeshua ha'Mashiach our King, and as priestly representatives for our nation and as heirs of the promises of God because of Yeshua, **WE AFFIRM OUR COVENANTAL BOND on behalf of** our people, the nation of Israel that dwells in the land of Israel, **WITH** the God of our fathers, the God of Abraham, Isaac, Israel, Moses, David, Elijah and the prophets, **the God who is the FATHER OF OUR LORD YESHUA HA'MASHIACH AND WITH THE NEW AND ETERNAL COVENANT** that ratifies and fulfills all other covenants made with our people. Israel shall no longer be called *Azuvah, Forsaken*, but she shall be called *Hephzibah*, "My delight is in her, a crown of glory in the hand of her God." (Isaiah 62:1-6)

WE AFFIRM THE COVENANTAL BOND of this City of Jerusalem, the City covenanted to David our father, the City in which God has placed His Name and which has been named, the City of the Great King **WITH David's promised messianic Offspring Yeshua**, David's ONLY legitimate Heir, the One chosen by the Father to build His House and to be seated on David's throne in Zion forever when He comes to reign over Israel and all its inhabitants and over all the nations in His coming Kingdom. **WE AFFIRM THE COVENANTAL BOND BETWEEN** the Land of Israel, the land that God calls *My Land*, the land upon which God's eyes are always fixed to care for it, (Deuteronomy 11:12) the land promised to our people Israel through the covenant made with our fathers Abraham, Isaac and Jacob and their seed forever **WITH** the God of our fathers, the God of Abraham, Isaac, Israel, Moses, David, Elijah and the prophets, the God who is the Father of our Lord Yeshua ha'Mashiach **WITH the New and Eternal Covenant** that ratifies and fulfills all other covenants made with our people Israel. We proclaim Yeshua as Lord, Heir and King over our people Israel, over Jerusalem His City and over all the biblical borders of the Land of Israel; we submit our lives and all that we are and have as a nation to His Kingship and Rule! Our Land shall once again become the *Holy Land* as the fountain of His Blood will be opened to cleanse Land and People from all sin and impurity. (Zech 13:1) The Land will be called *Beulah*, married in covenantal purity both to God and to Israel. We bow our knees before our King and beseech Him to take full possession by right of His inheritance, of all that is His, Jerusalem His City, Israel, His land and people, and all others who dwell together with Israel in peace!

We welcome You, King Yeshua, King of Israel, King of the Jews, back into Your Vineyard. May You be enthroned in Your restored Temple of living stones, Jews and non-Jews alike, in

Jerusalem and Israel, in the Sanctuary of our hearts and bodies! Blessed are You who comes in the Name of the Lord! Blessed are You who reigns in the Name of the Lord! (Matt 23:37-39)

(Reuven Berger and his brother Benjamin are pastors of Kehilat ha'Seh al Har Zion (Congregation of the Lamb on Mount Zion))

CHAPTER 42
PRAYER FOR PEACE

May we see the day when war and bloodshed cease, when a great peace will embrace the whole world.

Then nation will not threaten nation, and the human family will not again know war.

For all who live on earth shall realize

we have not come into being to hate or to destroy.

We have come into being to praise, to labor and to love.

Compassionate God, bless the leaders of all nations with the power of compassion.

Fulfill the promise conveyed in Scripture:

I will bring peace to the land,

and you shall lie down and no one shall terrify you.

I will rid the land of vicious beasts and it shall not be ravaged by war.

Let justice and righteousness flow like a mighty stream.

Let God's peace fill the earth as the waters fill the sea.

And let us say:

Amen

(Feld, Rabbi Edward, Senior Editor and Chair. Siddur Lev Shalem. New York, NY: The Rabbinical Assembly, 2016. Page 176.)

CHAPTER 43
PROCLAMATIONS ON BEHALF OF ISRAEL
BY DEREK PRINCE

He who scattered Israel is gathering him,
And keep him as a shepherd does his flock. (Jeremiah 31:10b)

Let all those who hate Zion
Be put to shame and turned back.
Let them be as the grass on the housetops,
Which withers before it grows up. (Psalm 129:5-6)

Destroy, O Lord, and divide their tongues! (Psalm 55:9a)

For the scepter of wickedness shall not rest
On the land allotted to the righteous. (Psalm 125:3a)

For the Lord will not forsake His people, for His great name's sake, because it has pleased the Lord to make you His people. (1 Samuel 12:22)

Let all the earth fear the Lord;
Let all the inhabitants of the world stand in awe of Him.

For He spoke, and it was done;
He commanded, and it stood fast.
The Lord brings the counsel of the nations to nothing;
He makes the plans of the peoples of no effect.
The counsel of the Lord stands forever,
The plans of His heart to all generations.
Blessed is the nation whose God is the Lord,
The people He has chosen as His own inheritance. (Psalm 33:8-12)

Show Your marvelous lovingkindness by Your right hand,
O You who save those who trust in You
From those who rise up against them.
Keep me as the apple of Your eye;
Hide me under the shadow of Your wings,
From the wicked who oppress me,
From my deadly enemies who surround me. (Psalm 17:7-9)

If it had not been the Lord who was on our side,"
Let Israel now say—
"If it had not been the Lord who was on our side,
When men rose up against us,
Then they would have swallowed us alive,
When their wrath was kindled against us;
Then the waters would have overwhelmed us,
The stream would have gone over our soul;
Then the swollen waters
Would have gone over our soul."
Blessed be the Lord,
Who has not given us as prey to their teeth.
Our soul has escaped as a bird from the snare of the fowlers;
The snare is broken, and we have escaped.
Our help is in the name of the Lord,
Who made heaven and earth. (Psalm 124)

CHAPTER 44
REES HOWELLS INTERCESSOR

Rees Howells was a humble coal miner who found the secret to receiving answers to prayer that altered world events. He founded a Bible College in Britain where he trained and led intercessors.

In 1940, while the Battle of Dunkirk raged, Rees saw a vision of God with His sword drawn at Dunkirk. As Rees and his team of 100 intercessors persisted in prayer, they asked God to bring "disaster on the Nazis."

As they waged war on their knees, a sense of relief washed over them. They felt something happened while they prayed. Hitler halted the German advance. It was a military blunder no one understood which gave the allies the time they desperately needed. In the miracle of Dunkirk, God rescued 338,000 troops.

(Grubb, Norman. *Rees Howells Intercessor*. Fort Washington, Penn.: Christian Literature Crusade, 1974.)

CHAPTER 45
REFLECTIONS ON CHANUKAH 2023

Chanukah (meaning "dedication" in Hebrew) is an annual 8-day celebration, commemorating the rededication of the 2nd Temple in 164 BC. The rededication was a culmination of a successful three-year campaign led by five sons (primarily Judas), of a priest named Mattathias Maccabee. The revolt was against an oppressive Syrian (Seleucid) regime, notably Antiochus IV Epiphanes, who had outlawed the Jewish faith, abused Jews with horrific violence, and defiled the Temple by erecting an altar to the Greek god, Zeus.

Today Chanukah is celebrated on the 25th day of Kislev (the ninth month of the Hebrew calendar. For eight nights, candles are lit in a menorah, a candelabrum with spaces for nine candles —one for each night plus a "servant" candle called the shamash. On each successive night, one more candle is added and lit. During the lighting, people recite special blessings and prayers. Songs are sung, and gifts are exchanged to commemorate the miracle in the Temple more than 2,000 years ago.

CHANUKAH PRAYERS

Blessed are You, Adonai our God, Ruler of the Universe, who makes us holy with Your commandments, commanding us to kindle (light) the Chanukah lights.Blessed are You, Adonai our God, Ruler of the Universe, who performed wondrous deeds for our ancestors in those ancient days at this season.Blessed are You, Adonai our God, Ruler of the Universe, who has kept us alive, sustained us, and brought us to this season.

Happy Chanukah! It is a Festival of Lights. This year's celebration in Israel has even more meaning as the battle of light over darkness continues.

Historically, there were two struggles going on:

- War between the Maccabees and the Greek Empire
- Cleansing and Re-dedication of the Temple and the re-Kindling of the Lampstand

In Revelation 1 it says the golden lampstand is actually a symbol for the people of God.

8 CHANUKAH PRAYERS FOR OUR ARAB FRIENDS

- Blessing over Arab believers;
- Freedom from demonic jihad;
- Protection for the innocent;
- Highest moral values to prevail;
- Right governmental solution for Gaza after the war;
- Light of Yeshua to shine;
- Salvation to be poured out;

- Cooperative relationships with moderate Arab nations going forward. (Asher Intrader)

The story of Chanukah describes how God protected and preserved His chosen people. If Antiochus IV Epiphanes had destroyed the Jewish population, then how would Mary have given birth to the Jewish Messiah, Jesus? In other words, "without Chanukah—there would be no Christmas!" (Mitch Glazer)

Without the victory won by the Maccabees, without the cleansing of the Temple, without the reigniting of the Lampstand, the promise of the Messiah would not have been birthed in its fullness. (Ariel Blumenthal)

As we light our Chanukah candles here in Israel in the midst of this present darkness, we remember our history, that "against all odds" the Lord enabled the Maccabees to triumph over their evil enemies and to re-dedicate the Temple. As believers in Messiah Yeshua, we are celebrating the victory of His Everlasting Light that shines in the darkness. "Rejoicing in hope, patient in tribulation, continuing steadfastly in prayer." (Romans 12:12) Thank you all so much for standing with us! (Karen Davis)

"When Jesus spoke again to the people, he said, 'I am the light of the world. Whoever follows Me will never walk in darkness, but will have the light of life.'" (John 8:12)

On the 25th Day of December we celebrate the birth of Yeshua/Jesus, beginning in the evening for the King of the Jews was born who is the Son of God. Is it not interesting that Jesus asserted His Deity during Chanukah? If there was no Chanukah and the Jewish people were assimilated into the Greek culture, could this assertion have even taken place? Chanukah was a historical event as well as a prophetic foreshadow of the last days. (June and Shelly Volk)

CHAPTER 46
REGARDING ISRAEL'S ENEMIES

While we are now engaging in vigorous warfare, we need to be mindful of The Lord's final victory.

> *It shall be in that day that I will seek to destroy all the nations that come against Jerusalem.* (Zechariah 12:9)

Why do the nations rage,
And the people plot a vain thing?
The kings of the earth set themselves,
And the rulers take counsel together,
Against the Lord and against His Anointed, saying,
"Let us break Their bonds in pieces
And cast away Their cords from us."
He who sits in the heavens shall laugh;
The Lord shall hold them in derision.
Then He shall speak to them in His wrath,
And distress them in His deep displeasure:
"Yet I have set My King
On My holy hill of Zion." (Psalm 2:1-6)

So the Lord will reign over them in Mount Zion From now on, even forever. (Micah 4:7)

CHAPTER 47
SERVING HOLOCAUST SURVIVORS
BY SUSAN HEAGY, NOVEMBER 30, 2023

I figured that the Holocaust survivors were going to be affected by the war, but I didn't realize how much, and what they needed until I started getting into their homes and talking to them. The very first thing we did was call all the survivors whose contacts I have, all of them, to ask, "How are you in this war?" And the very first thing that they said was, "I can't believe you called me, I can't believe you care enough. Somebody actually cares how I feel in this war." And so even though we have had contact with them for almost 20 years, they still reacted just by someone calling up. As we called, we began to find a little bit more of where their mind was at. As for myself, I could hear explosions all morning because I'm close to the Lebanon border. And then I heard a big boom, near here, which means that it was an interception.

Imagine a Holocaust survivor who was in the war for five years, and hearing explosions, telling us stories of being on trains that were bombed. As the train would stop, everyone would run into the forest. And then whoever lived through it would run back to the train. And sometimes a mother didn't come back, or a child didn't come back, or the children got left on the train, or the mother couldn't get on the train. These thing's happened, and there was a lot of trauma, and it's all coming back now, but it's reversed.

In the War, they lost their fathers who were fighting, they lost their mothers who were trying to take care of them, or they were simply older, their grandparents died or were murdered. Now they have their grandchildren going to war. And this is a whole new thing for them. And they have told me, "I came here to Israel to be safe. And there's disappointment and discouragement that I feel that now my grandchildren are being sacrificed to keep me safe." And it's a whole new perspective. And the things that I'm noticing is that many of them are nervous, much more nervous than before. One of them told me this is the eighth war she's been in!

Some of them are afraid to answer the door, until I say, "It's Sussanah." They say, "Ah, Ok, you can come in." They're very fearful. And what are they listening to? Most of them only speak Russian, so their source of information is Russian TV. Russian TV is not like getting everything from the Israeli government, so some of their information isn't good, or it's just not complete. So, they live with that information just like they did in in World War II.

One of them said, "I came to Israel so my grandchildren would not be in war because I was in war, and here we are." So, the trauma that they're feeling, is like if someone dies, the family is in need of somebody to come close, to come near, to hold them, to talk to them, or just be there. But most people are afraid. They're afraid for themselves, they're afraid for their families, and they're concerned that no one is thinking about the Holocaust survivors. It's only the people who are in this work that have a connection.

And so how do you handle trauma for someone? How do you handle their death, and everything that comes after? You are simply there. And people usually say, "Call me if you need me," but you're never going to call if you're in the middle of trauma. You're not going to call someone; you just have to be there. And so, we're increasing our contact with them. Some of them really need an extra something, so, we go out for coffee and cake. We're taking them out so they can forget everything for a time, and they get to talk, because when you get somebody alone with coffee, they start talking.

Sometimes I need a translator, but not every time. I've been delivering quilts, and I discovered I can do it all by myself because I have a letter that I made for Hebrew speakers, and for the Russian speakers. It's all about the quilt being their new heirloom, because they lost their heirlooms in the war. And so, I can go in, and I can give them a hug, and then I open up the quilt and cover them, and there's a big sigh, "Aah." They know it's for them, and they talk, and say "It's winter, it's winter, just in time!" And so, I give that to them, and I give them a letter that explains it, and I give them a hug and a kiss, and I tell them, "I love you," in Russian, and in Hebrew, if I need to.

We're not only making contact, we're calling them, stopping in, whatever is needed. We are there, and they know it. But one thing that really hit me was realizing, and it is one thing that I thought of right away, there are many survivors who cannot go to a shelter. Most bomb shelters here in the older buildings are downstairs under the building. It's on the bottom floor, the ground floor. But most of the survivors live in buildings four floors up, a walk up, and they can't go. We're here in Acco and in the north, we have 30 seconds to get to a shelter when we hear the siren. Well, it takes 30 seconds for them to stand up. They can't get anywhere, and it's only the newer buildings that have their own shelter to get to. So, what did they do? I asked them, "What did you do in the last war?" They said, "I watched the rockets come down." Can you imagine sitting there wondering if a rocket's gonna hit you. So, thank the Lord, He gave us the idea of what to do.

We have made up bags. I had this idea nine years ago, but the Lord didn't put it together until now. In these bags is everything you would need to survive for 48 hours, if you are in the rubble of a building that's been hit with a rocket. The likelihood of them needing this is very, very small, but the comfort of having it is huge.

So much has been given to us, and the funding was given to us as well. Thank you very much, you're making this happen. And so, everything is provided for them here. And the idea is that they can sit wherever they need to in their apartment, and hold the bag right to their chest, through the straps, and if anything happens, they have it. There's a medical kit, and water, and some protein bars, a flashlight, an emergency blanket, a little trash bag, socks, something to write on, whatever they need. This is giving them a real sense of comfort just to know that this is coming.

One woman who cannot leave her apartment was laughing and happy to have a quilt. And we will give her a bag as well so that she knows that she is safe. We also give birthday flowers. We gave them to a lady on her 85th birthday. She is a doctor and she has cancer. She's dying, but she had the most positive attitude. And what did she say? "I thank God for my life. I thank God for my husband to take care of me, and I thank God that He will watch over us during this war." We gave a quilt to a lady that is almost blind. Her daughter came to visit her from Russia, and she gave it to her. So, we gave her another one. We gave another quilt to this beautiful woman in a wheelchair, and it made her very happy. The important thing is being there.

We don't do things only for holidays; we want to do it every day, 365 days a year. Obviously, I can't be with them every day. I wish we had more volunteers who I could send out, like I used to do before COVID. Even if it's just to stop in, knock on the door, and hand them one carnation, and give them a hug. That is enough for them. And they will talk about that for weeks. And they don't even throw the carnation away. The next time we go, the dead carnation is there. But it's special, it means something to them.

What we really need are prayers for these people. I want them to find the peace that only God can give them. And I ask that you really pray for their health. I want to tell you; I have seen them age since this war started. I go to see them, and I have seen that they have aged during this time.

And it's unbelievable the ages of these people. We just went to see someone who turned 99. Now in December, we have a very special lady here in Acco who's going to be 101. And we have another one who'll be 100. We have another one who's turning 98. These ladies have all gone through the Holocaust, but they have such a strength about them, such a resilience. We can learn from them. But they need our prayers. As the sirens go off, as they read about this, as their grandchildren are going and fighting, please protect them and their families, please bring these grandchildren back to them safely. Amen.

(For more information about Susan's ministry, check out her Abundant Hope International web site at https://www.ahi-il.org/)

CHAPTER 48
SILVER TRUMPETS AND PSALM 91 BANDANAS
BY RICHARD AND CAROLYN HYDE, OCTOBER 22 2023

SAFETY OF ABIDING IN THE PRESENCE OF GOD

> *He who dwells in the secret place of the Most High*
> *Shall abide under the shadow of the Almighty.*
> *I will say of the Lord, "He is my refuge and my fortress;*
> *My God, in Him I will trust."*
> *Surely He shall deliver you from the snare of the fowler*
> *And from the perilous pestilence.*
> *He shall cover you with His feathers,*
> *And under His wings you shall take refuge;*
> *His truth shall be your shield and buckler.*
> *You shall not be afraid of the terror by night,*
> *Nor of the arrow that flies by day,*
> *Nor of the pestilence that walks in darkness,*
> *Nor of the destruction that lays waste at noonday.*
> *A thousand may fall at your side,*
> *And ten thousand at your right hand;*
> *But it shall not come near you.*

Only with your eyes shall you look,
And see the reward of the wicked.
Because you have made the Lord, who is my refuge,
Even the Most High, your dwelling place,
No evil shall befall you,
Nor shall any plague come near your dwelling;
For He shall give His angels charge over you,
To keep you in all your ways.
In their hands they shall bear you up,
Lest you dash your foot against a stone.
You shall tread upon the lion and the cobra,
The young lion and the serpent you shall trample underfoot.
Because he has set his love upon Me, therefore I will deliver him;
I will set him on high, because he has known My name.
He shall call upon Me, and I will answer him;
I will be with him in trouble;
I will deliver him and honor him.
With long life I will satisfy him,
And show him My salvation. (Psalm 91)

TWO SILVER TRUMPETS

And the Lord spoke to Moses, saying: "Make two silver trumpets for yourself; you shall make them of hammered work; you shall use them for calling the congregation and for directing the movement of the camps. When they blow both of them, all the congregation shall gather before you at the door of the tabernacle of meeting. But if they blow only one, then the leaders, the heads of the divisions of Israel, shall gather to you. When you sound the advance, the camps that lie on the east side shall then begin their journey. When you sound the advance the second time, then the camps that lie on the south side shall begin their journey; they shall sound the call for them to begin their jour-

SILVER TRUMPETS AND PSALM 91 BANDANAS

neys. And when the assembly is to be gathered together, you shall blow, but not sound the advance. The sons of Aaron, the priests, shall blow the trumpets; and these shall be to you as an ordinance forever throughout your generations.

When you go to war in your land against the enemy who oppresses you, then you shall sound an alarm with the trumpets, and you will be remembered before the Lord your God, and you will be saved from your enemies. Also in the day of your gladness, in your appointed feasts, and at the beginning of your months, you shall blow the trumpets over your burnt offerings and over the sacrifices of your peace offerings; and they shall be a memorial for you before your God: I am the Lord your God. (Numbers 10:1-10)

Hello. This is Richard and Carolyn Hyde. We're on top of our roof looking over the beautiful Galilee; the Sea of Galilee here. These last two weeks have been very difficult as you know. We've suffered quite a bit as a country, as a people. But we've also been drawn together. I've seen a lot of unity that has taken place even in our own neighborhood and among our neighbors. And we wanted to share with you some of the things we've been doing over the last two weeks.

Today's Parashat *HaShavua*, the Torah portion of the week, being Noah, isn't coincidental. In it, it's noted, "The world was filled with absolute wickedness (violence)." That's the word 'Hamas,' which is also the terror group who took hostages and brutally murdered so many in the kibbutzim near the Gaza Strip. As we have watched this unfold, it's been really hard to process this as believers. We've felt a mixture of love, shock, grief and anger. We're all processing it how we can.

As a result, our reserves have been called up, 300,000 or so of them. Perhaps you can imagine our roads are just full of soldiers, and tanks, and transport carriers. Especially on the

Northern and the Southern border. One day, we decided to actually go out and talk with some of these soldiers.

Last week we were carrying our Psalm 91 bandanas, and talking to the soldiers. As soon as we approached them, I'd tell them, "I have something to give to you. It's a Psalm 91 bandana." Then I would tell them the story. During WWI, there was a *pluggah*, a unit, that was from Texas, and they were on some of the worst front lines in France and Germany. They had very high mortality rates in the battles. And they prayed Psalm 91 every day together as a *pluggah*, and they didn't lose one person! And so, when I'd tell the troops this, they'd go, "Wow, can you give me more? I'll get one for my brother over here…" And so, we were handing these out like popcorn.

We'd see soldiers on the road, and we'd pull over to give them a bandana, and somebody else would give them like some socks and underwear. There was one particular time where they were given some sushi. So, as we were walking towards the guys eating sushi, I said to them, "Oh! We got here just in time!" And they held out a chopstick and said, "Yeah." It was a good connection. Yeah, sweethearts. But often times they would put them on their heads or around their necks or whatever.

There was another soldier, after I talked with him as we were walking off, he chased us down and said, "Are you guys' believers?" He was a believer himself. His dad was actually Jewish, so the son think he was Jewish. Of course, he is!

So, we were able to encourage him with that. If that's the mentality, then King David wasn't Jewish. Yeah, that's what we told him. So, we encouraged him.

There was another group of ones that were up on their soldier transport, and we gave bandanas to them, and they just grabbed them and were putting them all on their heads, and they were laughing and having fun. It was sheer joy. It was just really sweet to see because these guys have been sleeping in the field for like the whole time, and probably haven't had a bath this whole time.

So, they appreciated the hugs. And when I would ask them, "Could I give you a hug?" They'd say, "I'm all sweaty." It didn't matter to me. I would just give hugs. They got a lot of good food, but they are short on medical supplies. So, that's something else that we've been diving into to help with some ministries and organizations that are funding that.

So, this week we are doing similar things, going out and giving the bandanas to the soldiers, but also, we're doing something else. We have these silver trumpets. I was given these by a friend who said, when the North sees war, you are to blow these. And so, I've kept them in my home, and the day finally came when it was like, wow, we were looking at the scripture from Numbers 10:9.

It says, "When you are attacked by an enemy in your own land and you go to war, blow the silver trumpets." It's a way of gathering the soldiers together. And we actually came upon a whole group that was ready to be deployed. It actually says in Numbers 10:1: "The Lord spoke further to Moses saying, make yourselves two trumpets of silver, and you shall make them of hammered work, and you shall use them for summoning the congregation and breaking the camp."

We were driving yesterday in the Golan Heights, the GPS signal was blocked, and we didn't know where we were going. And so, we were trying to come down the Golan and we were traveling and going further and further and further, and finally we realized that we were close to the border of Lebanon. We were less than 10 kilometers from an area that had been hit. We were on these little roads and we came across a bunch of soldiers, about 150 of them. As it states in Numbers, they were gathered together so that they could be deployed. They had all their backpacks, their camouflage helmets, and their guns, and they were just about to take off when we arrived with our silver trumpets and the bandanas of course! Giving those out again and explaining what happened in World War I. The soldiers all loved these.

And then I showed Numbers 10:9 to one of the soldiers, and he read it out loud in Hebrew. And people were going like, "That's what we're doing. We're going. We've been attacked in our land and we're going to war against a nation that has attacked us." And so, they kept motioning, like are you going to blow the thing? So finally, I lifted it up and blew the trumpet. And you should have seen the smiles that broke out upon the soldiers faces. They were yelling, had their arms up in the air and screaming. It was so amazing that the Lord had brought us right to that place as they were just about to be sent out, and God gave us these scriptures and it was just perfect. Right on time.

So, we bless you this Shabbat. May you have a peaceful Shabbat. And may we see peace in Israel. Meanwhile, there's a huge table that's been set in Tel Aviv for 203 people; that's the number of hostages in Gaza. And they said, set a place at your table every Shabbat now, until they come home, so we'll be doing that tonight. We wish you Shabbat Shalom. God bless.

(Richard and Carolyn Hyde are Israeli-American citizens living in the Galilee who made Aliyah in 2003)

CHAPTER 49
THE CRY OF THE DAUGHTERS OF ISRAEL

"A voice was heard in Ramah,
Lamentation and bitter weeping,
Rachel weeping for her children,
Refusing to be comforted for her children,
Because they are no more." (Jeremiah 31:15)

We had a rocket hit and damage three houses in our neighborhood, not far from us. Right now, we just had a barrage in the center, and one went through a wall in an apartment building, it was quite large.

In Israel we walk with a lot of pain. We are heartbroken. We hear every day the stories. Every day! And we're angry too. We are angry with the organization the Red Cross. That red cross, it's hurting us deep inside, and we hurt, and we're angry with the U.N. We're angry with UNRWA. We're angry with what they've done, and how the world put's up with them. We're angry because we look and see, and my prayer is that all these organizations, these humanitarian organizations, who put up this big cry in Gaza. That they would be exposed for the darkness they have walked in. That God would expose it.

And also pray. Don't pray for a ceasefire. Please don't. We want to fight. We're ready to fight in our land. We're ready, and we're paying a price now. We're losing soldiers every day. Every time there's a pause or a ceasefire, and we get our people out, we're rejoicing, and joyful, and thanking God. Then we have tears and emotions; crying for those who are there, and those who are fighting, realizing that everyone around the world who cries for this humanitarian aid that Hamas is simply preparing to hit us hard. They know what they're doing. They have planned this out.

Israel is going through a shaking because we missed it. We missed it. There was intelligence, but we missed it. We were asleep, and Israel is going through a tremendous shaking. And you need to realize that one of the symbols in the land now is the Lion of the tribe of Judah. The Lion of Judah is Israel's symbol because Hamas attacked that day and Islamic Jihad and the Muslim world poked the Apple of God's eye – hard, and it hurt. And that's who God says we are in this land. We are the apple of His eye, the most sensitive tender part.

With God we have tremendous thanksgiving. We have resolved that we're going to persevere. We're going to go forward, and we need you to pray us through. You must pray us through. You must pray for us. We're taking care of a daughter with three small children whose husband right now is in the middle of everything. This is not just us; this is across the land, women are serving. Some are in strong battles, and some of the intelligence came from women here in Israel. There was a tank crew of women that killed 50 terrorists, and saved a whole kibbutz. They stood there, and stood their ground in a tank. The stories are amazing!

Amazing ones where we say, "God, thank you," and some where we just break down and cry. We have waves in the day time, tears that just roll over you, and we understand. There's a scripture that I've read many times in the Book of Job. It's where we get our seven days of shiva, to mourn for the dead. It ministered to my heart so deep.

> *So they sat down with him on the ground seven days and seven nights, and no one spoke a word to him, for they saw that his grief was very great. (Job 2:13)*

Job's friends sat with him as he wept over his loss, because it was great. Our pain is very great because almost every day they tell us that this soldier was killed, or they found another body of an Israeli that they thought was kidnapped as a hostage. So, it's not an easy time right now. It's a very challenging time when you see families mourning for the loss of the dear ones. Families are crying for loved ones who have been kidnapped. We are praying for their release.

We hear some of the stories from those who have been released. One 84-year-old woman in captivity didn't get any medicine, or any food. When they released her, they took her straight to the hospital and put her in intensive care because she was almost dying. And there are other stories of children who didn't get any food, and every time they wanted something, they beat them and told them to shut up.

One young boy was so happy to see his parents when he was released, but for days he was quiet. When the parents tried to talk to him, he said, "No, be quiet. We have to be quiet." He was so traumatized, and wouldn't speak because the terrorists would beat him whenever he would talk.

The psychiatrists are really helping the survivors from the trauma they went through while being in captivity. Sadly, there are many stories coming out about women who have been raped. There's a lot of pain, and a lot of challenges.

The distressing news we witness in the media deeply affects us here. Descriptions of beheadings, rapes, and people being burned alive evoke horror within us. The events of October 7th's final hours were truly terrible, and it's essential for believers worldwide to acknowledge this and respond with constant weeping and prayer—prayers directed fervently towards Israel. We must unite in prayer for Israel's victory, as defeating evil becomes imperative. God has a beautiful plan at the end of everything because He is God, and there is none other.

There are many amazing stories of women. One girl was hiding from the terrorists. She rubbed blood all over herself from another dead person, and just laid there, so they would think that she was dead. This happened while she'd been participating in a New Age Festival, part of a wild party, but she laid there covered in blood and cried out to God, the God of Israel, and said, "God I've done everything I know to do, and I put myself in Your hands," and she was saved. There are people who are crying to God, and what we need to know in our heart of hearts is that the Lion of Judah is Yeshua our Messiah.

We just received a travel alert, and we are being told not to go to different countries because they're saying we're not safe there. We won't be safe there because there's a lot of anti-Semitism now rising up in many countries, including America. Anti-Semitism is increasing, and there's many incidents of Jews that are in hiding, or even afraid to walk in neighborhoods because they feel they'll be persecuted. So, it's challenging times we live in, and we need to pray.

It's really important to know that the Jewish believers in the Land of Israel are not separate from our people. We're not separate; we're right along with them in all of this. During Corona, we decided to do a Women's Conference here in Israel in different parts of the country. One of the parts we went to was in the South, to Kibbutz in Sderot right by the Gaza border, where in 2014, terrorists came up in tunnels and attacked the soldiers in that base and were killed.

We went there for two years in a row. This kibbutz welcomed us as Messianic Jews. We worshipped God on that kibbutz, and we prayed. And every year we prayed a blessing over this kibbutz. We would ask God to take care of them because rockets were coming into this kibbutz. We prayed that God would protect them, protect their families, and that He would reveal Himself to them. We just prayed blessings upon this kibbutz.

On October 7th, a 25-year-old woman was in charge of the security of this kibbutz, and when she heard the siren and the rockets, they all went to the safe room. Something inside of her said, "Something is really wrong; it's bad." She didn't know why, but she felt something deep in what we say "her kishkes," in her gut. She called the 12 men who were with her to come in, and she opened up the weapons, and gave them all weapons. She and her commander told everybody to stay in the safe room because of the rockets, but in her heart of heart she knew she had to give them weapons. Then she put them all around the perimeter as watchmen. When the terrorists started approaching, these security forces stopped them, and not one person died in the kibbutz.

And I knew, at that moment that God had remembered every prayer that we had prayed for that kibbutz for two years.

CHAPTER 50
THE DANGER OF REPLACEMENT THEOLOGY

For over nineteen centuries the Jewish people have been an object of contempt and suspicion. What has come to be called "replacement theology" is widely perceived as being one of the causes of this attitude.[1]

So, what is Replacement Theology? International House of Prayer (IHOP) founder, Mike Bickle, laid this out in a recent teaching:

1. Replacement theology promotes the idea that God is finished with Israel as a nation and all the promises He made to Israel in the Old Testament have been given to the Church who is God's "new true Israel" who inherits all the national promises and blessings that God gave to Israel.
2. Replacement theology spiritualizes rather than interprets in a literal, plain sense way the prophetic promises given to Israel. It embraces a non-literal, allegorical interpretation of these promises and/or

insists that most of the end-time prophecies about Israel have been fulfilled in history.
3. Replacement theology views the Church as "spiritual Israel" and/or "spiritual Jerusalem." In the NT the term, *Israel*, is used nearly 70 times, always referring to the physical people of Israel, only once as a substitute term for the Church. The phrases, *New Israel* and *Spiritual Israel*, are not in the Bible.
4. Replacement theology has been taught by the Catholic, Eastern Orthodox, and Protestant churches for the majority of their history. Many Church Fathers—including Justin Martyr (AD 100-165), Augustine of Hippo (354-430), John Calvin, Martin Luther and more, espoused this doctrine.
5. There are 2 main approaches to replacement theology.
6. Israel's role as the people of God was **completed**. This says that after Jesus came, Israel's mission was completed. The Church took over as the people of God. In other words, in His redemptive plans, God is no longer working through ethnic Israel.
7. Israel's place as the people of God was **forfeited**. The Church replaced Israel because of God's permanent judgment on the nation for its rejection of Jesus.
8. **Literal interpretation**: The best Bible teachers in history embrace the **historical-grammatical** method of interpretation. This interpretative grid seeks to understand each passage according to the original meaning that was intended by the one who wrote it. Literal interpretation seeks to understand the "plain meaning"—what the author intended as conveyed by its *grammatical construction* and *historical context*, including the cultural background of the author and its readers.

1. Replacement theology is one of the most serious errors promoted throughout history by many who are reputed to be trustworthy Bible scholars by many over many centuries. There is serious contradiction in their teaching in that they insist on literal interpretation of Scripture *except when it relates to Israel* [2]

"Wherever replacement theology has flourished, the Jews have had to run for cover," notes biblical scholar Thomas Ice. "Wherever such a view has gone, it has always led to anti-Semitism." Another scholar says, "Replacement Theology has provided the basis for all sorts of mischief, persecution, and atrocities against the Jewish people throughout Christian history." [3]

Author Sandra Teplinsky shares her introduction to Christianity as an impressionable five-year-old:

"Flash back with me, if you would, to a childhood experience that seared my soul about "Christianity":

I stare in puzzled horror at a parade of living skeletons, sunken cheeks and bulging eyes, the subjects of macabre Nazi "medical" experiments. Seconds later, corpses-countless piles of them-are bulldozed and dumped into a gargantuan pit, like refuse heaped in a junkyard.

Then the film stops. The rabbi fumbles with the movie projector, and old reel-to-reel, and switches the lights on. He shuffles slowly around to share with the youth group from my synagogue in Chicago. Everyone is very quiet, and I can tell he has something important to say,

"This is what Christians will do to you, if you let them," he warns. "You must never let them; no, never again!" [4]

"Those in the Christian community who may feel the olive tree died about two thousand years ago and thus the root has no life now left in it must read Romans 11 again. There Paul emphatically says that God has not rejected his people (v.1). And though "some" (not all) of the branches of the olive tree have been broken off through unbelief (v.17), "God is able to graft them in again" (v.23). Israel, however remains a "holy" people, for "the root is holy" (v.16). Israel is yet "loved on account of the patriarchs" (v.28), "for God's gifts and his call are irrevocable" (v.29). The common belief today that gentiles have replaced the Jewish tree, rather than being grafted into it, is a position of post-New Testament Christian triumphalism that finds no support in Romans 11." [5]

"As for the Holocaust and the history of the church, we must recognize that the Holocaust did not come about *ex nihilo*, "out of nothing,' unfortunately, so-called Christian Europe at that time had been influenced by centuries of negative teaching concerning the Jewish people. Instead of the church affirming its Jewish heritage with a spirit of indebtedness and appreciation to Jewish people, over the centuries a spirit of apathy, indifference and hostility characterized its attitude toward the Jew. The toleration of negative caricatures, stereotypes, and mythic or cartoon-like images of Jews resulted in a lack of concern and a general malaise within the church toward the Jewish people. The cumulative impact of allowing centuries of religious anti-Semitism to go for the most part unchallenged helped to provide an environment or ethos where Hitler's targeting of the Jewish people for extermination was made possible.

Because the church had become largely cut off from the Jewish womb that had given it birth, anti-Judaism in the early Christian centuries eventually led to anti-Semitism. What an unbelievable paradox! The people who have given more of their rich heritage to the church than any other people have been most maligned by the church. The anguish of the Jewish people qt the hands of the institutional church is well documented in the teachings of the church fathers, in the works of reformers such as Martin Luther, and in events such as the Crusades and the Inquisition and expulsion from Spin. A spirit of arrogance, triumphalism, and supersessionism was allowed to fester within the church for centuries. This rot was never rooted out. Instead of non-Jews humbly seeing themselves as grafted into Israel (Romans 11:17), the church proclaimed itself to have replaced Israel. Instead of the church viewing itself as a remnant, it proceeded to define itself apart from Israel." [6]

The re-establishment of a Jewish state in the Promised Land caused some Christian theologians to do a double take. If the Jewish people were being restored physically to their homeland according to the prophecies in the Old Testament, could it be that God has not abandoned or rejected His people? Of course, such a radical thought would have been no surprise to the Apostle Paul, who made this a central pillar of his Messianic gospel in Romans 11:1-2: "I say then, God has not rejected His people, has He? Far from it! For I too am a son of Israel, of the seed of Abraham, of the tribe of Benjamin. God has not rejected His people whom He foreknew." (Avner Boskey)

---

1. Diprose, Ronald E. *Israel and the Church, The origin and Effects of Replacement Theology*. Rome, Italy. Instuto Biblico Evangelico Italiano. 2000. Page 29.
2. https://mikebickle.org/wp-content/uploads/2023/06/Refuse-To-Be-Intimidated-by-the-Error-of-Replacement-Theology.KD1_.pdf
    https://jij.org/news/replacement-theology
3. https://jij.org/news/replacement-theology
4. Teplinsky, Sandra. *Why Care about Israel?*. Grand Rapids, Mich.: Chosen Books. 2004.Page 111.
5. Wilson, Marvin. Our Father Abraham Second Edition. Grand Rapids, Mich.: Wm. B. Eerdmans Publishing Co. 2021.Page 30.
6. ibid. Page 351

CHAPTER 51
THE ISAIAH 19 HIGHWAY

In that day Israel will be one of three with Egypt and Assyria—a blessing in the midst of the land, whom the Lord of hosts shall bless, saying, "Blessed is Egypt My people, and Assyria the work of My hands, and Israel My inheritance." (Isaiah 19:24-25)

What a promise God has made, that those who have been historical enemies will be reconciled and blessed together! Egypt will be called "God's people," Assyria will be "the work of God's hands," and Israel will be "God's inheritance." Modern day Assyria would consist of the nations of Lebanon, Syria, Iraq and parts of Iran.

Recently a man shared about his involvement in this troubled area of the world. While the man was speaking, I saw a picture of a green iron braided stake that was planted behind him. As I considered this picture, the interpretation came into focus.

The stake

Stakes are for tents, which are temporary dwellings. We pray for those who are currently displaced from their homes by war. We are all pilgrim tent-dwellers in this life.

These all died in faith, not having received the promises, but having seen them afar off were assured of them, embraced them and confessed that they were strangers and pilgrims on the earth. (Hebrews 11:13)

Iron

Iron is a very strong metal.

Can anyone break iron, The northern iron and the bronze? (Jeremiah 15:12)

The back

Stakes provide stability, like a back bone. We don't look at present circumstances, but we stand firmly on God's promises.

Finally, my brethren, be strong in the Lord and in the power of His might. (Ephesians 6:10)

Braided

Three nations will be braided together for strength.

Though one may be overpowered by another, two can withstand him. And a threefold cord is not quickly broken. (Ecclesiastes 4:12)

Green

The color green speaks of fruitfulness. God will make this troubled and barren area of the world fruitful.

Is it not yet a very little while Till Lebanon shall be turned into a fruitful field. (Isaiah 29:17)

CHAPTER 52
THE ISAIAH 62 FAST

May 7 – 28 2023

Over five million believers engaged in prayer for Israel for at least one hour a day for 21 days (May 7-28) for the increase of God's salvation promises and plans for Jerusalem and Israel. Some prayed alone, and others prayed with two or more:

For where two or three are gathered together in My name, I am there in the midst of them." (Matthew 18:20)

—virtually or in-person—in their home, office, dorm, or at their church, etc.

A collaboration of ten thousand ministries—including Lou Engle, Jason Hubbard, Mike Bickle—called many believers to participate in a global solemn assembly (May 7-28) to fast in various ways and to pray for the Lord's purposes for Israel and to ask Him to raise up 100 million intercessors for Israel according to His promise in Isaiah 62:6 to sovereignly "set," "appoint," or "mark" intercessors who will remind the Lord of His promises for Jerusalem until Jesus returns. Isaiah 62:6 is an end-time promise that is now escalating across the earth.

I have set watchmen on your walls, O Jerusalem;
They shall never hold their peace day or night.
You who make mention of the Lord, do not keep silent,
And give Him no rest till He establishes
And till He makes Jerusalem a praise in the earth. (Isaiah 62:6-7)

In the first three weeks of announcing this fast on March 7, over 1,000,000 were set to participate in various ways. By May 7, over five million set their heart to engage in this 21-day fast in various ways (some fasted on water, some on vegetables, or juices, or taking one meal a day, and some "fasted media" instead of food, etc.).

We prayed for a greater manifestation of God's glory to be openly displayed in numerous ways including fulfillment of His covenant promises to Israel to make Zion a praise in the earth and to establish Israel as the leading nation on the earth that inspires all nations to work in justice and righteousness. Israel has been a blessing to the nations and it is our responsibility to be a blessing to Israel and pray, give, and serve Israel's calling until Jerusalem becomes a praise in the earth. God's honor is at stake in the fulfillment of His unique promises to Israel and our part is to agree with those promises and advocate for them.

In addition, Israel's national repentance:

Repent therefore and be converted, that your sins may be blotted out, so that times of refreshing may come from the presence of the Lord. (Act 3:19) and confession that Jesus is Messiah:

> *For I say to you, you shall see Me no more till you say, 'Blessed is He who comes in the name of the Lord!'. (Matthew 23:39)*

is deeply connected to Jesus' second coming, the Great Commission, and "life from the dead" for the whole earth:

> *For if their being cast away is the reconciling of the world, what will their acceptance be but life from the dead? (Romans 11:15)*

that comes when God fulfills His promises to Israel.

This was the first time in history that far more than one million will continue 24 hours a day for 21 days in praying for God's promises for Israel. The uniqueness of this prayer initiative is itself a sign of the times and an acceleration of God's "set time for a generation yet to be created" to engage together in His purposes for Israel.

> *You will arise and have mercy on Zion;*
> *For the time to favor her,*
> *Yes, the set time, has come.*
> *This will be written for the generation to come,*
> *That a people yet to be created may praise the Lord.*
> *(Psalm. 102:13, 18).*

This 21-day fast was a "global Esther moment:"

> *Then Esther told them to reply to Mordecai: "Go, gather all the Jews who are present in Shushan, and fast for me; neither eat nor drink for three days, night or day. My maids and I*

will fast likewise. And so I will go to the king, which is against the law; and if I perish, I perish!" (Esther 4:14-16)

that was a significant down payment for the final ultimate global Esther moment when millions of believers will engage in prayer, speak out boldly for God's purposes for Israel (as seen in Scripture), and stand with Israel as anti-Semitism increases until Jesus returns.

Behold, the day of the Lord is coming,
And your spoil will be divided in your midst.
For I will gather all the nations to battle against Jerusalem;
The city shall be taken,
The houses rifled,
And the women ravished.
Half of the city shall go into captivity,
But the remnant of the people shall not be cut off from the city.

Then the Lord will go forth
And fight against those nations,
As He fights in the day of battle.
And in that day His feet will stand on the Mount of Olives,
Which faces Jerusalem on the east.
And the Mount of Olives shall be split in two,
From east to west,
Making a very large valley;
Half of the mountain shall move toward the north
And half of it toward the south.

Then you shall flee through My mountain valley,
For the mountain valley shall reach to Azal.
Yes, you shall flee
As you fled from the earthquake

In the days of Uzziah king of Judah.

Thus the Lord my God will come,
And all the saints with You. (Zechariah 14:1-5)

This fast was very timely and important for Israel, as they were soon to face one of the most challenging conflicts in their history.

(https://isaiah62fast.com/)

CHAPTER 53
THE NIGHTMARE OF JIHADI RAPE AND MURDER
BY AVNER BOSKEY, DECEMBER 6 2023

There is a yawning gap between Hollywood movies and real life. Nevertheless, many prefer the drug of cinematographic fantasy to the simple truth, and lots of people in the West have been blinded by the silver screen, shying away from the hard facts.

It seems that a significant amount of people are willfully ignoring some uncomfortable truths – the brutal atrocities of the jihadi terrorist organization Hamas. Instead, some are choosing to support anarchist marches calling for 'jihadi justice.' They are participating in anti-Jewish demonstrations calling for genocide against Jacob's sons and daughters. Sometimes it feels like the inmates have taken over the asylum, and that the Nazis' spiritual descendants have taken over the United Nations. What's next as this world's dance turns into death?

On October 7, 2023 Hamas proudly filmed its slaughters, tortures, beheadings and mass rapes, broadcasting them live on social media. This monstrous footage is available on the internet, though many have not seen it. But to see such things is to look directly into the abyss, and I do not advise it. However, due to much of the world's incredibly short span of attention and its propensity to be so easily distracted, it is important to be aware that these atrocities actually happened. They are real. And they are an irreplaceable key to help people understand why Israel's population is unreservedly committed to wiping out – down to the last jihadi – that demonized evil called Hamas.

This newsletter takes a look at God's biblical perspective on rape, and then briefly describes Hamas' satanically motivated atrocities against Jews in their murderous pogrom of October 7, 2023. If you would prefer not to be exposed to descriptions of these events, feel free to only read the first part of this newsletter. But do pray with us based on the prayer guidelines at the end of the newsletter, in any case!

THE PUNISHMENT FOR RAPE IS DEATH

Moses instructs us: "But if the man finds a girl . . . in the field, and the man seizes her and rapes her, then only the man who raped her shall die . . . For just as a man rises against his neighbor and murders him, so is this case. When he found her in the field, the . . . girl cried out, but there was no one to save her" (Deuteronomy 22:25-27). The penalty for rape is the death sentence, says the God of Israel.

The rape of Jacob's daughter Dina happened 400 years before Moses, yet it was treated by her brothers Simeon and Levi as deserving of the same judgment. Unfortunately, it seems that her father Jacob was more concerned about how the Canaanites might react to divine justice, than about defending the honor of his own flesh and blood:

Now Dinah the daughter of Leah, whom she had borne to Jacob, went out to visit the daughters of the land. When Shechem the son of Hamor the Hivite, the prince of the land, saw her, he took her and lay with her and raped her . . . Now it came about on the third day . . . that two of Jacob's sons—Simeon and Levi, Dinah's brothers – each took his sword and came upon the city undetected, and killed every male. They killed Hamor and his son Shechem with the edge of the sword, and took Dinah from Shechem's house, and left. Jacob's sons came upon those killed and looted the city, because they had defiled their sister. They took their flocks, their herds, and their donkeys, and that which was in the city and that which was in the field; and they captured and looted all their wealth and all their little ones and their wives, even everything that was in the houses. Then Jacob said to Simeon and Levi, "You have brought trouble on me by making me repulsive among the inhabitants of the land, among the Canaanites and the Perizzites; and since my men are few in number, they will band together against me and attack me, and I will be destroyed, I and my household!" But they said, "Should he treat our sister like a prostitute?" (Genesis 34)

A few hundred years after Moses, certain wicked Benjaminites from the town of Gibeah attempted to gang-rape a male Levite who was spending the night in their town as a guest. Hospitality has nearly sacred dimensions in the Middle East; there are parallels between this incident and how the men of Sodom attempted to rape the angels visiting Lot (see Genesis 19:4-16):

While they were celebrating, behold, the men of the city, certain worthless men, surrounded the house, pushing one another at the door. And they spoke to the owner of the house, the old man, saying, "Bring out the man who entered your house that we may have relations with him." Then the man, the owner of the house, went out to them and said to them, "No, my brothers, please do not act so wickedly. Since this man has come into my house, do not commit this vile sin. Here is my virgin daughter and the man's concubine. Please let me bring them out, then rape them and do to them whatever you wish. But do not commit this act of vile sin against this man." But the men would not listen to him. So the man seized his concubine and brought her outside to them. And they raped her and abused her all night until morning, then let her go at the approach of dawn (Judges 19:22-25)

The entire nation of Israel was shocked at this atrocity which has carried out on one Jewish women – she was raped to death by a group of wicked Jewish men. The entire army of Israel gathered together to insist on justice, "so that when they come to Gibeah of Benjamin, they may punish them for all the vile sin that they have committed in Israel:"

So all the men of Israel were gathered against the city, united as one man. Then the tribes of Israel sent men through the entire tribe of Benjamin, saying, "What is this wickedness that has taken place among you? Now then, turn over the men, the worthless men who are in Gibeah, so that we may put them to death and remove this wickedness from Israel." But the sons of Benjamin would not listen to the voice of their brothers, the sons of Israel (Judges 20:10-13)

In the battle which followed, triggered over the rape and murder of one Jewish woman, a total of over 60,000 Jewish fighting men were killed. This was a very sober price to pay to purge out wickedness in the Jewish nation.

In 2 Samuel 13:14, David's son Amnon raped his half-sister Tamar (see 1 Chronicles 3:1-9). In due time, Absalom arranged for his half-brother Amnon (the perpetrator of the rape) to be killed:

And Yonadav, the son of Shime'ah, David's brother, responded, "Let my lord not assume that they have put to death all the young men, the king's sons, for only Amnon is dead; because this has been set up by the intent of Absalom since the day that he violated his sister Tamar" (2 Samuel 13:32).

In Bible times, whether rape was carried out by Gentiles or by Jews, the death penalty was the same for both – the death sentence. The honor of God demanded holiness and purity of sexual intimacy from God's people. Sexual violence and impurity were anathema both to the God of Israel and to His Jewish people.

A FOUNTAIN OF TEARS

The prophet Jeremiah wept over how anti-Jewish enemies murdered and raped their way through the cities of Judah. His tears mingle with those of today's Israelis who have suffered similar atrocities at the hands of Hamas jihadis:

> *Remember, YHVH, what has come upon us! Look, and see our disgrace! Our inheritance has been turned over to strangers, our houses to foreigners. We have become orphans, without a father. Our mothers are like widows . . . They violated the women in Zion, the virgins in the cities of Judah. Leaders were hung by their hands; elders were not respected . . . Elders are absent from the gate; young men from their music. The joy of our hearts has ended; our dancing has been turned into mourning. The crown has fallen from our head . . . Because of this our heart is faint; because of these things our eyes are dim – because of Mount Zion which lies desolate (Lamentations 5:1-18)*

> *Oh, that my head were waters and my eyes a fountain of tears,*

that I might weep day and night for those slain of the daughter of my people! (Jeremiah 9:1)

DEDICATED TO THE ONE I HATE

The God of Israel commanded Joshua to raze Jericho to the ground due to its idolatries and abominations. The Hebrew word used in Joshua 6:17-18 is cherem (חֵרֶם); it means dedicating or appointing something to utter destruction. To put Canaanite cities 'under the ban' meant that they would be dedicated to total destruction (see Leviticus 27:28-29; Number 21:2-3; Deuteronomy 7:1-5; 13:16-17; 20:16-17; Joshua 11:14).

Dr. Gleason Archer notes in his A Survey of Old Testament Introduction: "In view of the corrupting influence of the Canaanite religion, especially with its religious prostitution . . . and infant sacrifice, it was impossible for pure faith and worship to be maintained in Israel except by the complete elimination of the Canaanites themselves" (see Revelation 18:20-21). God's severe mercies are far removed from 'politically correct' and 'woke' perspectives. His judgments on Canaan, on the world in the days of Noah, and on Hamas might not be the same as that of the United Nations, the European Union, or Qatar – but they are 100% God's take on what needed (and needs) to be done.

YHVH made an oath that He would have war with Edom from generation to generation. He also took a vow to blot out the people descended from Edom's son Amalek. In our day we are observing this ancient biblical promise coming into fulfilment. Though many do not know either Biblical teaching or history in this regard, the majority of today's Palestinians are descendants of these Edomite forefathers (see https://davidstent.org/yhvh-will-have-war-against-amalek-from-generation-to-generation/ and 'Jews, Arabs and the Middle East: A Messianic Perspective').

The pronouncement of the word of YHVH to Israel through Malachi: "I have loved you," says YHVH. But you say, "How have You loved us?" "Was Esau not Jacob's brother?" declares YHVH. "Yet I have loved Jacob; but I have hated Esau, and I have made his mountains a desolation and given his inheritance to the jackals of the wilderness." Though Edom says, "We have been beaten down, but we will return and build up the ruins"; this is what YHVH of armies says: "They may build, but I will tear down; and people will call them the territory of wickedness, and the people with whom YHVH is indignant forever." And your eyes will see this, and you will say, "YHVH be exalted beyond the border of Israel!" (Malachi 1:1-5; see also Romans 9:11-13).

PART TWO: HAMAS ATROCITIES

> *"God created man in His own image, in the image of God He created him. Male and female He created them" (Genesis 1:27).*

One of the main goals of Satan is to disfigure, mutilate and destroy anything or anyone who reflects the image of God. Messiah Yeshua taught that "the thief comes only to kill and destroy" (John 10:10). The atrocities that Satan catalyzed (through Hamas and its partner Palestinian Islamic Jihad) had a triple purpose – to release a wave of fear and terror throughout the world; to catalyze a tsunami of anti-Semitic hatred across the face of this planet; and to blot out the image of God by desecrating that image through murdering, torturing, raping and mutilating Israelis on that day.

The foundational need for these bestial actors to be taken down is connected to justice – God's justice in His word, and mankind's justice as codified in centuries of jurisprudence.

In Judges 5:28-30 the mother of Israel's Canaanite enemy is anxiously waiting for her son General Sisera to return from his slaughter and plunder of the Jewish people in the Jezreel Valley. She waxes poetic about how he will bring with him the spoils of war, including rare colored fabrics and a few Jewish women to rape: "Out of the window she looked and wailed, the mother of Sisera through the lattice: 'Why does his chariot delay in coming? Why do the hoofbeats of his chariots delay?' Her wise princesses would answer her – indeed, she repeats her words to herself – 'Are they not finding, are they not dividing the spoils? A womb, two wombs for every warrior!'" The Hebrew word for 'womb' here is 'rachama / rechem' ('uterus' or 'vagina'). Rape as part of Middle Eastern warfare has ancient roots. Though rape may still be common practice throughout the Middle East, it is not the case with the Israel Defense Forces, who have no reputation for raping Arab women.

The following are links from news media sources considered responsible and accurate in their reporting. They can be consulted for more details about Hamas atrocities on October 7, 2023:

1. https://www.ynetnews.com/article/s14ccafrp
2. https://www.ynetnews.com/article/hjhumxb4t
3. https://www.jpost.com/arab-israeli-conflict/gaza-news/article-776347
4. https://en.m.wikipedia.org/wiki/Sexual_and_gender-based_violence_in_the_7_October_attack_on_Israel
5. https://www.christianpost.com/news/hamas-raped-women-grandmothers-children-israeli-official-says.html
6. https://www.thetimes.co.uk/article/ten-hamas-fighters-were-raping-the-woman-she-begged-for-death-6ldlmh8sp
7. https://www.timesofisrael.com/kill-behead-rape-inter

rogated-hamas-members-detail-atrocities-against-civilians/

8. https://www.timesofisrael.com/global-womens-rights-groups-silent-as-israeli-women-testify-about-rapes-by-hamas/amp/

9. https://www.dailywire.com/news/israeli-official-hamas-raped-women-grandmothers-children-so-violently-they-broke-victims-pelvis

10. https://www.israelhayom.com/2023/11/08/she-was-gang-raped-then-they-executed-her-horrific-testimonies-from-oct-7-atrocities-emerge/

11. https://www.timesofisrael.com/liveblog_entry/report-police-receive-witness-testimony-of-gang-rape-murder-of-a-woman-during-oct-7-onslaught/

12. https://www.timesofisrael.com/taken-captive-naama-levy-hands-of-peace-project-alumnus/?fbclid=IwAR31zvM6MjTSeunluigX2boan9x--DFKAHgcDt9R8VZ9iuz4g4X-B1FH7EA_aem_Ae9kMbY5IDC1R6GbWwuyTLTmkz5P8GlG2xsIoaTik_NahOQ80rMHjIS8jIuTr_GUxmY

13. https://www.jpost.com/israel-news/article-776654?utm_source=ActiveCampaign&utm_medium=email&utm_content=Israel-Hamas+war%3A+IDF+readies+to+flood+Gaza+tunnel+network&utm_campaign=December+5%2C+2023

These articles describe in greater detail interviews with eyewitnesses to Hamas massacres, gang-rapes, tortures and murders. There are interviews with medical professionals – those who found the bodies of victims; those who applied forensics to the vast crime scenes; those pathologists who performed autopsies on bodies, pieces of bodies, and teeth, etc.

Without going into great detail, the credible eyewitnesses, medical professionals and Hamas video footage reveal:

1. Gang rapes, one of which involved ten Hamas men against one Jewish woman. In most cases the rape was followed by murdering the victims. In some cases, the woman was murdered during the rape

2. Corpses found of rape victims of both sexes and all ages with broken pelvises

3. Necrophilia (sexual relations with the corpses of murdered Israelis)

4. Rape of men and women and children of all ages, followed by castration and mutilation of private parts, limbs, faces to the point that one could not tell if the victim was a man or woman

5. Decapitation of people who were still alive

6. Murdering victims with hammers

7. Women shot in the crotch, or having their breasts cut off and kicked around like a soccer ball, before being executed

8. Rape and murder of teenage girls in their own bedrooms

9. Arabic notes found on Hamas terrorists clearly indicated that the raping of Jewish women was a direct operational goal

10. Hamas jihadis explaining that they were given instructions by commanders to kill, behead and crush the skulls of everyone, and to cut off people's legs

11. Jihadis were instructed to kill young men and teenagers, and to kidnap the elderly, women and children

12. An unborn baby was cut out of her mother's womb and then beheaded with the umbilical cord still attached – and then the mother was beheaded – all of this filmed live

VIOLATING THE DAUGHTERS OF ZION

"They violated the women in Zion, the virgins in the cities of Judah" (Lamentations 5:11).

History sometimes repeats itself. What was common in Jeremiah's day, was common on October 7, 2023 when Hamas jihadis raped, tortured and murdered innocent women, teenagers, babies and pensioners of both sexes as they carried out their pogrom in the Israeli farms and kibbutzim bordering Gaza. At a US State Department briefing, Spokesman Matthew Miller was asked a question by a reporter: "The Israeli Government is conducting this investigation to look at Hamas using rape as a weapon of war against Israeli women and girls on the 7th. They say they've now collected more than 1,500 eyewitness accounts of sexual assault, sexual violence, including rape against women and girls that day." Miller responded:

"Hamas has committed sexual violence. They've committed rape. We have no reason at all to doubt those reports. When you look at all of the atrocities that Hamas carried out on October 7th and the atrocities that they've carried out since, the fact that they continue to hold women hostages, the fact that they continue to hold children hostages, the fact that it seems one of the reasons they don't want to turn women over that they've been holding hostage and the reason this pause fell apart is they don't want those women to be able to talk about what happened to them during their time in custody – certainly there is very little that I would put beyond Hamas when it comes to its treatment of civilians, and particularly its treatment of women."

Part of the reason Hamas violated its hostage deal mid-way is connected, said Miller, to its damage-control course correction. Hamas has no problem raping, torturing and murdering Israelis or all ages and sexes. But when it realizes that it might lose some public sympathy over blowback issues here, it has no problem making use of what Goebbels and Hitler called 'the big lie.' In Mein Kampf Hitler explains:

"In the primitive simplicity of [average people's] minds, they more readily fall victims to the big lie than the small lie, since they themselves often tell small lies in little matters but would be ashamed to resort to large-scale falsehoods. It would never come into their heads to fabricate colossal untruths, and they would not believe that others could have the impudence to distort the truth so infamously. Even though the facts which prove this to be so may be brought clearly to their minds, they will still doubt and waver and will continue to think that there may be some other explanation"

Yesterday, according to the Saudi al-Arabiya channel, Hamas dismissed claims by women and advocacy groups regarding documented eyewitness, medial forensic and video proofs of rape, murder, torture and sexual war crimes against Israelis on October 7, 2023. Hamas charged that the allegations were part of "Zionist campaigns which promote unfounded lies and allegations to demonize the Palestinian resistance," and that they are part of "a series" or Israeli "lies" since the start of the war.

As the OSS (precursor to the CIA) stated in their psychological profile of Adolf Hitler: "His primary rules were: never allow the public to cool off; never admit a fault or wrong; never concede that there may be some good in your enemy; never leave room for alternatives; never accept blame; concentrate on one enemy at a time and blame him for everything that goes wrong; people will believe a big lie sooner than a little one; and if you repeat it frequently enough people will sooner or later believe it."

ISRAEL CANNOT LIVE WITH HAMAS OR THE EQUIVALENT NEXT DOOR

The horror of having demonized neighbors living next door who are murderers at the level of the SS and ISIS, makes some points crystal clear, at least for Israelis:

Hamas and their fellow travelers in the Palestinian Authority can no longer walk and breathe in Gaza.

Any world leader who pushes for either one of those above options for Gaza does not seek the good of the Israeli people.

Prime Minister Ariel Sharon's Disengagement from Gaza (2005) is dead. It has turned into a wide-open back door for jihadis and enemies of Israel to regain strength, power and murderous influence.

The Oslo Accords (1993 – Clinton, Rabin, Arafat) are also dead, for the same reasons. The Palestinian Authority has the same philosophy, and approach to terror and the validity of the Jewish state, as does Hamas.

The explosion of anti-Semitism connected to the wicked deeds of Hamas and Iran is a flashing light and a benchmark that the prophetic pace of world events is picking up speed.

God warns the world that He will judge the nations based on how they will divide the Land of Israel (see Joel 3:1-12) and conquer it with great cruelty (see Zechariah 14:1-2). These dynamics indicate that we are drawing much closer to the return of Messiah Yeshua.

(https://davidstent.org/the-nightmare-of-jihadi-rape-and-murder/)

Avner and Rachel Boskey live in the Beersheva region of Israel, and are dedicated to stirring up the creative arts, worship, intercession, evangelism and the prophetic gifts within a Jewish and Israeli matrix.)

CHAPTER 54
THE SPIRIT OF AMALEK
BY PETER TSUKAHIRA, NOVEMBER 24, 2023

The background with Hamas and Hezbollah goes back to ancient times because of the spirit that is motivating them, but let's look at recent history. In the year 2000 Israel withdrew from Southern Lebanon. Then in 2005 there was an event in Israel called "Disengagement" when thousands of Israelis were forced by their own government to leave Gaza. We remember those heartbreaking television stories where we watched Israeli soldiers dragging Israeli citizens out of their homes in Gaza. And two years later, Hamas took control, and that's what we're dealing with in Gaza today.

Why did Israel do things like that? Because in the 1990's, the majority of Israelis believed in something called "land for peace." In the 1990's, the majority of the Israeli electorate believed if we gave up territory, we would receive peace in exchange. So, we pulled back to the internationally recognized borders in Lebanon, and immediately a group called Hezbollah took over. What's happening today on Israel's northern border is the result of that decision, because land for peace would never work because Hamas and Hezbollah are not fighting for land, they're fighting to destroy Israel.

Let's look at the spiritual roots of this conflict, and how we as the people of God have a calling to stand in this spiritual battle. At the core of this conflict, from a human perspective, lies something simple yet potent—a spirit of jealousy. The underlying force behind it, in my understanding, is what I'd describe as the spirit of Amalek. But today, the spirit Amalek has gone global. Today we don't deal with Amalek as a people attacking Israel; we deal with a deadly spirit that today is attacking Jews all over the world.

Let's delve into the background story. God chose a man named Abraham and made promises and a covenant with him. God told him that he would be a great nation and that he would be a blessing to all the peoples of the world, and that this people of Israel would have an inheritance in this particular land, and that the promise of this land was an everlasting promise throughout all generations. These promises in this covenant were passed down from Abraham to his chosen son Isaac, and to his chosen grandson Jacob. Jacob's name was changed to Israel, and from him and his 12 sons we get the people of Israel. From this people of Israel, we received Moses and the law, the judges, the kings, and the prophets of Israel. And from this one people, we receive Yeshua, the 12 apostles and the New Testament.

It's very important to understand our roots, and why this is a battle we are not exempt from, and can't ignore. When we say that we serve the God of Abraham Isaac and Jacob, we need to recognize that we are reciting a series of choices that God made one generation after Abraham. In Genesis chapter 17, God made a choice between two of Abraham's sons, his firstborn Ishmael, and Isaac who was born about 13 years later. Although Abraham prayed that Ishmael would live before the Lord, the

Lord told him that Sarah would bear a son in her old age, and that he would be their heir.

Ishmael was blessed. He was made a prince of nations, and was given a huge territory, and wealth and prominence, but the covenant, and the redemptive promise to be a light to all the world went to Isaac. A generation later Isaac and his wife had twins, and before they were born, God said it is the second one He has chosen for that particular inheritance. In Genesis chapter 25, the Bible says God chose Jacob and not his older brother Esau. Esau was given a territory. His name was changed to Edom, and God gave him Mount Seir and the territory that is today in modern Jordan and Saudi Arabia.

It is clear in the Book of Genesis that Ishmael and Esau were both older brothers who were passed over by God. They were given great things by God that we read about it in the Book of Genesis. They were blessed by God, but the promise to be in Abraham's redemptive line was given to Isaac and Jacob.

We know now that there has been a rivalry with the people of Israel and all of their neighbors, the people of Ishmael and Esau, ever since the Book of Genesis. After God chose his younger brother, Esau married Ishmael's oldest daughter, and their families were joined. Eventually Ishmael and Isaac reconciled, coming together when their father died, but their descendants have been rivals ever since. In the beautiful story in Genesis 33:4, Jacob and Esau come together, embrace one another, and are reconciled. But the grandson of Esau never reconciled, and in him was found a spirit of jealousy and hatred that he refused to let that go. His name was Amalek.

That spirit is alive today! It is not something rational, political or even religious. This is a spirit as dark as darkness can ever be. It's a spirit of jealousy that doesn't want to take what it has, it wants to take your life. So, let's follow the spirit of Amalek beginning 3000 years ago in Exodus chapter 17.

Then Amalek came and fought against Israel at Rephidim. So Moses said to Joshua, "Choose men for us and go out, fight against Amalek. Tomorrow I will station myself on the top of the hill with the staff of God in my hand." Joshua did just as Moses told him, and fought against Amalek; and Moses, Aaron, and Hur went up to the top of the hill. So it came about, when Moses held his hand up, that Israel prevailed; but when he let his hand down, Amalek prevailed. And Moses' hands were heavy. So they took a stone and put it under him, and he sat on it; and Aaron and Hur supported his hands, one on one side and one on the other. So his hands were steady until the sun set. And Joshua defeated Amalek and his people with the edge of the sword.

Then the Lord said to Moses, "Write this in a book as a memorial and recite it to Joshua, that I will utterly wipe out the memory of Amalek from under heaven." And Moses built an altar and named it The Lord is My Banner; and he said, "Because the Lord has sworn, the Lord will have war against Amalek from generation to generation." (Exodus 17:8-16 NASB)

Let's go to Deuteronomy chapter 25.

Remember what Amalek did to you on the way when you came out of Egypt, how he confronted you on the way and attacked among you all the stragglers at your rear when you were tired and weary; and he did not fear God. So it shall come about, when the Lord your God has given you rest from all your surrounding enemies in the land which the Lord your God is giving you as an inheritance to possess, that you shall wipe out the mention of the name Amalek from under heaven; you must not forget. (Deuteronomy 25:17-19 NASB)

3,000 years ago, the people of Israel were coming into the Land of Promise to claim it as their inheritance, and now again the people of Israel are coming back to this land, to the promised land that God has given them, and once again this spiritual enemy is rising up. It's not the Palestinian people, it's the spirit that is driving many, but that spirit today is being found all over the world, and before this generation that spirit was found in Europe. What drives this is a deep unresolved jealousy. Why should you be the people chosen by God from all the other people of the world? How can it be that that you were chosen, and my people were not? How can it be that you have this promise from God. I will change that. It is difficult to grapple with, but there are people who want to kill every Jewish person and everyone who supports them. God says don't ever forget that.

Many of us grew up in times of peace in loving countries, and it's unthinkable that there are people less than 100 kilometers away who think it will be a good day if all of us would die. In our spiritual warfare, we don't wrestle with flesh and blood. We need to understand the darkness and the serious nature of this enemy spirit. That's why it really makes a difference when we gather to worship the God of Israel. We are reporting for duty, and standing in our spiritual calling.

We're not called to be soldiers in Gaza who today are putting their lives on the line for their assignment. Our assignment is to proclaim the word of the Lord; to stand as his people; to resist the anxiety and the fear of our day, and to let the light of God shine upon us and to stand against this spirit of hatred, born of jealousy that's sweeping the world today. God says don't forget. Don't sweep this under the rug as some political issue or some military issue, or some type of religious conflict. God says you belong to me, and you have to fight to defeat this spirit.

Let's turn to 1 Samuel chapter 15, 300 years after Moses.

Then Samuel said to Saul, "The Lord sent me to anoint you as king over His people, over Israel; now therefore, listen to the words of the Lord. This is what the Lord of armies says: 'I will punish Amalek for what he did to Israel, in that he obstructed him on the way while he was coming up from Egypt. Now go and strike Amalek and completely destroy everything that he has, and do not spare him; but put to death both man and woman, child and infant, ox and sheep, camel and donkey.'" (1 Samuel 15:1-3 NASB)

Then we read that Saul and the people spared the Amalekite king Agag and the best of the sheep, the oxen, and the lambs, and all that was good. They were not willing to utterly destroy them, but everything despised and worthless they utterly destroyed. Then the word of the Lord came to Samuel saying "I regret that I made Saul King for he's turned back from following me and not carried out my commands." (1 Samuel 15:11)

Samuel was distressed and cried out to the Lord all night. God calls us to destroy this entity, this spiritual darkness and ancient hatred. God's word says we have to stand against this every generation, and not just stand and resist it, you have to fight this, and you have to be willing to destroy it from your midst. That's the hard lesson of war; war requires the destruction of your enemy. God makes it very clear: you don't make some type of deal with this spirit. This spirit you have to fight and break.

Look what the prophet Ezekiel says about this spirit in chapter 35:

> 'This is what the Lord God says: "Behold, I am against you, Mount Seir, And I will reach out with My hand against you. And make you a desolation and a waste. I will turn your cities to ruins, And you will become a

desolation. Then you will know that I am the Lord. Since you have had everlasting hostility and have turned over the sons of Israel to the power of the sword at the time of their disaster, at the time of the punishment of the end, therefore as I live," declares the Lord God, "I will certainly doom you to bloodshed, and bloodshed will pursue you; since you have not hated bloodshed, therefore bloodshed will pursue you. (Ezekiel 35:3-6 NASB)

This is an ancient hatred born of jealousy. Jealousy is when you want what someone has. It is or connected to the sin of covetousness. If someone is jealous of you and hates you, there's nothing you can do about it. It's not a matter of what I can give you, or you how we can work this out, because nothing will satisfy that spirit. We should fight it when it's small, not when it gets big.

You should thank God for how he made you. I'm thankful for what He made me. I don't want to be you, and you should never want to be me. I thank God for me, and I thank God for you. Each of us have our calling, each of us has our assignment, each of us has our place in God. But when you want something that belongs to someone else, that's the spirit of Amalek! God says you have to recognize that, and you have to learn to stand against it, and when I tell you to destroy that spirit, you must destroy it.

Search your heart, and ask the Lord to show you if you are jealous of anyone, or if you secretly wish you could be different than what He created you to be. Are you jealous of someone because they have what you can never have or because they are what you can never be? The spirit of Amalek is the deepest darkness, and a hatred for which there is no remedy. God says don't forget. I will blot out that spirit, and it will never stand before me. So, let your heart be ready to do battle with the sword of the Spirit. Our job is to put that spirit of jealousy and hatred to death.

That's why Saul was rejected by God. He won a great victory in an important war. He defeated the Philistines and he fought against Amalek and defeated them, but he didn't bring it to an end. And that's the kind of spirit we need when we talk about spiritual warfare. You don't enter into spiritual warfare in order to do warfare, you enter into spiritual warfare to kill the enemy spirit. Then the warfare is over.

In Ezekiel 35:3-4 the Lord says:

> *"Behold, I am against you, Mount Seir,*
> *And I will reach out with My hand against you*
> *And make you a desolation and a waste.*
> *I will turn your cities to ruins,*
> *And you will become a desolation.*
> *Then you will know that I am the Lord.*

The Lord says why in verses 5-6:

> *Since you have had everlasting hostility and have turned over the sons of Israel to the power of the sword at the time of their disaster, at the time of the punishment of the end, therefore as I live," declares the Lord God, "I will certainly doom you to bloodshed, and bloodshed will pursue you; since you have not hated bloodshed, therefore bloodshed will pursue you.*

This is the spirit that is motivating the enemies of Israel today. You hear them say that they're not giving up. They want more October 7 massacres again and again and again. And their statements saying that Israel is weak, isn't that exactly what Amalek did in Moses' time? They looked for the weakness of Israel and killed off the weak and the defenseless. God says "I'm never going to forget that and I will destroy that spirit."

Here's what Psalm 83 says:

> *God, do not remain quiet;*
> *Do not be silent and, God, do not be still.*
> *For behold, Your enemies make an uproar,*
> *And those who hate You have exalted themselves.*
> *They make shrewd plans against Your people,*
> *And conspire together against Your treasured ones.*
> *They have said, "Come, and let's wipe them out as a nation,*
> *So that the name of Israel will no longer be remembered."*
> *For they have conspired together with one mind;*
> *They make a covenant against You:*
> *The tents of Edom and the Ishmaelites,*
> *Moab and the Hagrites;*
> *Gebal, Ammon, and Amalek,*
> *Philistia with the inhabitants of Tyre;*
> *Assyria also has joined them;*
> *They have become a help to the children of Lot. Selah*
> *Deal with them as with Midian,*
> *As with Sisera and Jabin at the river of Kishon,*
> *Who were destroyed at En-dor,*
> *Who became like dung for the ground.*
> *Make their nobles like Oreb and Zeeb,*
> *And all their leaders like Zebah and Zalmunna,*
> *Who said, "Let's possess for ourselves*
> *The pastures of God.*
> *My God, make them like the whirling dust,*
> *Like chaff before the wind.*
> *Like fire that burns the forest,*
> *And like a flame that sets the mountains on fire,*

So pursue them with Your heavy gale,
And terrify them with Your storm.
Fill their faces with dishonor,
So that they will seek Your name, Lord.
May they be ashamed and dismayed forever,
And may they be humiliated and perish,
So that they will know that You alone, whose name is the Lord,
Are the Most High over all the earth.

In our day the spirit of Amalek isn't just these nations and these people groups today. The spirit of Amalek has gone global. Voices around the world are being raised in praise of the massacre that took place on October 7th. Governments are aligning themselves politically with them. It's awful to say this, but phrases like: "Kill the Jews, send the Jews to the gas chambers" are being heard in capitals and university campuses around the world.

It's really important to understand that we're in this struggle. We can't be passive. We have to stand. We have to fight. We have to win. As it says in Ephesians 6:12, Our struggle is not with flesh and blood, but against rulers and powers, principalities and spiritual wickedness. We need to take up the weapons of our warfare. Chiefly the weapon of worship. Worship is so powerful! The Hebrew word for worship simply means to bow down. Singing is an important part of worship, but the heart of worship is bowing down.

In the days of King David, godly worship is what released the hostages. In 1 Samuel 30, King David was fighting the Amalekites, and they came and took his family and the families of his warriors' hostage. His own people were embittered and they were blaming him. What did King David do? Did he defend himself? Did he fight back? Did he try to find someone else to blame? No. David fell on his face before the Lord and worshipped, and he said "Lord, what do you want me to do?" And the Lord said, "Go after them. If you go after them, you'll get them all back," and that's what he did. That's The power of worship! That's our weapon!

Another weapon is prayer with fasting. In the days of Esther, she had an adversary who wanted to kill all the Jews. His name was Haman the Agagite. Haman was a descendant of Agag, the

Amalekite king that Saul refused to execute. He had a plan to destroy all the Jews. And what did Esther do? She prayed, she fasted, and she spoke out about these things. The weapons of our warfare are worship. We pray with fasting, and we speak out.

While people are saying what they're saying around the world, we don't attack those people. We don't hate those people. We love those people enough so that we want them to be saved. Each one of us has a circle of influence. Don't try to change the world, but speak out to your world. Speak the truth that this is a globalized spirit of Amalek. These students that chanting, "From the river to the sea!" are calling for the destruction and the punishment of Israel. These people aren't any eviler than anyone else. They're just in deep darkness. We have the light, and we are called to be the light of the world. So, let's speak up!

(From a message given by Peter Tsukahira, Co-Founding Pastor, Kehilat HaCarmel given November 4 2023)

CHAPTER 55
THE WAY OF THE OIL
דרך השמן

BY CAROLYN HYDE, OCTOBER 15, 2023

A word of encouragement for intercessors:

"I am so impressed with the inner strength that יהוה has placed in each of you. You are all overcomers who carry an abundance of oil in your lamps! And I hear יהוה calling each of us to begin imparting The Way of the Oil to others who have empty or partially filled lamps. We can't give them our oil, but we can impart The Way of the Oil. Thank You L-rd and teach us what exactly is The Way of the Oil!"

I was shown to search for the א and ת – the first and last – of these two words: דרך השמן – The Way of the Oil.

דֶּרֶךְ

way, road, direction, journey, path, manner, a course of life, of moral character

א: Genesis 3:24

So He drove the man out; and at the east of the Garden of Eden He stationed the cherubim and the flaming sword which turned every direction to guard the WAY to the tree of life.

ת: Malachi 3:1

Behold, I am sending My messenger, and he will clear a WAY before Me. And the L-rd, whom you are seeking, will suddenly come to His temple; and the messenger of the covenant, in whom you delight, behold, He is coming," says the L-rd of armies.

שֶׁמֶן

fat, oil, as a staple, medicine for healing, for anointing, the fat of fruitful land & valleys

א Genesis 28:18

Jacob got up early in the morning, and took the stone that he'd placed as a support for his head, and set it up as a memorial stone, and poured oil on its top.

ת: Haggai 2:12

If someone carries holy meat in the fold of his garment, and touches bread with this fold, or touches cooked food, wine, oil or any other food, will it become holy?'" And the priests answered, "No."

We can't give away the oil that we've been given but we can show others The Way of the Oil. It's all related to the anointing and the Tabernacle. As Reuven Berger proclaimed during the historic WTKOG – Welcome the King of Glory – conference, "We, the people of יהוה, are a moving, living Tabernacle."

And I heard יהוה say, "Those who walk in The Way of the Oil are called to live, walk and breathe Haggai 2 from now until the end!"

When יהוה begins to shake the heavens and earth, the sea and dry land and all the nations, they will come with the wealth of all nations, and יהוי will fill this house with glory! The gold & silver belong to Him (His supernatural provision will come in the midst of desolation) The latter glory of this house will be greater than the former,' says the L-rd of armies, 'and in this place I will give peace (this is the fruit of The Way of the Oil)

Immediately after these verses, we see the timing:

On the twenty-fourth of the ninth month, in the second year of Darius, King of Persia.

In the Second Year of Darius:

Ezra 4:24 – Then work on the house of G-d in Jerusalem was discontinued, and it was stopped until the second year of the reign of Darius king of Persia.

1. The enemies initially offered to help rebuild the T but were turned down

2. So, they appealed to Persia's Xerxes and got permission to stop the rebuilding by force.

3. Rebuilding resumed in Darius' 2nd year.

4. The Jews rebuild with repentant hearts, citing Cyrus

5. Darius Found Cyrus' Decree

6. Full cost was paid from the Persian treasury to the Jews to offer acceptable sacrifices to G-d of heaven – this is the true destiny of Persia – to stand with Israel!

7. Those who stand in the way will become a heap of ruins like AI.

8. They successfully rebuilt through the prophecy of Haggai and Zechariah

And I clearly heard, "The true destiny of the Persian people will rise up during this time."

Haggai 1:1 – In the second year of Darius the king, on the 1st day of the 6th month (ELUL = Aug 18, 2023 & Sept 4, 2024, the word of יהוה came by Haggai to Zerubbabel, governor of Judah & Joshua, high priest:

1. Build The House

2. Drought & famine on new wine, grain, oil

3. The nation obeyed & revered יהוה

Haggai 1:15 – on the twenty-fourth day of the sixth month (ELUL = Sept 27, 2023 which was the final day of the (PAJ)? Prophetic Artists Journey) in the second year of Darius the king:

1. stirred up the spirit of Zerubbabel, governor of Judah, the spirit of Joshua, the high priest, the spirit of all the remnant of the people

2. They began work on the house of יהוה of armies, their G-d.

Haggai 2:1 in the twenty-first of the seventh month (Tishrei = Oct 6, 2023, the last day before the current war)

1. "Take courage; I am with you"

2. I will shake the heavens & earth, the sea & dry land.

3. I will shake all nations to bring their wealth

4. I will fill this house with glory!

5. The latter glory of this house will be greater & I will give peace.

Haggai 2:10 – On the twenty-fourth of the ninth month (Kislev = Dec 7, 2023, first night of Chanukah, which is all about the

Letts missing in words 'God & Lord' incomplete
not in the Bible
not in Bible

miracle of the oil!), in the second year of Darius, the word of יהוה came to Haggai:

1. From the 24th day of the ninth month (Kislev); from the day when the temple of יהוה was founded – from this day on I will bless you. (Dec 7, 2023)

2. Haggai 2:20 on the 24th day of the month: I will overthrow the thrones of kingdoms and destroy the power of the kingdoms of the nations; & I will overthrow chariots, their riders, horses and their riders will go down, every one by the sword of another. On that day,' declares יהוה, 'I will take you, Zerubbabel, son of Shealtiel, My servant,' declares יהוה, 'and I will make you like a signet ring, for I have chosen you,'" declares יהוה.

Zechariah 1:1 – In the eighth month (Cheshvan) of the second year of Darius, the word of the L-rd came to Zechariah the prophet…

1. "Return to Me and I will return to you"

2. True repentance came

Zechariah 1:7 – On the twenty-fourth day of the eleventh month, that is, the month Shevat (= February 3, 2024), in the second year of Darius, the word of the L-rd came to Zechariah the prophet:

1. The four horses appeared with a report, the ones whom יהוה sent to patrol the earth.

2. Adonai said He will return to Jerusalem with compassion; "My house will be built in it and a measuring line will be stretched over Jerusalem. I will again comfort Zion and again choose Jerusalem."

3. Zechariah was given the vision of חרשים Charashim – artisans who are called to terrify, scatter & destroy Israel's enemies.

This is the foundational Scripture, along with Exodus 25:40 for the PAJ. Thank You, Father for the anointing and restoration of the true Tabernacle and thank You for giving this confirmation of the date of the next PAJ, Prophetic Artists Journey on the 24th of Shevet!

(https://heartofg-d.org/the-way-of-the-oil/)

CHAPTER 56
TRY TEARS

Jesus wept at the tomb of Lazarus. (John 11:35)

Jesus wept over the city of Jerusalem. (Luke 19:41)

God puts our tears into His bottle. (Psalm 56:8)

Those who sow in tears shall reap in joy. (Psalm 125:6)

Weeping may endure for a night, but joy comes in the morning. (Psalm 30:5)

Several young Salvation Army officers asked their leader, General William Booth, "How can we save the lost?" They had felt like they had exhausted everything that they knew to do. So, Booth tore off a piece of brown paper sack and wrote two words and he handed it to these young zealous leaders and the note read, "Try tears."

Hannah was in bitterness of soul about being barren, so she prayed to the Lord and wept in anguish (1 Samuel 1:10), and God gave her a son Samuel, and many more children.

When Jesus was on the Earth, He offered up prayers and supplications, with vehement cries and tears to Him who was able to save Him from death, and was heard because of His godly fear. (Hebrews 5:7)

"O Jerusalem, Jerusalem, the one who kills the prophets and stones those who are sent to her! How often I wanted to gather your children together, as a hen gathers her chicks under her wings, but you were not willing! See! Your house is left to you desolate; for I say to you, you shall see Me no more till you say, 'Blessed is He who comes in the name of the Lord!'" (Matthew 23:37-38)

Pray for the peace of Jerusalem: "May they prosper who love you. (Psalm 122:6)

I tell the truth in Christ, I am not lying, my conscience also bearing me witness in the Holy Spirit, that I have great sorrow and continual grief in my heart. For I could wish that I myself were accursed from Christ for my brethren, my countrymen according to the flesh. (Romans 9:1-3)

Brethren, my heart's desire and prayer to God for Israel is that they may be saved. (Romans 10:1)

For the children of Israel shall abide many days without king or prince, without sacrifice or sacred pillar, without ephod or teraphim. Afterward the children of Israel shall return and seek the Lord their God and David their king. They shall fear the Lord and His goodness in the latter days. (Hosea 3:4-5)

And I will pour on the house of David and on the inhabitants of Jerusalem the Spirit of grace and supplication; then they will look on Me whom they pierced. Yes, they will mourn for Him as one mourns for his only son, and grieve for Him as one grieves for a firstborn. (Zechariah 12:10)

For I do not desire, brethren, that you should be ignorant of this mystery, lest you should be wise in your own opinion, that blindness in part has happened to Israel until the fullness of the Gentiles has come in. And so all Israel will be saved, as it is written:

> "The Deliverer will come out of Zion,
> And He will turn away ungodliness from Jacob;
> For this is My covenant with them,
> When I take away their sins." (Romans 11:25-27)

We offer our prayers and our tears for Israel's salvation to You, oh Lord.

CHAPTER 57
24 HOURS OF WORSHIP

As the war in Israel continued, the Global Watch called several 24-hour worship watches to worship the Lord in the spirit of King Jehosophat in as described 2 Chronicles 20. Each hour was hosted by worship leaders from around the world. The nations that participated included Russia, Turkey, Norway, Singapore, Lebanon and Australia. The following are prayers and reflections by worship leaders and participants about what God did during the November 10-11 watch.

And when he had consulted with the people, he appointed those who should sing to the Lord, and who should praise the beauty of holiness, as they went out before the army and were saying:

"Praise the Lord, For His mercy endures forever."

Now when they began to sing and to praise, the Lord set ambushes against the people of Ammon, Moab, and Mount Seir, who had come against Judah; and they were defeated. (2 Chronicles 20:21-22)

MJ: Our Father we're so grateful that we can come before the throne of mercy, and we thank you Father for guiding us all and bringing us together from glory to glory. Father, we thank you for Your plans that are good, for a hope and a future. Thank you, Father, for helping us all to come through this assignment by Your grace and bringing us as watchmen all across the globe, doing the will of the Father on the Earth as it is in heaven. Abba, we bless you for this hour, to hear what the Spirit is saying as we all were called in our positions as watchmen in this time to bring our offerings of a sacrifice of praise. Father, we pray that it was a sweet aroma and an incense before the throne, and Father for beloved Israel and Your people and for all that the Holy Spirit is doing right now. Father, we ask for Your mercy, Your grace, and Your Spirit of wisdom and revelation to help us understand as You sharpen each one to hear what the Spirit is saying through each one of us. We bless everyone, and we thank you for the leaders you have given each one in this watch. We bless them, and we thank you Lord in Yeshua's name. Amen.

FR: The 24 hours of worship that we just recently completed was very important because worship is a very powerful weapon in the hands of the Lord. Praise is perhaps one of the most powerful weapons that there is in terms of spiritual warfare. It's also about us coming together and joining together across the nations to worship Him, with our eyes focused on Israel.

The joy of the Lord is our strength, and joy is a supernatural weapon in His hands. We can have joy in the midst of stress, in the midst of warfare, in the midst of sorrow. Joy does several things: it gets us up into the third heaven, into the throne room with the Lord, and it helps us to focus on things from His perspective. God is not anxious. He's not taken by surprise by any of the things that are going on. We can war with that incredible peace, that incredible shalom of God.

Given the joy we're experiencing, it's important to acknowledge that we're embodying the spirit of Psalms 100. We enter His gates with thanksgiving, and we enter His courts with praise. We can in fact be walking in the presence of the Lord every day, all day long, with hearts of thankfulness. This is so important for all of us in the watch.

I just want to say a tremendous thank you for everybody who participated in any parts of the 24 hours of worship. We were in unity, and we were in agreement with what was going on. We especially want to thank the people who were worship leaders during that time. It's just amazing to us, and it just blesses our hearts that we can with very short notice get people around the globe in different nations to come on. Some of them with groups, some of them with just one person with the guitar or with the keyboard, and worship the Lord, coming into His presence and going from person to person to person to person. It is just amazing! So, we want to thank each and every one of you. We were not just observers, but you were participants for this, and we believe that it shook both the heavens and the earth when we came together for this purpose.

SR: I would really like to hear from some of the worship leaders. What was your experience? We've not been this way before. We've done it once before internationally. This is the second time around, and I have some thoughts about smoothing out the process and helping you guys with this.

WV: I think it was an extremely important time not only for me to engage in this place of worship at a certain moment. It was like worshiping from heaven. It was not to open up the heavens; the heavens have been open for 2000 years. For me, I worship from heaven, and everything flows out of that. I really felt that we've been in this prayer mode since the 7th of October.

We were recently in Egypt for three weeks of intense 24/7 prayer with hardly any sleep. Our friends are in Gaza fighting, as we were worshiping. I felt that sound, and as we were worshiping at a certain point we were in the tunnels of Gaza. That sound penetrated the deepest layers of that conflict. As we worship, the tabernacle of God, the presence of the Lord, the glory of God is so huge that it can cover that whole place and every soldier. We heard of a Messianic soldier losing both legs and fighting for his life in the hospital. It breaks my heart, honestly.

There was a dynamic in our worship. It's not even music anymore, it's beyond that. It's just engaging God, and the justice of God, and the courtroom of God to see the justice of God released, and to see the head of the snake being cut off. I think in the coming months we're going to see some incredible stuff happening not only in Gaza, but all over the world. I felt that as we were worshipping here, shockwaves went off all over the planet. Simply as a child I believe that. I just believe that. I just believe that.

AV: I felt at one point the frequency of the sound wave was resonating through that whole structure of the tunnels underneath Gaza. We have been on this journey for already 30 years. When we started off, to be honest, we had no clue what we were doing, and sometimes we still don't have a clue what we're doing, but it's by faith that we just step out and release that sound believing that God uses that to shift situations. That's how I felt during those 24 hours. It was powerful, and that unity is still resonating today, we release those sounds over Israel and over Gaza today. That's what I believe. When we agree and we are in unity to release those sounds over Israel, over Gaz, that still resonates today. And I thank God for this massive opportunity to have this done.

RW: Things are just shifting to a higher level. Just a few days earlier we were in another gathering locally, and as I was in worship, one of the pastors saw the sound falling over Gaza. That sense of like we may be worshiping in whatever country we're in, but it's like the sound is transported where the Lord wants to take it. I was really aware that the decrees and scriptures the Lord had given us were literally happening in real time.

Whether it was the tunnels, singing about the wisdom of God being released to the soldiers and to the crews, it was as if they knew where to go, and what to do. It was the revelation the Lord was giving. It was almost beyond just doing it by faith, there was a very strong connection between heaven and earth, and there was that sense of it actually happening right there.

Even though we may not know exactly what it is until some of the stories come out, but it was that sense of like you could tell it was actually taking place. And the other thing is how quickly it was able to come together, that sense of unity across the nations of being the shields of iron. There was a real sense we had locked shields. We are standing together on the walls, and it's not a metaphoric thing, it's actually very real, we've locked shields together. It's like we've locked shields together, and heaven and earth are aligned together working in sync together.

And though we know some of these things, it's like it's shifted into another gear. We've come up higher, and so there's a sense of really being aware of the angelic activity as we're in the worship space, as we decree the word. It's like some people will actually see it, but it's actually happening. So, I want to bless you for taking hold of that, and for everybody that was involved because this has been on our heart for so long to see this happening. And I see in the days ahead there's going to be a multiplication of this.

TT: For me it's very interesting that I never plan for joining the worship because of the ministry here. I miss some of the daily updates, but somehow, I just checked on the Global Watch and Sue mentioned that maybe we should do 24 hours worship again on November 11. It's hitting me, "Oh no, I need to join somehow." I just sent a message to Sue that I need to join for any reason because November 11, 11/11, is always on my heart. J

For me, it's like we all are bringing the wood to the mountain of the Lord, and we are just preparing our sacrifice, but we won't bring the fire, because the fire will be poured out from the Lord from heaven. So, it's something I'm not doing myself, but with the others.

This is very early morning to me, and at the same time I have been joining the training for becoming a trainer to help the Muslim background believers to be set free. So, we've actually learned some of the Muslim background and how Muhammad formed the Muslim Islamic belief. What I am seeing is something I really need to use, to just simply declare the blood of Jesus to face the thing because how Muhammad responded to the rejection, and how he formed Islam is very broken and evil. He used a lot of manipulation and violence, but what Jesus did to respond to the rejection is to sacrifice himself for us for the rejection, and that the blood can solve every problem.

I've been meditating on Isaiah 60 verse 18, and especially to go deeper in the study about the meaning of Hamas, especially how your walls will be called salvation. Salvation in Hebrew is Yeshua. So, this is one thing I can proclaim that is the name of Jesus that salvation is for us, and what we can do is call the gate praise. I am really thankful for the 24 hours that we can lift up our tehilah (praise) together with all the nations and to pray for our brothers in Israel. So, it's really my privilege to be part of that. Thank you.

SR: This morning I woke up to that song "New Jerusalem", and I cannot get it out of my head. In thinking about these 24 hours that we did, I feel like we hit a moed time, or in Hebrew otherwise known as a set time in the Spirit, and something really did shift. We're in a time of shifting. Iceland is shifting. The plates are shifting up there, and I'm not sure we can fully articulate it yet.

I went back to Amos 9:11, which was a central scripture for this 24-hour watch. Amos 9:11 is a very key verse for me personally, because after I had the open vision of 9/11 in October of 2000, within a couple weeks of when I landed on this verse, 9/11/2001 was when modern day Islam was again introduced to the world for what it is. It's just pure evil; it's violent, and it wants to kill people.

I believe that God is preparing us to move into this tabernacle, and in many ways, we've been moving into that with the 24-hour expressions that are going on. I'm not dissing them at all, but I think we're in a shift to the tabernacle of God being with men—being with us—and He's expanding our vision beyond the four walls of a church or a house of prayer. It's about an expression of God walking with us and within us in the world. So, I want to read (Amos 9:11-15):

> *"On that day I will raise up*
> *The tabernacle of David, which has fallen down,*
> *And repair its damages;*
> *I will raise up its ruins,*
> *And rebuild it as in the days of old;*
> *That they may possess the remnant of Edom*
> *And all the Gentiles who are called by My name,"*
> *Says the Lord who does this thing.*
> *"Behold, the days are coming," says the Lord,*
> *"When the plowman shall overtake the reaper, (that's revival)*

> *And the treader of grapes him who sows seed;*
> *The mountains shall drip with sweet wine, (that's revelation)*
> *And all the hills shall flow with it.*
> *I will bring back the captives of My people Israel;*
> *They shall build the waste cities and inhabit them;*
> *They shall plant vineyards and drink wine from them;*
> *They shall also make gardens and eat fruit from them.*
> *I will plant them in their land,*
> *And no longer shall they be pulled up*
> *From the land I have given them,"*
> *Says the Lord your God.*

The other scripture was Daniel 7:21-22:

> *I was watching; and the same horn was making war against the saints, and prevailing against them, until the Ancient of Days came, and a judgment was made in favor of the saints of the Most High, and the time came for the saints to possess the kingdom.*

I believe we are in that time, and how do we possess the kingdom by expanding our spirits to be more filled of Him. I believe God is working toward Revelation 21:3:

And I heard a loud voice from heaven saying, "Behold, the tabernacle of God is with men, and He will dwell with them, and they shall be His people. God Himself will be with them and be their God.

We're in that transition of God encompassing us, and all the pain and the sorrow of the mantles of crap that people carry from experiences in their past is being released into the hands of God, and he's pouring out the Tabernacle of God upon us. We don't have to be in a big fancy building. We've witnessed that. There were times in that 24-hour expression that you could feel the expansion of the kingdom, and so we're wanting to begin to understand what that is, and what is Revelation 21:3. We're being prepared as his bride, and it has to go beyond the confines of our hour of worship of our house of prayer, to an expression of us walking with Him, and He's going to have us as His bride. That's the transition I see, and I'm just walking into this revelation and waking up. The "New Jerusalem" song, sing it today, or listen to it. The tabernacle of God is me. Amen.

FR: That time is fast approaching. Pray a blessing over all the worship leaders, all the people that participated in the 24 hours. They need covering too, that there's no backlash from the enemy.

LM: Father Your kingdom come; Your will be done. Father, we thank you that you are the God who desires relationship, desires fellowship and intimacy with Your children, Father. We thank You for the ones that You have set aside, and You have anointed for worship for this expression, this wholehearted expression. How we love You with all our hearts and all our minds and all our strength, Father. Thank You that you have anointed and raised up the worship leaders for this purpose, Lord. We bless them with an increased devotion, an increased revelation of the beauty of Jesus, an increased measure of understanding, of revelation, of Your heavenly ways, the heavenly realms, the heavenly truth. Lord, the spiritual truth that is beyond even what our mind could comprehend. Father, take them into Your deeper measures of your presence to know you in the secret place, and for that expression of worship to be richer with the knowledge of You.

Father, we ask for the days that their worship will even be like prophesy, that their worship will draw the harvest even more. Lord, move hearts to change and enter in to that place of worship, Father. We bless them, and we ask for Your protection on every single one of them, and on their families. We plead the blood of Jesus, Lord. We understand that we don't come because of our own righteousness. It is Your righteousness that covers them and their families, all that is theirs and belonging to them we bring under Your authority, Your reign, Your covering. You are the refuge that they have trusted in, we trust in that faithfulness. Lord, in Your faithfulness You are a refuge that is sufficient for them and You're the covering over them even in the days to come. Lord, protect them in Jesus' name we pray. Amen.

MF: Good morning. Thank you for the 24 hours of worship. I don't think I was able to join one single time, but I was praying with all of you for the release of the hostages, and for the ongoing prayer of support for Israel. So, as we go into communion, I want to read to you from the First Nations version of the New Testament from First Corinthians 11:23-26. This is a version that has been translated by the different tribes across Turtle Island.

"This is the sacred tradition that came from our Honored Chief, a tradition that I have received and passed on to you: On the night that Creator Sets Free (Jesus) our Honored Chief was betrayed, he took some frybread.

He then gave thanks to the Great Spirit, broke the frybread into pieces, and said, "This is my body, broken for you. Eat it to remember me."

In the same manner, when the evening meal was over, he took the cup of wine, gave thanks to the Great Spirit, and said, "This cup represents the new peace treaty, brought into being at the cost of my lifeblood. Whenever you drink this cup, drink it to remember me."

For until our Honored Chief returns, each time you ceremonially eat from this frybread and drink from this cup, you are retelling the story of his death and its full meaning and purpose."

First Letter from Small Man to the Sacred Family in Village of Pleasure 11:23-26 FNVNT

https://bible.com/bible/3633/1co.11.23-26.FNVNT

SZ: I know we were praying in particular times regarding the hospital, and the surrounding things that were taking place, and I got up in the middle of the night last night to see a message from Josie where she had posted the nurse that had broken through with communication from the hospital, and it was so powerful. And as I watched that, I just thought of how God was moving amongst the Palestinians that are not in line with the god of Hamas, and how the prayers were even moving in that.

So, Father I just want to thank you God. It is such a humbling place to be, and such an honor to be prostrate before Your throne Lord with these that are crying out Lord in unity, singing Lord Your words, singing Lord the prophetic sounds. And thank You Lord for the advancing of Your kingdom, Lord in each of our nations. Thank You that You are advancing Your kingdom in Israel and even in Gaza that Your glory is rising that You will shine. Israel is going to shine and be the light Lord that You've called her to be originally. She is going to enter into the fullness of her destiny for all to see, where You are glorified and magnified, and so thank You Lord for giving each and every one of us Lord the ability to cry out, to travail, and to walk as one. And we just thank You and praise You even for this time, this morning together in the name of Yeshua. Amen.

CHAPTER 58
ZINZENDORF AND THE MORAVIANS: MESSIANIC TRAILBLAZERS

The story of Zinzendorf and the Moravians goes like this. The rich, young Nicholas Ludwig von Zinzendorf stood transfixed before a painting of Yeshua being presented to the people by Pilate, whipped and crowned with thorns. The painting was entitled "Ecce Homo" (Behold the Man), and written below were the words, "This have I suffered for you; now what will you do for me?"

Count Zinzendorf would be forever changed from that moment. His response was to offer his life and all that he owned in return, and so God (never one to turn down an offer like that!) used him to launch one of the most influential movements in history. Zinzendorf and the Moravians not only restarted the defunct engine of world mission and initiated their famous 100 years of continuous prayer, but they also were world pioneers for the Messianic movement way back in the early eighteenth century. Here's what happened.

THE SITUATION WAS RIPE FOR A MAKEOVER

For centuries, Yeshua's mandate to take the gospel to the nations had been all but abandoned, along with an understanding about what the gospel even really was, since most ordinary people had no access to the word in their own language. The advent of Bible translation and the invention of the printing press brought the Bible had to be translated and printed before people could discover God's plans for Israel about a Bible reading revolution, and by the sixteenth century, believers could finally read for themselves what it really meant to follow Yeshua, and also about God's plans for Israel.

Before those events, a man called John Huss had been calling people back to Biblical truth in what is now the Czech Republic. He was eventually burned at the stake, but his followers continued with his call for a departure from man-made religion, back to the simple truths of the Bible, and like him, they were hounded and persecuted. Many years later, a large group of these faithful Moravian Hussites fled up to Germany, seeking refuge. It is at this point in the story that our friend, Count Zinzendorf, appears.

ZINZENDORF AND THE MORAVIANS

The Moravian believers needed a place to settle, and Count Zinzendorf was a wealthy nobleman with a heart for Jesus and plenty of land to share. Land he had already dedicated to God long ago. It was on this very estate in Herrnhut that a movement began with Zinzendorf and the Moravians that would be truly ground-breaking—both in church history and also in the story of Messianic Judaism.

The first tree was felled to start building accommodation for the Moravian refugees on 17th June 1722. When Zinzendorf came to see how the building was coming along, "He joyfully entered it, welcomed them cordially, fell upon his knees with them, returned thanks to God, and blessed the place with a warm heart." [1] At the dedication of the house, they read Isaiah 62 together:

"On your walls, O Jerusalem, I have set watchmen; all the day and all the night they shall never be silent. You who put the Lord in remembrance, take no rest, and give him no rest until he establishes Jerusalem and makes it a praise in the earth". (Isaiah 62:6-7)

"Count Zinzendorf was undoubtedly one of the most extraordinary personages", wrote his friend and biographer, "He was a lover of Jesus, and a friend of man... a man of original genius... a sound, though occasionally eccentric theologian" who "could not be prevailed upon to do anything contrary to his conscience".[2] He would often give two or even three sermons a day to anyone who would listen – sometimes just his extended family, other times many others. He wrote hymns and poetry, and would travel often, and inspire others to do so, preaching the gospel wherever he went.

The movement that started with Zinzendorf and the Moravians on the Count's estate became quite remarkable for a number of reasons. After multiple conflicts in the community, a contract of peace was created, with every household agreeing to the covenant of how to treat one another. A system of prayer was instituted, praying literally around the clock in shifts, 24 hours a day, 7 days a week. They kept this up for one hundred years. ONE HUNDRED YEARS of continuous prayer!

THE EFFECT OF 100 YEARS OF PRAYER

Perhaps unsurprising then, that many other fireworks erupted from within this bunch of dedicated believers. In what was otherwise a lull in proclamation of the gospel among the nations, the Moravians sent over one hundred missionaries all over the world. Possibly the most remarkable story being that Zinzendorf had met an African man who had escaped captivity in the Americas, and after hearing his harrowing story, brought him back to tell the Moravian community.

The Moravians were so moved by what they heard that some of them even offered to sell themselves into slavery, so that they could share the good news with those immiserated in bondage as they worked alongside them. Unlike the Africans who had been kidnapped and stolen, these crazy Moravians volunteered themselves willingly to be shipped over the ocean as slaves, simply to take the gospel of freedom to those trapped in the hell of slavery.

That level of loving sacrifice is hard for us to even imagine.

There is another wonderful story of a group of Moravian families on a boat to America who had set out bearing the Good News, when suddenly they hit terrible weather and were all in mortal danger. To the amazement of the rest of the ship's passengers, the Moravians—men, women and children—sang songs of praise to God with no trace of fear. This so impacted one of the passengers (who already believed himself to be a Christian) that he underwent a powerful spiritual transformation and arrived in America like a new man. His name was John Wesley. God later used Wesley to spark an evangelical revival in the UK and to raise up hundreds of evangelists who would travel round preaching the gospel. [3]

A FORERUNNER FOR THE MESSIANIC MOVEMENT

According to Christiane Dithmar's work on the subject [4] this Zinzendorf became convinced from the Scriptures that reaching the Jews first was a necessity of world mission according to Romans 1:16, and so sent people to the Jewish community in Amsterdam straight away.

Zinzendorf added prayers for Israel to the community's litany in 1740 – the first-time intercession for Israel had ever been made a regular part of liturgy in the whole of the Western church. The petition asked that God would "restore the tribe of Judah in its time and bless its first fruits among us."

He also introduced the keeping of Yom Kippur as a way of remembering the Jewish roots of the faith, and even tried to keep kosher to make it easier for Jewish people to live with them in their Moravian settlement. He criticized the Western church for adopting the name "Oester" (Easter) instead of holding to the original "Pasch," which is closer to the original festival of Pesach (Passover) during which Yeshua was crucified and rose again. Lamb was the preferred Easter dinner for many Moravian families throughout the 19th century, in reference to the Passover lamb that was slain.

Over the years, Zinzendorf and the Moravians made several attempts to establish a Jewish "Kehila" (congregation or community). Zinzendorf arranged for the marriage of Jewish-Christian couples according to Jewish rites, but there was never a large enough group to establish a separate community. Not many Jewish people were coming to faith in Yeshua at that time in history, but I personally know of at least one Jewish family who joined the Moravians, and whose descendants later became missionaries to Tibet, and there were certainly others. However, numerous Gentiles were touched by this amazing movement and the gospel they were offering, and by key influencers like John Wesley who were so impacted by them.

A DIFFERENT END TO THE STORY OF THE RICH YOUNG RULER

The story of Zinzendorf and the Moravians shows what can happen when the rich young ruler doesn't walk away from Yeshua with sadness, but joyfully embraces the challenge to surrender everything he has and serve the needy. Yeshua chose just twelve ordinary men to turn the world upside-down; men who became unafraid of death, suffering or sacrifice. They had walked with Yeshua and seen his willingness to pour out everything for them, and were willing to dedicate everything to him in return. The man in the picture throws down the gauntlet to us all: "This have I suffered for you; now what will you do for me?"

In our time there is still a community of believers living in Herrnhut who love Israel and the Jewish people, and pray for them continually. This community of believers have loved the Jewish people and Israel since the seventies, while they were still in the socialist East Germany. Since the fall of the wall, many have been serving Jewish people in Israel in various ways, including helping Holocaust survivors there and in Eastern European countries.

---

1. The Life of Nicholas Lewis Count Zinzendorf, tr. by S. Jackson – By bp. August Gottlieb Spangenberg (1838) pp.ix – xiv
2. ibid, page 40
3. Christianity Today Magazine – "The Moravians and John Wesley" posted 1/01/1982

4. Christiane Dithmar: Zinzendorfs nonkonformistische Haltung zum Judentum (Univ. of Heidelberg, 2000)
   (https://www.oneforisrael.org/bible-based-teaching-from-israel/zinzendorf-the-messianic-trailblazer/)

CHAPTER 59
ZION'S FUTURE GLORY
A WORD FOR THE WATCHMAN

Watchman, what of the night?
The watchman said,
"The morning comes, and also the night. (Isaiah 21:11-12)

And let us not grow weary while doing good, for in due season we shall reap if we do not lose heart. (Galatians 6:9)

But You, O Lord, shall endure forever,
And the remembrance of Your name to all generations.
You will arise and have mercy on Zion;
For the time to favor her,
Yes, the set time, has come.
For Your servants take pleasure in her stones,
And show favor to her dust.
So the nations shall fear the name of the Lord,
And all the kings of the earth Your glory.
For the Lord shall build up Zion;
He shall appear in His glory. (Psalm 102:12-16)

. . .

CHAPTER 60
THE LAST WORD ON THE MIDDLE EAST
BY DEREK PRINCE, 1982

THE CLIMAX

For the final dramatic climax of Zechariah's predictions concerning Israel and Jerusalem, we must turn to chapter 14:

> For I will gather all the nations to battle against
>   Jerusalem;
> The city shall be taken,
> The houses rifled,
> And the women ravished.
> Half of the city shall go into captivity,
> But the remnant of the people shall not be cut off from the
>   city.
> Then the Lord will go forth
> And fight against those nations,
> As He fights in the day of battle.
> And in that day His feet will stand on the Mount of
>   Olives,

> Which faces Jerusalem on the east.
> And the Mount of Olives shall be split in two,
> From east to west,
> Making a very large valley;
> Half of the mountain shall move toward the north
> And half of it toward the south.
> Then you shall flee through My mountain valley,
> For the mountain valley shall reach to Azal.
> Yes, you shall flee
> As you fled from the earthquake
> In the days of Uzziah king of Judah.
> Thus the Lord my God will come,
> And all the saints with You. (Zechariah 14:2-5)

In all probability, this passage depicts the final outcome of the gathering of all nations against Jerusalem, which was referred to first in Zechariah 12:3. It also seems reasonable to set these events in the period described by Jeremiah:

> *Alas! For that day is great,*
> *So that none is like it;*
> *And it is the time of Jacob's trouble,*
> *But he shall be saved out of it. (Jeremiah 30:7)*

It is not my purpose to examine all the details that are depicted so vividly here. Suffice it to say that the climax comes with the direct, personal intervention of the Lord Himself.

Anticipation of this glorious climax continues among God's people in the New Testament. In II Thessalonians, for example, Paul looks forward to this same event:

> *And to give you who are troubled rest with us when the Lord*

Jesus is revealed from heaven with His mighty angels, When He comes, in that Day, to be glorified in His saints and to be admired among all those who believe, because our testimony among you was believed. (2 Thessalonians 1:7,10)

In Revelation 22:13, Jesus declares Himself to be "the Alpha and Omega" of all history. As the Alpha, He set history in motion. Therefore, other persons and agents have played their various parts. But when the end comes, it will again be Jesus who reappears as the Omega, and brings history to its divinely ordained consummation.

In the consummation, the severed strands of history are reunited. The invisible becomes visible; the spiritual blends with the natural. Prophecy becomes history. The written word of Scripture merges into the personal word – the Lord made manifest. The merging accomplishes the full and final outworking of the last word on the Middle East.

In this closing scene, all the actors in the drama of establishing God's kingdom on earth are brought together on stage. It is the same stage on which every previous crisis of the same drama has been enacted: Jerusalem and the mountains that surround it. Angelic hosts glorified saints and the preserved remnant of Israel take their respective places.

But the central figure, outshining all the rest and drawing them together around Himself, is that of Messiah, the King.

I believe with perfect faith in the coming of the Messiah, and even if he tarries, still I will wait every day for him to come.

Thus, too, will heaven answer the prayer of the aged apostle John on the isle of Patmos – the prayer echoed by every true

Christian as he closes his New Testament:

Amen. Even so, come, Lord Jesus!

1

---

1. (Prince, Derek. The Last Word on the Middle East. Grand Rapids, MI.: Chosen Books, 1982. Pages 141-142.)

ABOUT THE AUTHOR

Michael grew up in a Conservative Jewish home in New York City. He came to faith in Messiah in Eugene Oregon in 1970. He worked in business for 40 years, including 28 years as a systems engineer and project manager with IBM.

During this time, Michael served as a congregational and teaching leader in Minnesota, Arizona and New York.

He earned a BA from Bethel University, and an MA in Human Resource Development from the University of St. Thomas.

He is the author of four books, and is a National Board-Certified Health and Wellness Coach (NBC-HWC). He has also completed 15 marathons and 60 half-marathons in 10 different states.

His passions are prayer and teaching, and he serves on the leadership team of Five Stones Impact, an international church planting and development network. He lives in Eden Prairie, Minnesota with his wife Cheryl. They have been married for 50 years.

Made in the USA
Columbia, SC
17 April 2024

34511603R00189